LOST

IN

YOU

LOST

IN

YOU

HEIDI MCLAUGHLIN

Edited by Fallon Clark at SnowEditing.com
Alyssa Minger at Precision Copyediting & Proofreading
Cover Designed by Sarah Hansen at © OkayCreations.net
Interior Design by E.M. Tippetts Book Designs

ISBN-13: 978-0-9893738-9-0

Other Books by Heidi McLaughlin

The Beaumont Series:

Forever My Girl - #1
My Everything - #1.5
My Unexpected Forever - #2
Finding My Forever - #3
Finding My Way - #4

FOR
Ryan Michael

chapter
one

RYAN

Beads of sweat drip down my face. My shirt is soaked and filthy, but I can't stop to change or find something else to wipe away the grime. The lawn needs to be mowed and raked before my dad comes home from work if I want any semblance of a weekend.

It's not like I have plans, but something may come up and I don't want to give my dad an excuse to say no, not that he'd need one.

My parents are strict. Well, my dad is. My mom is okay for the most part as long as my dad isn't around. We live on the outskirts of town away from the high-traffic life of Brookfield. You know when you look in the magazines and see the town that time forgot? That's us – except time didn't forget, it just passed over, and when it did – my dad stayed with it. He said his life was simple when he was growing up and ours would be too.

With the lawn finished, I pull out my pre-paid cell and look at the time. It's all I can afford and half the time I don't have any minutes on it. I use it strictly for emergencies or when I want to look like I belong.

Neither of which happen very often.

Scooping up the last of the grass clippings, I push the wheelbarrow to the back corner of our lawn. We have a pile of dead grass near the fence that my dad uses in the spring to reseed the yard. He refuses to haul it off to the dump or have the garbage company pick it up.

Removing my shoes and grass-stained socks outside, I step into our sweltering house. I hate not having air conditioning, especially when the temperatures are over one hundred. If we're lucky, the air will cool down enough and we can place the box fans in the window tonight and try to cool down the house. I'm not counting on it though. We're in the middle of a heat wave and it's not supposed to stop any time soon.

My school is air-conditioned. Thank God. If it wasn't I'm not sure how we'd survive. School starts in a few days and I'm probably the only kid in town who is looking forward to it. I'm counting the days until I'm done. I want out of here, away from the dirt and brown grass. Away from the quiet and almost desolate life my parents lead.

I don't know where I'm going. I just want to go. My plan is to catch the six o'clock bus one morning and never come back. I just need to make sure I have enough saved by then.

I look around the house, making sure everything is picked up. The dishes are done and put away. The newspaper is centered on my dad's placemat, just like he requires. I'm thankful I'm not asked to cook; flipping burgers at Stan's three nights a week is enough kitchen time for me.

I straighten out the pillows on the couch before heading to the shower. It's just one less thing for my parents to look down on when they come home. I'm allowed five minutes in the shower. My dad says any more time is just wasteful.

I set the egg timer and get in. I learned a long time ago to shower in the cold and enjoy the little warm water I can get toward the end of my allotted time. It's just best this way. I'm done before the timer goes off; too bad I can't accumulate the extra time and use it for my next shower. I would ask, but hearing no and receiving lectures all the time gets old.

When I get out of the shower, my best friend, Dylan, is laying on my bed. Her long dark hair is spread across my pillow. Her right leg is propped up on her left, her foot bouncing. I know she's listening to music; she always is. She peers at me over her leg, her foot stops bouncing as her eyes move up and down my body.

"Damn, Ry."

"What?" I ask, suddenly self-conscious standing in my room naked except for the towel covering my lower half.

She continues to stare. I have to look away when my cheeks become warm.

"Damn, Ry." This time when she says those words her voice is raspy. "For being almost eighteen you're freaking hot."

I shake my head and grab some clean clothes and head back to the bathroom to get dressed. She's never said that before, not sure why she's saying it now. I've seen the guys she dates and I look nothing like them.

I've lived in Brookfield all my life. So have my parents and their parents, too. I didn't meet Dylan Ross until halfway through sixth grade. She found me eating alone one day and flat-out told me she felt sorry for me. It took me two months to say something to her, but once I did she never shut up. With her came other friends, but Dylan dubbed me her best one that year. The ironic thing is that her friends have known me for years, but we've never hung out. I'm on the wrong side of Brookfield. There is a small group of us that hang out, but most of the guys play sports and I don't fit in, mostly due to my social status. I would like to play some sport, maybe football or basketball, but I have to work and there is no way my dad would ever agree to pay for something like basketball shoes. I don't fit in, never have.

Most of the guys we hang out with like Dylan and want to date her. A few of them have asked how many times I've been with her and think I'm bullshitting them when I tell them we are strictly friends. I've never looked at her that way. Don't get me wrong, she's beautiful and any guy will be lucky when she finally looks in his direction. But it's hard for me to see Dylan as more than a friend. Even if we did date, what would happen if things didn't work out? Besides, I wouldn't stand a chance with her. I'm her go-to guy when she's having problems.

I tap Dylan on the foot when I'm back in the room. She pretends to ignore me, likely waiting for her current song to finish. I sit on the edge of the bed and wait for her. I know this game – I've become the master. There is no interrupting Dylan and her love for music.

She sits up, her eyes gleaming. I know this look – she's up to something. She pulls out her ear buds. "Guess what I won?" she asks. I'm never going to guess so I shrug. Dylan wins everything even though her parents give her anything she wants.

"Aren't you going to guess?"

"No, you're going to tell me anyway," I reply. I scoot back on my bed, crossing my ankles. Dylan moves closer, matching the way I'm sitting. Her long, tan legs are pressed against mine and I don't like it; it's too hot to be touching anyone. I shift slightly, only for her to put her hand on my leg.

"I won tickets to the Hadley Carter concert and not just any tickets, but backstage passes and a meet and greet."

"Cool, but who is Hadley Carter?" Dylan knows I'm not up-to-date on the music scene. I don't have a fancy music player like she does or even a computer where I know she gets most of her music. Sure we listen to music in her car, but I try not to get attached to something I can't have. It's the devil's music, or so my mom says. Unless the band is on public access television, it's not allowed.

Dylan turns her body so she's facing me. I can tell that she's excited about these tickets she's won. "Hadley is like the biggest music star out there right now and she's coming to town. Well not here, but to Jackson and I've got us tickets!"

"Us?"

"Of course us! Who else would I want to go with?"

"I don't know, D, Rachel, Sarah, or Jill. I'm sure they'd all want to go with you. I don't. Hell, even the new guy that moved here last week. I saw him watching you the other day when you were at Stan's. I think he drooled on his burger when you bent over." Dylan hits me in the arm. I act like it hurt, but it didn't. She's too tiny to cause much damage. "Come on, I don't know any of this singer's music. I'll be bored."

Dylan sticks out her bottom lip and bats her eyes slowly. "Please, Ryan. It'll be a great night and I want to spend it with you. You're my best friend and this is a once-in-a-lifetime experience. You're the one I want to share it with."

When she gets like this I can't say no. Even if I tried, she'd find a way to make me feel guilty and remind me of something she did for me or tell her I owe her a favor and that she's collecting now. I'm in a no-win situation with her and I know it.

"When's the show?" I ask while rolling my eyes. She knows it's pretend and that I'd do anything for her.

Her face lights up and she starts clapping. I can't help it. I smile too and look away from her so she doesn't see it.

"The show's tonight, but don't worry. I stopped by your mom's office and asked her if you could go and she's okay with me driving us to Jackson."

Dylan is like the daughter my mother always wanted and never had so I'm not surprised she said I could go. Had it been anyone else she would've made me ask my dad and that is usually an automatic no.

I look at my alarm clock and cringe. My dad will be home in twenty-minutes; my mom not for another hour. I don't have any money for dinner if I go to the concert.

"I haven't gotten paid yet, D. I don't have any money."

"Oh, don't worry about that. I got it. You can pay me back later." She says this too eagerly. I owe her a million dollars already.

"We should go before my dad gets home. Is what I'm wearing okay?"

Dylan jumps off my bed, heads to my closet and pulls out one of my Sunday church shirts. Fear creeps up my spine – if I ruin it, I'm in trouble. She hands it to me with a huge smile on her face. Sometimes I wish she knew exactly how things were in my house. No, I take that back, I wish I had the carefree attitude and the ability to do whatever I wanted that she has. I wish that my check went to me and not my parents. Most of all, I wish my life was different.

chapter
two

HADLEY

Alex braids my hair. She does this because she knows it pisses off *Anal Anna* and loves to watch her huff and puff while she's trying to get out the kinks. I don't understand why I can't perform in a braid. It would be so much easier and would keep my hair out of my face. But what do I know? I'm just the talent surrounded by people paid to know what's best for me.

Alex moves from my hair to my shoulders and massages them. My head falls forward as she works the muscles in my neck. Having my best friend on tour has so many perks, this being one of them. And I have someone to talk to when I'm lonely. Which is all the time. She ends up being my everything – my confidant, my shopping buddy and even my date to the movies when I want to see something. I lean on her for everything.

She taps me on the shoulder to let me know I'm done. I open my eyes and look at her. The bright lights surrounding my vanity mirror are making her dark skin pale. I hate that because her dark complexion and caramel-colored eyes are beautiful.

Alex and I switch spots and I do her make-up. This has become our ritual. Not that anyone is going to see us like this. She'll remove the make-up before we leave the bus and head into the arena. This is the only time I can be a kid again, even though at twenty-two, those days are over. I just missed them by performing and sometimes I want them back. I miss the days where I didn't have to do anything. I didn't have to be "on". When I could go to the mall and hang out, eating at the food court and not having to worry if paparazzi are lurking in the dressing room next to me. Those days have been gone for so long, I wish for one moment I can be normal again.

A knock on the bus door makes us both groan. Sometimes performing every other night and traveling in between is too much. I long for my soft bed and stuffed animals. Yes, I know, I'm too old for stuffed animals, but every so often I need them.

Alex goes to get the door. She sashays as she walks, flipping her hair over her shoulder every few steps, mimicking *Anal Anna*. It's something we've practiced night after night either on the tour bus or in our hotel room.

"Oh look, if it isn't the hair dresser." Alex walks back toward me, rolling her eyes. When Anna spots my hair braided she sighs heavily causing Alex to laugh. I bite the inside of my cheek to keep from smiling.

They have a love/hate relationship. Actually, I think it is more hate/hate because I don't remember them every really loving each other.

"Are you ready?" she asks.

I don't answer her. I fall into step behind her, Alex behind me. Outside my bus is a security guard. He's not mine, but someone that the venue hired to stand here and block my door. He looks me up and down and smirks. Not sure why. Maybe he's a hard-core rocker fan or something. Alex mutters something under her breath and starts laughing, earning us a look from Anna. I swear she thinks we're twelve years old.

The venue is bursting with people. The opening act is about to go on. They are an up-and-coming boy band that has been traveling with me for a few months now. One of them, the lead singer, Smith Michaelson, hits on me after every show. At first I was flattered, but it quickly got old. If I don't buy what he's selling, he moves on to some bopper that somehow made it into our after-party. I've been with only one musician and that was enough to last me a lifetime. They're nothing but trouble. Pure heartbreak waiting to happen, that's what it is. When men have women throwing themselves at you night after night you seem to forget about the commitment you made to someone else. I swore off relationships like that, which is why I'm single. I want "normal" but "normal" definitely isn't knocking on my door.

He's persistent though. I'll give him credit for trying, but if seeing him talk to me and then walk to the first willing girl is supposed to make me want him more, it doesn't. It makes me feel sorry for him. I've taken to carrying handiwipes with me so after he touches my hand I can disinfect my skin.

Anal Anna opens the door to my dressing room. I have a bouquet of sunflowers sitting on the table along with magazines for Alex. My rack of possible outfits sits in the corner and all of Anna's make-up is stacked on the table in front of the full-length mirror. I sit down and plaster on a fake smile so Anna knows I'm ready. The last thing I need is for her to tell my uncle Ian, who doubles as my manager, that I don't have my game face on. A lecture from him is something I can do without.

There are more flowers, roses this time, on each side of this vanity, no doubt set up by Ian. I don't know why he insists on having more flowers. They go to waste each and every night. It's not like we can take them with us when we leave, so why have them here? This is supposed to be my sanctuary.

Alex lounges on the couch, reading the newest *People* magazine. I'm in this issue as one of the top one hundred most beautiful people. I wanted them to use Alex, but she's not famous enough. She mocks me when she comes to my page and reads the quote from Smith, "*Being with Hadley on tour has been an amazing experience. When we aren't on stage, we are together. She's such a lovely and sweet girl.*"

I glare at her through my mirror. Anna has my hair in big rollers, the pins digging into my scalp. While my hair sets, she does my make-up. She's only been with me for two months. She was highly recommended by some tart that was dating my uncle. When the tart got kicked to the curb, Anna stayed. I suspect she's doing my uncle, but I don't ask. I think if I knew, I'd fire her and that would piss him off.

Anna picks out my outfits for tonight. A couple of dresses, which I love because I can wear my cowboy boots with them; a pair of jeans with rhinestone tank tops in various colors; and my least favorite is an uncomfortable leather number with stiletto heels. I hate the leather outfit, but Ian says it gives me sex appeal, which apparently I need. I refuse to have my shows staged. I hate it. I want my fans to expect the unexpected and that includes my clothes. Wearing the same thing over and over, night after night, is boring and lacks creativity. I want my shows to be fresh.

When Ian walks in, he's on his phone. He doesn't say hi to Anna and her face drops. If they aren't doing it, she wants to or they did and he's ditched her. That's usually how he operates.

He hangs up and looks at my outfit, very Sandy from *Grease*. I want to fire whoever suggested this idea. "Are you ready?"

"Yeah, I am. Are the contest winners here?"

He rolls his eyes. He hates the contest winners, but I love them. They make this all worth it. To know that they've won tickets by repeatedly calling a number to enter a contest shows a lot about a person's character. Ian thinks it's too charitable and Alex says it's not enough so she usually invites them to an after-party. This just pisses Ian off even more because he says he's stuck babysitting all night when he should be able to enjoy himself.

"Yes, they're here, are you ready?" he sighs heavily. He's frustrated and angry about something. What else is new? Ian is good at his job, but his interpersonal skills need a lot of work.

"Where are they?" I need to know because I like to focus on them during the concert.

"Front row and one girl answered all your trivia questions right so she has a backstage pass."

"Did you—"

Ian puts his hand up for me to stop talking. "I told her she and her guest can come and go as they please, but to wait until after the show is over before approaching you."

"Perfect." I kiss him on the cheek, earning a tiny smile from him. I know deep down he loves me, but loves the money and power he has more.

He opens the door. I take a deep breath and step out. I'm flanked by my bodyguard, Jones, and the rent-a-cops as they push us through a wall of reporters who all have press passes. They never get it. I don't do interviews before a show. This is my rule, not Ian's. I hate having my fans wait. They expect me on the stage at eight and that's where I'll be.

Alex holds my hand as we walk the long hallway. The chanting gets louder the closer we get. She squeezes my fingers. She gets so excited before each show. Me, I just get nervous. Not the butterfly nervous – no, I've never felt that – but the I'm-going-to-hurl nervous.

We stand on the side of the stage and I can see some of the fans. There are signs that say *I love you, Hadley* hanging from the second floor seats. Little girls are standing, looking for any sight of me. Sometimes I just want to run out there and sit on the stage and talk to them. Each and every one of them, but I'll never get that opportunity.

The lights go down and the crowd gets louder. 'Hadley, Hadley' echoes throughout the venue. My band starts up and that's my cue in this tight leather contraption and hair sticking out everywhere to get on stage, all for my first three songs.

I kiss Alex and give her a hug before doing our secret handshake. I can barely see it's so dark. I count the steps I took earlier, remembering my movements so I don't trip or walk off the front of the stage. When I'm in center, I take a deep breath and count to three. My foot starts moving to the beat of my song.

When the spotlight comes on, it's just me and the light. I sing with my eyes closed. When the first verse is over all the remaining lights come on and I can finally see my fans here to sing with me, and I'm reminded why I'm up here.

I love it.

chapter
three

RYAN

The things I do for friends. Well, actually just one friend. If anyone else had asked me to attend a concert where there are five men – or are they boys? – dancing around and gyrating their junk in our faces, I would've given them a resounding *hell no.*

Yet I stand here, for Dylan, while she paws at these dudes in white pants. What guy wears white pants anyway? She freaks out each time one of them touches her and yells loudly in my ear that she's never washing her hand. I want to remind her that she has other peoples' germs on her because they've touched a lot of people and themselves throughout their performance. Watching Dylan sing the lyrics while I stand stiff-legged, being jostled between her and the girl on the other side of me, is a bit annoying. I should step out into the aisle and allow them more space to get closer, but Dylan would freak.

It's times like this that I want to be different. I want to be in the center of the crowd, jumping up and down and singing along. I want to be able to walk out to the concourse and buy a hotdog or even a t-shirt to remember the night like every other teenager in the country. Why my parents are so strict about money, I'll never know. Both of them work, so where does all their money go to?

When the group leaves the stage, Dylan grabs my hand with the hand she said she was never going to wash, sharing the boy band germs with me. She pulls me through the crowd, saying "excuse me" each time we bump into someone else. Once we clear the row, she turns and faces me.

"Are you having fun?"

"Of course," I lie.

"Isn't the front row the most amazing thing ever?"

"Yeah, it's pretty cool." I will give her that. Being in the front row at a packed concert is definitely an experience. Something I would've never had the opportunity to do if it wasn't for her. "Are you thirsty? You were singing your little heart out."

"I am," she says, pulling us through the entryway. Instead of turning left where the concession stands are, she turns us right and we smack into security. She shows him the lanyards that hang from our necks and he signals for us to go through. She drops my hand as soon as we come to another door with another security guard. With our lanyards shown again, we enter.

The room is bustling with people. I look around and notice it's the group we just watched, the *white pants boy band*. The guys are loud and animated. There's a table full of food that Dylan leads me to. She hands me a plate and takes hers and starts filling it up.

"Are you sure this is okay?"

"Totally, it's part of the package."

I follow behind her, trusting that what we're doing isn't breaking any rules. When our plates are full we find a place to sit down. We're eating just finger foods, but I don't care; everything tastes amazing when you're hungry.

"Do you want to meet the band?" she asks in between bites.

"You go ahead." I don't want to hold her back from enjoying this experience. It's just not for me. She looks at me, her face almost sad. I smile, letting her know everything is okay, but she's not buying it. She stays with me, finishing our snacks.

When my plate is empty she takes it from me and throws them away. When she turns and looks at me, I know she's about to pout so I stand up and follow her to meet the *white pants boy band*.

The girls in front of us gush and make annoying sounds. I poke Dylan in the side. "If you do that, I'm walking home." She laughs and elbows me in the ribs.

It's our turn next. I take a picture of Dylan with the band on her iPhone, but decline when she offers to take mine. My prepaid doesn't even have a camera and I'm not sure I want to remember this as much as she does.

After a few minutes of small talk, the room starts to clear out for the next show. Dylan promises me that I'll *just love* Hadley Carter. I don't want to remind her that she's the one that *just love's* everyone and anything that has to do with music.

I'm simply her companion for the evening.

When we step back into the venue I'm surprised to see more seats filled. Clearly she is far more popular than the *white pants boys*. Dylan moves in between people and back to our seats. We sit on the uncomfortable, yet cushioned seats until the lights go out completely. The crowd roars much louder than before. Both girls and guys are jumping up and down chanting 'Hadley'.

I stand and stare off into the pitch-black stage. Music starts, the crowd gets louder. I can barely see the guitar player but can feel him close to me. It's almost as if they want us blind for this show.

I join in. I can't help it. I start chanting and clapping right along with everyone else. Dylan looks over winks. I may just have a good time after all. I don't think the crowd could get any louder, but the moment the spotlight shines on who I'm assuming to be Hadley, the venue erupts.

Her song starts immediately. She sings softly, all while standing in one spot. Suddenly all the lights come on and she's all over the stage. I don't know what she's singing, but I move to the music. Dylan and I bump hips occasionally, causing her to smile at me.

Hadley is dressed in what looks like a cat woman costume. Guys are reaching for her, but she stands just far enough way that they can't touch her. When she stands in front of me, I sort of want to reach out, but the thought of rejection keeps my hands safely at my side.

My neck hurts from watching her, the constant looking up to follow her around the stage is straining. She plays three songs in her leather contraption before returning in a dress and cowboy boots. Her hair is pulled back and she's sitting on a stool. She looks comfortable and relaxed, like she's not playing in front of thousands of screaming fans.

The show goes on for over an hour. It seems the louder we are the longer she'll stay on stage and we keep cheering. When the venue lights come on and the stage is clear, Dylan grabs my hand and rushes us in the same direction as before.

There is a large group trying to get past the security guard. Many of them yelling Hadley's name down the long hallway, hoping she hears them, I guess. We flash our passes again, this time to a different guard who lets us through. We squeeze by him and walk down the hall where we are directed by another guard.

We enter the door marked Hadley. It's much larger than the previous room and with a lot less people.

"Hadley will be with you guys in a minute." We're told this by the guard at the door. I walk around, looking at wall hangings. There are pictures of other famous people who have come through Jackson on their tours and played here. I take a seat in the corner while Dylan talks with another contest winner.

Hadley comes bursting into the room, sort of like she's still on stage. She greets each of her fans with hugs and introduces them to the girl standing behind her. She acts as if they have all been friends forever and haven't seen each other in years.

Music is turned on and drinks are passed out. I take a can of Coke from the server. I watch as Dylan and Hadley talk, noticing how pretty Hadley is when she's just in a dress and not on stage. She's very short. Her blond hair is almost white and fairly long. It makes me wonder if she's required to keep her hair long so she can do all those crazy hairstyles she had tonight.

Dylan looks over and points at me. I smile shyly and study my Coke can; it's suddenly become very interesting. When I look up, Hadley is looking at me. Our eyes meet and she smiles, causing me to sit up a little straighter. She looks away and whispers something in the ear of her friend. She's watching me the whole time.

Her friend comes over to me, she's probably about to ask me to leave. Maybe I remind her of an ex or something. I try not to look at her as she approaches; instead I'm watching Dylan's back.

"Hey, what's your name?"

I clear my throat. "Ryan Stone."

She extends her hand and we shake. "I'm Alex Graham, Hadley's best friend. I just wanted to say hi since you were sitting over here by yourself. Feel free to mingle or whatever, okay?"

"Okay, thanks."

Alex Graham walks right back to Hadley and leans into her, whispering again. Hadley's eyes catch mine and I look away, feeling completely out of place.

chapter
four

HADLEY

Rushing off stage before my fans are ready for the concert to end does not sit well with me. I hate that the band listens to Ian. I'm the one who is up there singing and putting on the show. They should want to do what I want. But he has rules and they listen only to him.

Alex meets me with a bottle of water that I chug down. She pats my forehead and hands me some lip gloss to apply. No time to freshen up as the local press is waiting. We rush down the hall, fans yelling my name. I want to stop and turn around, but Ian's hand is clamped on my elbow steering me in the direction of the media room.

He drops my arm once the flash bulbs start. Gosh forbid a picture of him cattle-herding me makes the news. He knows my mom will throw a fit. I sit down at the long table, Alex on my right and Ian on my left. Ian points to a reporter and the questions start.

"Hadley, will you be visiting Jackson?"

"Yes, Alex and I plan to visit. Take in a few of the sights while we are here."

"How long will you be in Jackson?" Alex whispers the answer to me. It's not that I don't know, but my schedule is crazy and it's Alex's job to help me remember.

"For at least three days. I will be attending the Johnson Foundation Children's Ball."

"When will we get a new album?"

"That will be early next year," Ian speaks up. Good to know. I was hoping to spend some time overseas before recording a new album. Guess that will have to wait.

"We'll take one more question," Ian says suddenly. I look at him out of the corner of my eye and wonder what he's up to.

"Hadley!" They all yell. I point to a woman in the back.

"Your show was great tonight. Will you and Smith be happy when the tour is over?"

I deadpan and look at Ian, who isn't answering. I don't know what he's playing at, but this question should not be allowed. Not only is there no relationship between Smith and me, but I never talk about my social life.

I look back at the reporter who is smiling. This must be her million-dollar question and it makes me wonder what Smith said during his interview.

I sit forward and clear my throat. "The relationship between Smith and me is strictly professional. Once the tour is over, I'm sure I'll see him at an awards show." I get up and push my chair forward with some force, shaking the table. Alex is on my heels as the questions from the reporters become shouts.

I slam my dressing room door open, my hands clenched. I hear Alex lock the door, giving me time to cool down. It's only a matter of time before Ian comes knocking on the door. I run a brush violently through my hair, until Alex takes it from my hand and directs me to my chair. I sit and she starts brushing.

"You know how he is. The tour is almost over and he needs some headlines."

"At what expense, Alex?"

"He means well. He's just trying to keep you in the spotlight. That's all."

Alex helps me fix my make-up and I change back into a dress with my boots. I want to be comfortable with these few fans, not some stuffy, pissed-off rock star. I sigh when the knocking starts. I know it's Ian and he's either pissed or about to be pissed. He hates meet and greets, doesn't understand why I feel the need to spend time with people beneath me. The more he bitches, the more I have Alex schedule.

Alex opens the door. Ian stands in the doorway, one eyebrow raised. He's asking if I'm ready. I nod and follow him and Jones down the hall. There are still fans lingering behind security. I give them a little wave before disappearing behind another door.

This is how I love a meet and greet. Music is turned on as I enter the room, playing softly in the background. Everything is relaxed. A few fans, milling around talking to each other, enjoy complimentary drinks on me. It's me giving back. Tonight I have four sets of fans who won a chance to meet me from the tickets they purchased and one fan and a lucky guest are here because of a radio trivia game.

I introduce Alex and myself to each of the fans, giving them ample time to ask questions and for us to get to know them. The questions center around touring or what it's like to be on stage. I'm thankful there aren't any personal questions.

"Hi, I'm Hadley and this is my best friend, Alex." I shake the girl's hand in front of me. Her eyes are a bit glazed over and I wonder if I'm about to be attacked.

She shakes her head. "Sorry, I'm Dylan."

"It's nice to meet you. You're my radio winner, right?"

My words make her face light up like she's just won the lottery. This is why it's so important to know your fans. "I am. I'm so glad I won."

"Did you come alone? Wasn't your package for two people?" I always have a concern with someone keeping the extra ticket for themselves and only giving the winner one. It's happened before.

"Oh no, I brought my friend. He's sitting down over there." She turns and points to the guy sitting on a stool in the corner of the room. His eyes are wandering around until he looks right at me, through me. My smile is automatic, nothing forced. He sits up a little straighter before dropping his eyes to his suddenly very interesting can of Coke.

My face falls when he looks away. Why did he do that? When he looked at me, my heart began racing so fast I thought I was going to pass out. Different from the exhilaration I feel on stage. This is real, like the sun shining on just the two of us, our hands a magnetic force field bridging the gap. My palms sweat just thinking about being able to hold his hand. The rush I'm feeling now is like no other. I've never been one to believe in love at first sight. Can it exist after one simple look? I keep staring, hoping that for one brief moment he'll look up, but he doesn't. Can he feel my eyes trying to get him to look at me? I want to know more – no, I need to know more – about this girl's friend. I take a step forward, the gravitational pull too strong for me to resist. Alex's hand comes down on my arm, halting my progress. I turn to Alex. "I have to know him. I have this feeling, Alex. I can't explain it."

"He's very cute," she says, looking over my shoulder. I follow and have to agree. Although cute doesn't describe him fully, I want to say gorgeous and I need to know him.

"Can you find out his name for me?" Alex nods and walks over toward him.

His eyes go wide as Alex approaches. He quickly looks at his friend for help, but she's talking my ear off. I'm not listening, I can't. I'm studying him and his reaction to Alex. He opens his mouth to speak and they shake hands. He looks so nervous and out of place. I want to rush over there and talk to him, just to hear his voice.

Alex comes right back to me, the look on her face is priceless. "His name is Ryan Stone and he's extremely shy," she whispers. I look at him out of the corner of my eye. He's looking at me, but looks away as soon as I make eye contact.

"Excuse us for a minute," I say to his friend. Alex and I move to the side, away from unsuspecting ears. "He's cute, Alex."

"Very. What are you thinking?"

I look back toward Ryan. He's still watching me, but this time doesn't look away. "After party in my suite," I say to Alex without breaking contact with Ryan.

"Ian is going to flip," Alex reminds me. She's right, he will, but I don't care. I want to know who this Ryan is and this isn't the place.

Looking back at Alex, I shrug. "We're here for three days. I want to meet some locals. He can't fault me for being hospitable."

"Oh, sweetie," Alex says as she pulls me into a hug. "He'll fault you for anything that he didn't suggest." Alex chuckles. We talk about who to invite and I say screw it and invite all of them over. Maybe I can let loose tonight.

"Listen up," Alex says loudly. The music is turned down and the chattering stops. "As you know, Hadley loves her fans and is happy you guys came out to the show tonight, so we're extending an invitation for her after-party. If you'd like to keep your evening going, come see me."

Ian storms over to me and grabs my arm, pulling me into the corner. "What are you doing?"

"What?" I ask innocently. "I'm not tired and want to hang out. It gets sort of boring for Alex and me just hanging out with each other."

"You've got to be kidding me. You're Hadley Carter. You don't get to just invite people over to your hotel whenever you want."

I rip my arm out of his grip. "Thanks for reminding me, but in case you've forgotten, I sign your paychecks."

"You pay me to protect you."

"No, Ian, I pay Jones to protect me, *Anal Anna* to do my hair, make-up and pick out my clothes and you to handle my affairs. I'm an adult. If I want to have people come over to a hotel room that I've paid for, I can."

Ian rubs his face, clearly set off by my little temper tantrum. "I don't get you sometimes, Hadley. One minute you are itching to get home and the next you're doing something like this. I'm looking around here and can't fathom how any of these people interest you. Each one is beneath you."

"Really? Is that my uncle or my manager talking?"

"Both."

I look around and try to see the image he's seeing: I see a mom and daughter; girlfriends who are laughing and meeting others, something I've made happen; and I see Ryan, sitting in the corner, content to let his friend bask in meeting a celebrity. I look back at Ian and shake my head.

"I'm sorry, but I don't see what you're seeing. I'm here for three days and if I want to entertain, I'm going to."

Alex signals that we are all set. When I look at her and nod my head toward Ryan she nods and smiles. I'm about to get to know a fan, something I've vowed I'd never do.

"Alex says everyone is ready to leave. So I'd like to go now."

Ian walks away and starts talking animatedly with Jones. His eyes get big as he looks over the people. If anything I should've consulted with him first, but

I wasn't thinking. All I really wanted to do was get Ryan alone so we can talk. Somehow I don't think he'd open up in a room full of girls.

But maybe he'll open up when it's just him and me on my balcony. At least that is what I'm hoping.

chapter
five

When Alex announces that everyone is invited back to Hadley's suite, I groan. I'm not interested in hanging out with people I don't know, but Dylan will want to and I can't let my disposition affect her happiness. She earned this.

I *am* worried about curfew though. My parents are expecting me home at some point and it's already approaching midnight.

Dylan comes bouncing over to me when Alex says it's time to leave. She pulls my hand into hers. The grin on her face must be hurting because it's been permanent since Hadley walked into the room.

We rush to her car, running through the now-empty parking lot. Dylan cranks the radio once she has the car started and pulls out of the spot. I roll down my window and let the breeze wake me up a bit. I can't help but laugh at Dylan; her attitude is infectious.

"You know I'm going to get into trouble," I tell her. Her face drops as she looks at me. She pulls out her phone and presses on the screen.

"Hi, Mrs. Stone. Sorry for waking you, but Ryan and I are really tired so I think we're going to grab a hotel for the night."

My mouth drops as she blatantly lies to my mom.

"Yeah… no, I've got it covered. Okay, see you tomorrow."

Dylan puts down her phone and starts laughing. I'm staring at her, shocked that she just did that.

"There, now you aren't late."

"I can't believe you did that."

Dylan shrugs and looks at me quickly. "I'm willing to do just about anything if it means I can party with Hadley Carter."

"You're freaking crazy, Dylan Ross."

"Yes, but you love me." She drives us to the hotel. It's an expensive one with two valets. Something I've only read about in books. Two men with long black coats and hats open the car doors. One extends his hand, helping Dylan out. The doorman pulls open the main door and smiles as we pass by. I've never had such treatment before.

I follow Dylan up to the front desk. She asks for a room for the night. She pulls out her credit card that her dad gave her. I hate that I can't help her pay. She's always footing the bill for me.

The clerk hands Dylan two room cards and she gives me the spare. Now I can ditch this after-party and hang out in the room. Dylan also gives her name for the list that Alex said would be waiting. She's handed another key and quickly turns for the elevators.

I'm standing in front of gold elevators… gold. When the car dings, signaling its arrival, Dylan starts bouncing on the balls of her feet. She's way too excited. She skips in, causing the other patrons getting in to look at her funny. I shrug and skip in behind her.

We stop on the thirty-fifth floor. I step out first and look left and right. I motion for her that it's safe. She slides against the wall until the next opening, waving her hand that the coast is clear. We started doing this at about the sixth floor, pretending we are spies. I come around the corner and a door opens, causing Dylan to start laughing. She falls into me, gripping my arm, just like the last time she had gotten drunk and I had to babysit her.

We straighten up as an older couple walks by us. Their stern look is enough to keep our faces from cracking under pressure. They watch us as we walk to Hadley's room, probably wondering if we even belong on this floor. Dylan does, but definitely not me.

"I'm only going to stay for a few minutes, okay?" Dylan rolls her eyes as she knocks on the door.

"You'll have fun." I can't respond because the door swings open and a very tall and extremely large man is standing there glaring at us.

"Names?" his voice is deep and rough, like he's been screaming all his life.

Dylan gives him our names and he moves aside to let us in. This room is larger than my house. The people here don't even take up an inch of the space. I don't know if women like this kind of stuff, but I can tell you I'd never decorate my apartment like this; way too much gold.

Dylan spots one of the girls she was talking to earlier and heads toward her. I guess she thinks I'm okay by myself. An older lady walks by and tells me to help myself to food and drinks. I see others eating so I make a plate, grab a soda and sit down away from everyone. Other than the guy at the door I'm the only male in the room.

I'm trying not to watch the clock, but I can't help it. I'm bored and this is just awkward. All these women are giggling and talking fashion and I could really use the sleep. Dylan is in an in-depth conversation so I really don't want to bug her. I pull out my phone and text that I'm heading to the room.

"Leaving so soon?" I turn and find Hadley… a girl I didn't know existed until tonight, behind me. She caught me sneaking out of her party, not that I think she'd miss me.

"I was just going to my room." My hand finds the back of my head but I quickly pull it down remembering how much Dylan hates it when I pull at my hair.

"I didn't get a chance to introduce myself earlier. I'm Hadley Carter," she says extending her hand. When my hand touches her, I feel a jolt, like when you rub your socks on carpet and touch someone to shock them. I drop her hand immediately and put it in my pocket. "Would you like to go outside and talk? I've had a chance to speak to everyone but you."

"Oh, I'm just here with my friend; she's your fan."

"And you're not?"

I feel like I've been caught red-handed in the cookie jar. I didn't mean to offend her. But the look on her face shows that I did.

"I'm—"

"It's okay, we can still talk." I nod for fear of hurting her feelings anymore. My luck, she'd write a song about some rude boy she met in Jackson who didn't like her music but had the nerve to show up at her after-party and eat her food. She turns away and takes a few steps before looking at me from over her shoulder. I step forward and she smiles.

She fixes a plate of snacks and grabs a couple sodas.

"Want me to carry those?" I ask, holding my hands out for the soda. She places them in my hand, her fingertips lingering on my skin a bit longer than normal. I feel the charge again and wonder if she's feeling it too.

She slides open the balcony door and closes it once I've stepped through. I don't know if anyone else has noticed, but the curtains have been drawn so no one can see us out here. Whoever closed them clearly didn't see us walk out.

She sits down, pulling a chair close to her. I set the sodas on the small table and sit down across from her. Our knees are almost touching and close enough that we've created a table for her to place the plate on our knees. I feel this energy pushing me toward her, as if my body is telling me that I need to touch her.

"So, back to my music. You don't like it?"

"No, it's not that. This was the first time I've heard it… or maybe the first time I've actually listened. Your show was really good though."

Hadley's eyes haven't left mine since we sat down. She squints a bit when I tell her this is the first time I've listened to her sing.

"Have you lived under a rock? Sorry, that was rude. I'm just used to everyone being the *biggest* fan, so I don't often run into someone who doesn't listen."

"It's not just your music; I don't listen in general."

This time her eyes widen and her mouth drops even though she keeps her lips sealed. "How can you not listen to music?"

I shrug. "My parents don't like it and I don't have a radio. I mean, I listen when I'm in the car with my friend, but I can't say I pay attention enough to know who I'm listening to."

"Wow, that's just so—"

"Odd, stupid, strange. That pretty much sums up my parents."

Hadley reaches into her pocket and pulls out her phone. Of course it's just like Dylan's. She turns on some music and sets it down on the table.

"Well, your parents aren't here now, are they?"

"No, definitely not."

"So tell me about yourself, Ryan."

I look at her questioningly. "How do you know my name? I didn't introduce myself?"

She bites her bottom lip and looks away from me. Her cheeks turn pink and I can't tell for sure, but I think she's trying not to laugh. "Alex told me," she says without looking at me.

"Oh." I'm not sure how I should feel about that. Do I like it that she asked or what? I'm not sure what I'm supposed to tell her. What does one tell someone when he or she says "tell me about yourself"? Are they looking for a specific answer? "Um, well, Dylan is my best friend. We live in Brookfield, which is about two hours from here. On Monday I'll be a senior in high school."

When I say high school her head snaps up. She studies me as if I'm joking, her eyes moving around my features. My hands rest on the side of the chair and wait for her to say something.

"How old are you?" she asks.

"I'm seventeen."

"When will you be eighteen?"

"In December."

"Oh wow, I didn't think… Crap this isn't good."

The awkwardness increases tenfold. She moves away from me. I scramble to catch the plate before it tumbles to the ground.

"Shit," she says. "I'll be right back."

She gets up, leaving me, with a plate of half-eaten food and her phone playing music.

chapter
six

Why can't things in my life just go as I imagined? Ryan and I getting to know each other, finding out if this connection I'm feeling is real or just my imagination. No, it's not my imagination. The pull is there. I feel it, that magnetic force that people always talk about. I felt it the moment we made eye contact from across the room.

Why does he have to be underage? Eighteen I can deal with, but not seventeen.

I left him sitting on the chair. Just upped and left. He must think I'm rude. I have this party as a front to get to know him. I stop him from leaving, knowing that if he did, I'd never see him again. I would never have the opportunity to hear his voice or experience the feelings going through me right now when he answers my questions. I knew sitting there that I wanted to keep him talking.

Now I stand at the other end of my balcony. My head rests on my hands as I lean against the cold concrete wall – a wall that is currently preventing me from jumping over the side while I figure out what to do. I need to talk to Alex, but she's occupying the guests while I hit on Ryan. Or try to. Maybe he doesn't even like me. Hell, he didn't even know who I was until tonight.

I stare out into the night sky, the stars twinkling as I ask them for some sign on what I should do. Never have I been in a relationship where I've felt this strongly about someone. I should be scared. I should be kicking him out of here and hopping on my bus to get out of dodge.

I know that starting something with him is wrong, but we can be friends. I can be his friend. That's what I tell myself as I walk back toward him. I remind myself that we'll be friends, pen pals or texting buddies. We'll keep things platonic until he's eighteen and if he wants, then maybe we'll share a kiss or hold hands.

Over and over again, I say this as I round the corner and look at him. He sees me and stands up. His short, dark hair is now standing on end, likely from endless pulling, no doubt wondering where the crazed rock star ran off. My fingers like his hair like this. They twitch with desire to run through his locks. I close my eyes to remove the image of my lips pressed against his while he's pulling me close, his hand guiding my leg over his hip.

My mind is saying get over him, but my heart is speaking loud and clear. I need to have him in my life. I want to know him.

With my game face on I take the last few steps back to the chaise lounge. Ryan steps back, his legs bumping into the chair. He wobbles a bit and I reach out to catch him. Big mistake. My hands feel as if they are on fire. It's small and manageable, yet I don't want to let go for fear the sensation will stop. I know I have to. I'm an adult, I very sadly remind myself.

Letting go of his arm, I sit down in my same spot as before. I look at him, my head tilted back as I take in his tall stature, his eyes never leaving mine as he sits back down. He's tense, I can tell, his posture rigid and uncomfortable. I made him this way and now I need to fix it.

"I'm sorry about before, about leaving. That was rude."

"It's okay." He says this so politely it makes me want to pull him into my arms and hug him.

"No, it's not." I lean forward so that I can peer into his eyes. They're a beautiful combination of blue and green. I can't help but want to get lost in them for hours.

I straighten when Ryan clears his throat. He looks down, clearly shy or surprised by my gawking. I need to control myself. I'm a professional and need to act like one. I sit back and extend my legs in the chaise, turning so I can look at him. I want to tell him to make himself at home, but he doesn't seem like the type that would do that.

"Who is this singing?" he asks, effectively breaking the awkward silence. I pick up my phone and show him my picture. The song is a ballad I did two years ago. It never went anywhere, but it's always been one of my favorites.

"It's me."

"You're very pretty." He says this so quietly I almost didn't hear him. His cheek turns a pleasing shade of pink. It's a good thing I'm this far away from him because I want to run my fingers along his cheekbone. I want to feel the heat from his blush.

There is something seriously wrong with me. I tell myself to snap the hell out of it and come back down to reality. Friends, Hadley… that is all you can be. There will be no touching of any kind.

"Thank you." I say this in hopes to open some conversation, anything to hear his voice.

"You weren't supposed to hear that," he mumbles his reply. Ryan mirrors my position on his chaise, turning his body to look at me. I'm lost in his beauty. I hope he doesn't mind me staring because I don't think I can stop.

"I think you're handsome." He looks away. He starts picking at the hem of his shorts and I fear I've said the wrong thing. Everything has come so natural to me until now. "Is that the wrong thing to say?"

Ryan shrugs. "No one has ever said that."

"Girls don't tell you that you're hot?"

"No, definitely not."

"That's such a shame."

Ryan looks away from me and I don't like it. I get up and move to his chaise. I sit toward the middle, where his knees are bent. With my legs under me, I lean toward him so that we're touching. He doesn't pull away or shift so we aren't touching. But he's still not looking at me.

"I'm sorry for embarrassing you. I just call things like I see it."

Ryan shakes his head and stalls briefly before turning back to me. His eyes are focused and in control of my beating heart. How can one person make me feel this way after only knowing him for such a short time?

"You have a very nice voice. I like listening to you."

"I'll take that compliment any day, especially if it's coming from you." I expect Ryan to look away, but he doesn't. He holds my gaze, driving home the fact that I'm already in too deep. There is no backing away from this.

For a moment I can see myself leaning in, him meeting me half way. Just a small touch of the lips, enough to quench my desire, is all I need. I imagine him pushing his hands into my hair, capturing me with soft lips.

I can hear muffled sounds, his lips are moving, but I can't make out the words. I clear my head of the lust-filled images. "I'm sorry, what did you say?"

"I said, do you like what you do?"

"Oh yeah, I do actually. Performing has always been a passion for me. I started in county fairs when I was about twelve and got noticed when I was fifteen. What about you, what's your passion?"

"To leave Brookfield," he says with such sadness it makes me wonder why he'd want to leave.

"How long have you lived there?"

"All my life," he says. His fingers go back to pulling on his shorts. For the first time I get a good look at him. His shorts aren't new and the edges are frayed. He wears generic sneakers that look old. His black dress shirt is the only thing that looks new.

"Why don't you like it?"

Ryan adjusts so he's sitting up a bit more, but doesn't move his leg from touching my arm. I like that he made sure we were still touching. "What's to like? The town is divided. Half is these upper-class mansions and the other half is industrial with a working mill and small clapboard homes that were built to house the millworkers."

Without even asking I know that is where Ryan lives and, while that would matter in my group of friends (Alex not included), it doesn't matter to me. If he lived under a bridge I'd still want to know him.

"So what do you want to do when you graduate?"

"I'm going to leave. Get on a bus and not look back. I want my life to be different from my parents'. My dad, he expects me to start at the mill when I finish school and work my way into becoming the fourth-generation Stone crowned foreman, but that's not me." Ryan gets up and moves over to the wall, peering over the side. I spin so that my eyes are on him, afraid to miss a moment.

"I want to live in a place that is loud and busy. Somewhere where I can walk down the street at night and not need a flash light."

"Like New York City?" I ask, hoping the answer is yes.

"Exactly like New York City or Las Vegas. Any place as long as the town never sleeps. I get so tired of listening to the cicadas and the coyotes in the middle of the night. I want to hear horns honking and people yelling."

"That can be annoying too," I add. Even though I love the city and wouldn't want to live any place else, there is something to say for the solitude of a small town.

Ryan turns and looks at me, his arms resting on the wall. If I was brave, I'd stand and walk up to him and live out one of the many fantasies I've started to have about him, but I'm not there yet. Ryan pushes off the wall and comes back over to the chaise we've been sharing, albeit for a few brief minutes. He sits, his legs touching mine. He places his hand down on the cushion, centimeters from my bare leg and looks at me.

"I've never met someone famous before. Why are you spending the night out here with me when you could be inside with your fans?"

chapter
seven

RYAN

I don't know where this small bit of confidence came from, but watching her sit there, the way the moonlight is shining off of her, makes me want to be next to her. Never have I had the notion to sit this close to a girl. No, that's not right, Hadley is anything but a girl. She's a woman and she wants to talk to me. For the life of me I can't fathom why.

Someone like Hadley Carter can have anyone she wants. She's having this after-party and yet she's out here on her balcony keeping someone like me company. For all I know she's taking pity on me because I was alone and about to leave. I suppose leaving her party would've made her look like a fool.

I'm close to her, so close that I can touch her if I wanted. I could move my fingers slightly and let her skin light mine on fire. I want to ask her what it feels like for her when we touch because for me it's as if her skin is full of electricity and my body wants to know what it's like to be touched by her repeatedly.

Hadley shifts, her knee brushing lightly against my fingers. I don't move, afraid that she'll notice. There is a light tingling sensation coursing from her to me. I look down, briefly. She moves closer.

"I shouldn't tell you this since we just met, but when I saw you across the room I knew I had to know you."

"Is that a line you use to pick up people?" I blurt this out without thinking. Talking to a beautiful woman is all new to me. I know I've offended her when she pulls away from me, making sure we are no longer touching. Hadley adjusts herself so she's turned away from me. I can no longer see her soulful brown eyes, just her golden hair, which is pulled tight into a ponytail.

"I'm sorry," I say, hoping to diffuse the situation. Normally my response would be to clam up and ignore the person next to me. Find something to tinker with or just look away. But with Hadley, for some reason I hate knowing that I've upset her and I don't even know her. It's not like I'll see her after tonight.

"It's okay. I'm sure that is what a lot of people think of celebrities." She turns back, gracing me once again with her beauty. "But no, Ryan, it wasn't a line. I don't show emotion because a lot of people want to take advantage of that weakness. I've never done a lot of the things I've done tonight."

"Like what?" I'm asking purely out of curiosity.

"Like throw a party so I could get to know someone." Hadley adjusts so her leg is touching my fingers again. They twitch when her skin touches mine. If she notices, she doesn't say anything. I swallow hard.

"Is that what you did tonight?"

Hadley nods, leaning closer. "I wanted to talk to you away from everyone else. Earlier, you were in the corner and we were pressed for time, so I decided to have this party. The only problem is I only wanted to invite you, but that would've looked awkward. Would you have come?"

"No." I shake my head.

"Why not?"

I run my hand through the back of my hair. I'm not really sure how to answer her without hurting her feelings. "I came here with Dylan." This is the answer I give her, which is apparently the wrong one because we're no longer touching.

"I didn't realize Dylan was your girlfriend. I thought she said she was your friend."

I move closer, determined to keep touching her. "She's my best friend, but we aren't dating or anything like that. I don't have a girlfriend, never have."

I wish I hadn't said that because the look on her face is definitely one of pity. Her eyes study me, likely curious as to why I would say something stupid like that. I turn away, only to have her fingertips pull my chin toward her. I should've told her that I haven't found anyone interesting enough to spend time with aside from Dylan and she's the only one because she made the effort. The rest of the girls just look at you, wondering if you're going to be the one that they end up with after a prom night mishap.

"I don't care that you've never had a girlfriend."

I have to turn away so she doesn't see me blush. She laughs quietly, which in turn makes me laugh. For having just met her, I'm feeling like I've known her for years.

"Are you a good boy, Ryan, or is there a bit of bad boy hiding in there?"

This question takes me by surprise and I play with the hem of my shorts thinking about how I'm going to answer. I look at her and try not to smile, but have a feeling I'm failing terribly.

"I'm a good boy. I do as I'm told."

"Good boys are nice." I think she's flirting with me, but I'm not sure. But the way her voice changed when she said that makes me think that she is. I wish I wasn't so lost when it comes to girls.

Nice? I hope she's not one of those girls who allow the men in her life to treat her like crap. I see the way my dad treats my mom and that's not something I'd ever want to do.

"But there is something definitely appealing when that nice boy brings out the bad that he has buried deep inside."

I nod and make a note of what appeals to girls if I'm ever faced with a decision on whether to be good or bad.

"Tell me, what would a dream date be like for you, staying at home or on the beach?"

I rub my hands over my shorts, wiping away the sweat. "Beach, definitely the beach. I try not to spend a lot of time at home. Can I ask you a question?"

"Yes." She says this with a smile like this is the best thing she's ever done.

"Do you like guys who dress casual or preppy?"

"I like both. Casual is nice because it shows their relaxed side, but there's something sexy about a guy who dresses up." I'm curious if she likes how I dress. I'm neither casual nor smart. I'm a hand-me-down kid who can't afford to buy jeans at a discount store. I can't even believe she's talking to me. Can't she see I'm nothing?

"Okay, my turn. Do you prefer girls in sweats or dresses?"

I look at her and her long legs and know the answer. "Dresses. I like legs. I mean, if you have legs you should show them off, especially if they're like yours. Not that I'm constantly looking at your legs. Okay, I'll shut up now." I can't believe I actually said that out loud and want to internally hit myself for my inability to control my verbal filter. I turn away from her so she doesn't see the embarrassment showing all over my face. Dylan has always said that I turn a lovely girly shade of pink when I say something stupid.

Hadley reaches out, her fingers caressing my chin. She turns my chin toward her. Her eyes are smiling, if that's even possible. "It's your turn to ask a question."

I swallow and hate that she's let go of my face. "Do you prefer singing songs or writing them?"

"I prefer singing. I'm not very good at writing down how I'm feeling, so singing is much easier for me."

I wouldn't have thought that about her. She seems pretty expressive. I could probably write a song about how I'm feeling. I'd have to title it 'Confused, Lost and Freaking the Hell Out' because I have this gorgeous girl sitting next to me and talking to me and not because she has to, but because she wants to.

"Do you like girls with long or short hair?"

I look at her and know my answer is based on what I'm looking at.

"Definitely long, but without all that crap that girls put in it, ya know? I think I like the loose and natural look."

Hadley runs her hand through her hair and for the first time ever, I want to reach out and touch someone's hair. I can feel my hand twitching and it takes all I have in me to stop it in fear of rejection. I need a distraction so I decide to ask her about her career.

"If you weren't a famous singer, what would you be?"

Hadley thinks about this for a long time before answering and I use this time to study her. How she scrunches her nose while she contemplates her answer, how her fingers delicately play with the chain she has around her neck and how I really like the look of her perfectly formed lips. I can't stop looking at them as she starts to answer.

"Oh wow. I'm not sure. I've been performing for so long I don't think I had the aspirations others did, but maybe a teacher like my mom."

"You'd be a good teacher."

"Why do you say that?" she's giggling when she says this. I like that I've made her laugh.

"Because you've already taught me a few things like how to find out what girls like and how to talk a bit more."

Hadley's smile turns serious. She leans forward, her eyes traveling from mine to my mouth and back. This is about to be my first kiss and all I can think is that I should be the one making the first move. I lean forward, hoping to meet her half way. A throat clears behind us, she turns and I save myself from my face hitting her shoulder.

The server is standing there with a plate of food and drinks. It's amazing how they just know the right time to interrupt something that maybe shouldn't happen even though I wanted it.

The party in Hadley's suite has quieted down, but neither of us wants to see what they were all up to. Each time the door opens I fear it's Dylan coming to take me away. I know I shouldn't feel like that, but I'm having fun. Okay, not fun, but I like that I'm able to sit out here and learn. Hadley isn't judging me like the other girls in school do. She isn't giving me sideways glances or snubbing her nose at me. Last year I tried to talk to this girl, Jenna, but she wouldn't give me the time of day. I heard her tell some of our classmates that she didn't date beneath her. I knew what it meant and it hurt. Dylan tells me I'm good-looking, but I guess sometimes that's not enough.

Until now.

I yawn and stretch my arms up over my head. Hadley takes this opportunity to poke me in the stomach. I grab her hand quickly and her fingers lace with mine like it's the most natural thing to do. I look down at our conjoined hands and realize that I don't want to let go.

"Are you tired?"

"I am," she replies. "But I don't want this night to end. I'm not sure what the morning will bring."

I pick up her phone and look at the time. It's about three in the morning. The sun is going to be coming up soon. I'm curious as to why Dylan never came out here to get me. Did she even know I was gone?

"I can leave you if you want to go to sleep." I offer this solution, praying she'll say no.

"No, but I have an idea." If her idea is letting go of my hand, I'm not a fan. She stands quickly and walks to the back of the chaise lounge and pulls the top portion down until it's reclined. She's back before I can comprehend what is going on. She's kneeling in front of me, before she sits down. She pulls her dress down as far as it will go. I wonder if she's cold and wish I could offer her a jacket, but I just have on my dress shirt.

I watch as she lays down, her eyes on me the whole time. She's on her side, on the edge, leaving space for me. I unbutton my shirt and pull it off, thankful that I'm wearing a t-shirt underneath. I lay it across her legs before turning on my side to lie next to her. She immediately pulls my hand into hers and sets them between us.

"The sun is almost up."

"That means the night is almost over and I'm definitely not ready."

"Me neither," I say. "Can I try something?"

"Sure."

I sit up slightly and pull her up a bit with me. I slip my arm under her head and she falls into the curve of my elbow. I lie back down and pull her closer until her head is resting on my shoulder. For the first time I'm holding a girl in my arms. Something I've only dreamed of.

"Is this okay?" I only ask for confirmation. She seems very comfortable with me holding her like this. I know I like it, I just hope she does too. I dread the sun coming up because that means everything ends. At least right now I feel like I'm someone special with her.

"This is perfect," she says, wrapping her arm around my waist. I set my head on top of hers and hold on for this emotional ride I'm about take myself on. I already know I'm going to miss her tomorrow when I have to face reality.

I fight the urge to close my eyes, but it's a losing battle. I want to prolong this night because I know that when the sun rises, it's all over and tonight has been one of the best nights of my life. She's going to go on to her superstar life and I'll return to the dirt road and house that I share with my parents. School will start and I'll just be another body in the cesspool of high school. Back to wearing clothes from the second-hand store and eating lunch at a table in the corner.

Hadley will return the stage and find herself a man that is capable of and deserving of being seen with her. I know I shouldn't be thinking like this, but I can't help it. What if... what if *I* was Hadley's boyfriend? Images of us standing side by side while she gets her photos taken flood my mind. They call her name and she looks only at me while flashes of white light go off repeatedly.

Her image quickly changes to dust as realization slaps me in the face. I can never be that guy on her arm. She'd be embarrassed by me. She needs someone who can complement her in every way and that is just something I can't do.

Tonight is a fantasy. Something everyone dreams about, but only few can enjoy. No one will ever believe me. Not that I have anyone to tell. Dylan probably knows, but she won't say anything. Or maybe she will. For all I know she could be jealous that I've spent all this time outside with Hadley while she's been stuck inside. It didn't escape my attention that only the server came out here. No other fans or her best friend.

I rest my head upon her and breathe in her scent. I don't know what perfume she's wearing and I can't describe what I smell. I've never been this close to a girl to learn all the things I should know about them. Seventeen years old and I've never been kissed. You'd think that is something a girl would say, but sadly that is my life. Having Hadley in my arms is surreal. I close my eyes and think about what it would be like to do this every night.

chapter
eight

I have never felt so warm before in my life. The early summer heat is flickering down on my arms and back. I open my eyes carefully so the sun doesn't blind me. I'm met with a white shirt as it stares back at me. My eyes trail up, squinting as the sun becomes brighter. I slowly emerge from his cocoon. He looks peaceful and content.

I would've never imagined him as the man he portrayed himself to be last night, especially when he took off his shirt and used it as a blanket to keep me warm. No one has ever done something like that for me. And he did it after only knowing me for a few hours.

Looking at Ryan, I've come to the conclusion that I need him in my life. I definitely want to spend time with him because last night was not enough. I'm not sure how to make that happen, but I will. Ian is going to flip. The age difference alone is enough to cause issues, but I don't care. Ian is going to have to accept that Ryan is my friend… for now.

I shift closer hoping to remember what his body feels like against mine. He sleeps so softly as if he doesn't have a care in the world, but I know that's not true. He has dreams, even if it's just to move to a city, they are still dreams he should follow. My hand inches higher up his back and I wonder at what point in the past few hours did my hand move under his shirt and if he minded. I know that I don't. Feeling his soft skin and the outline of his shoulders against my fingertips drives my thoughts to places they shouldn't go. He whimpers softly and I remove my hand, not wanting to wake him. I'm enjoying the calmness that he's sharing with me.

My hand doesn't stay still for long as I find his hair. It's a bit shaggy, the in-style right now with teens. He at least has that going for him, aside from the fact that he's gorgeous and makes my heart flutter every other second. My fingers push through his mane, massaging his scalp. He adjusts, leaning somewhat into my hand. I feel his body relax as he tries to move closer to me. His hand grips my hip tightly. I realize that this is turning him on. I know I should stop, but I can't. Knowing I can do this to him, for him, encourages me.

Has anyone ever done this for him? It's a question plaguing my mind, but also one I don't want to know the answer to. I know he said he hasn't had a girlfriend, but what about a fling or a hook-up? I want to be the one who fulfills every fantasy that he has. Ryan buries his head into the crook of my neck, his nose skimming along until he's rested by my ear. If I had any reservation about him, it's gone. I thought he'd wake up and wonder where he is, but he knows. I have to fight the urge to take over, to guide him. I know nothing can happen. I have to remind myself over and over again. It has to become my mantra.

"Can I try something?" he whispers, clearly awake and aware of what I've been doing. I nod, unable to find my voice. I don't know what he's going to try, but I'm eager and afraid all at once to find out.

His lips touch just below my ear in the softest of kisses. He does it again and this time his fingers spread over my back, holding me to him. I know I should stop him. My mind is yelling for me to put on the brakes, but my heart is screaming for me to turn just slightly so that when his lips touch me again they will be pressed against mine in what's surely going to be the most sinful kiss I'll ever experience.

I do as my heart commands, turning slightly. When his lips touch mine, he pulls back. His eyes are questioning me. I offer only the smallest of smiles and nod, hoping he understands that he can continue. That I want – no, I need – him to continue. I won't be able to make the first move, but I can't resist him if he does.

Ryan's kiss is soft and hesitant. He's unsure of himself. As much as I want to take over, I don't. I want to learn with him as he explores. He's shaking, his nerves trying to get the best him. He kisses me once, twice, before pulling back. His eyes shine in the early morning sun as he stares at me. No words, but I can see the emotion written across his face. My fingers leave his hair and trail down his face, along the scruff of his cheek.

"Was that okay?" he asks shyly.

"Yeah, it was."

"Can I kiss you again?"

Ryan doesn't wait for me to answer, not that he needed to, my eyes and body are telling him yes even though my head is screaming no, but the moment his lips touch mine again my brain shuts up. I could get lost in him with these delicate caresses. He's not intrusive or needy, nor is he slamming his tongue into my mouth and demanding attention.

His large hand cups my face, holding it to his as his lips work over mine. I need to feel more, but I don't dare break him of his trance. A throat clears behind me. He drops his hand suddenly and moves as far away as he can get from me. The chaise is still holding him close enough that I can feel his body heat, although I can tell that he'd rather be across the room from me than get caught kissing and I don't blame him, but for other reasons. I'm sad and extremely disappointed that we were interrupted.

I turn and find Alex standing just far enough way. I sit up and adjust the top of my dress and pat down my hair. I don't even want to know what I look like right now.

"Good morning." My voice is hoarse and tired from singing last night. My usual home remedy of hot honey tea did not happen, but I wouldn't change anything that happened in its place.

"Thought you'd like to know that breakfast is here and that Dylan is looking for you, Ryan."

I sneak a glance at Ryan. He's a statue. I need to talk to him, tell him that I want to see him again, tonight, tomorrow and all the time in between.

"We'll be in soon."

I wait until Alex is behind closed doors. Once the door is shut, Ryan is off the chaise. He picks up his shirt and puts it on hastily. His fingers fumble with the buttons. I can't stand watching him like this. I stand up and wrap my hands around his. He stills, his head hanging low. I so want to look into his beautiful eyes, but he's not looking at me.

I push each button into their respective slots; stalling the closer I get to his chest.

"Ryan, please look at me," I all but beg.

His head rises slightly. There is torment in his eyes. I rise up and kiss him softly. His hand finds purchase on my hip and pulls me closer. My hands, flat on his chest, move to his neck and then the back of his hair. He pulls away first, releasing his hold on me, much to my dismay.

"I sh-should go."

"Can I say something first?"

Ryan's hand finds the back of his head. He rubs his hair, pulling most forward. "You don't have to say anything."

"Yes, I do." I step forward, hoping he won't step back. He looks at me briefly before looking at the door leading to the hotel room. "I'm just going to cut to the chase. I want to see you again before I leave."

Ryan's eyes are sharp when he looks at me. There's a hint of a smile forming, but he's fighting it. "You do?"

"I do." I step even closer so that we are touching. His knees are touching my thighs, our hands brushing against each other. "I'm not ready for you to leave, but I know you have to."

"I don't know what I'm supposed to say."

"Tell me you'll come back tonight and stay with me." I'm asking for trouble, I know this.

"I'd be stupid to tell you no because I want to see you, but I'm just me and you're you. You can have anyone you want."

He's right, I can and have, but it's always the same. I want something different, real. Ryan can offer me so much more than any of the other guys interested in me. He can bring me serenity when I need it with just his touch.

"I have a charity ball tonight. Will you accompany me?"

Ryan shakes his head adamantly. "I can't afford clothes like that, Hadley."

I have to tread lightly because I know this is a sensitive subject. "Because I'm asking on short notice, I'll have a tux sent up. I'm not asking because I need a date, I'm asking because I need to spend more time with you."

Ryan looks around as he shuffles his feet. He looks at the ground before setting his eyes back on mine. "Dylan is my transportation. I can't offer her gas money. I'm sorry, I really am, but I'm not the guy who can just spend money like you're used to. I don't even know what I'm doing here. I mean… we spent the night together and I kissed you and it felt like the best thing ever and now you're asking me to come back. I'm confused."

Ryan's little monologue takes me by surprise. I didn't think he'd question everything at once and I'm not sure I'm ready to tell him exactly what's going on in my head. Maybe after tonight, after he's held me on the dance floor.

"I'll send a car or I'll pick you up—"

"You think I want you to see where I live? No thanks." Ryan starts to walk away. I run and jump in front of him.

"I'm sorry, Ryan. I don't have the right answer except I need to see you tonight. I'm just asking for one more night."

chapter
nine

Silence.

Completely uncomfortable and awkward silence as Dylan speeds down the highway. Her posture is rigid, nothing like her usual self. The music is off and for the first time I wish we were listening to it. I've taken to looking out the window since she's not talking or even singing.

She hasn't said much. She doesn't need to. Her eyes said it all when she saw Hadley and I walk in from outside. If I didn't know better I'd think that I hurt her, but I don't know how that could be. I didn't approach Hadley or even want to come to the concert.

Although I'm glad I did.

My phone vibrates in my pocket. I hesitate for a moment before pulling it out. My movements catch Dylan's attention. I see her look at me out of the corner of her eye. I flip it open and look at the message from Hadley. I can't help but smile at the heart she added at the end of her text.

"Is she going to pay your phone bill?" Dylan asks in a very sarcastic tone.

I shut my phone without replying. "Are you talking to me now?"

Dylan shrugs. She maneuvers her car to our exit and makes a turn taking us away from Brookfield.

"Where are we going?"

"To talk."

"We've had two hours to talk." I look behind me and shake my head. "You want to talk now that we're five minutes from home?"

She doesn't answer me, just keeps driving until she reaches the old abandoned high school. The one our parents graduated from years ago before our new state-of-the-art school was built on the hill overlooking the town.

Dylan shuts off her car and rests against the headrest. Her eyes are closed, but her lips are moving. I can't tell if she's talking to herself or singing whatever song is playing in her head. Either way, she's not talking to me.

I open the door and get out. She says something, but I slam the door and start walking. I'll walk home from here. Anything to get away from whatever she has going on in her head. When I hear her door open I walk a bit faster.

"Where are you going?" she yells. The gravel behind me crunches. She's coming after me. We've never fought before and I'm honestly not sure how to handle her when she's quiet like this.

"Home, Dylan." I say, turning around to face her. She stops short, putting her hands on her hips. She doesn't look at me, but past me, toward the road.

"I just… I'm just trying to process everything. It's…you ran off with Hadley Carter last night. I sat up waiting for you and you never made it to the room. At first I thought you got lost so I went back up and her friend, Alex, said you guys were still talking. Who talks all night long?"

"I guess we do." I shrug and stuff my hands into my pockets. I feel my phone resting there. I'm almost desperate to pull it out and see if she's texted me again. I told her more secrets in one night than I've told Dylan and I've known her for years. But with Hadley things just feel differently, like I'm supposed to know her.

When she asked for my number I didn't tell her it was a prepaid phone. I told myself that I'll pick up an extra shift or mow some more lawns to keep my phone stocked with minutes. I'll do whatever I can to talk to her, even if it's just once a week.

"That's the thing. When you walked in, her hair was a mess. It looked like… you and her…" Dylan looks away, maybe she's embarrassed. "Did you do something with her?"

My gaze had been on Dylan until now. I look away, not sure how I want to answer that question. It's really none of her business. I definitely don't ask her what she does with guys so why should I tell her about me and Hadley? Hell, I can't even believe most of it happened. But I definitely know I kissed her first. I made that move and she didn't turn me down or away. She accepted it and wanted more.

"You're avoiding my question."

"No, I'm not sure what you want me to say."

Dylan steps closer, her hands balled into fists. I know I'm missing something. It wouldn't be the first time she's called me dense or dumb. All boys are dumb, she says. Her eyes are searching for a sign, anything to tell her what she wants to know. The only problem is that I don't know girls. I don't understand the facial expression or the dramatic sighs they let out every other minute. It's not like I can ask my dad; he just pushes a book in front of me and tells me the answer is in there… somewhere.

"I didn't realize you even knew who she was."

"I didn't, Dylan. I was about to leave the party when she stopped me. We went outside and started talking. It was better than sitting there by myself all night long."

"You talked all night long?"

"Mostly, I don't know." I hate being questioned. My hand finds the back of my hair as I walk away from Dylan. People wonder why I choose to stay home. Simply put, solitude in my bedroom, surrounded by the dingy white walls is better than being analyzed under a microscope because I spoke to a girl all night long.

"How do you not know?"

I shake my head, wishing she'd let this go. I don't want to talk about what Hadley and I did out on the balcony. I'd rather remember the way I held her in my arms or how she slept on my shoulder. How we didn't need blankets. How kept each other warm. I don't want to cheapen my memories of being brave enough to kiss her. My first kiss and I experienced it with a beautiful woman who wanted me to kiss her, repeatedly.

"Are you not going to answer me?"

"I don't know, D. I don't want to talk about what happened."

"Why not?" she asks, moving closer to me. "You're my best friend. We tell each other everything."

No, she tells me everything. I sit and listen and nod when it's appropriate. I've never had anything to tell her and I'm not sure I want to start now. Besides, what if Hadley doesn't want anyone to know what we did.

"You tell me everything. I've never had anything to tell."

"So nothing happened between you and Hadley Carter?"

I shake my head.

"You spent all night with her, on a balcony where none of us could see what was going on and *nothing* happened?"

I shake my head. This time I bite my tongue to keep from speaking out. I hate lying, but protecting Hadley seems more important right now.

Dylan sighs as she looks away. She turns away and starts walking back to her car. I think she's upset. I guess she has a right to be. I did end up ditching her at the party in favor of Hadley. I just wanted to be with her, she made me feel… special. For the first time, I felt wanted.

I walk back to the car, slowly. I'm waiting for Dylan to speed away leaving me standing here in a cloud of dust. When I reach for the door, the car starts. I hesitate. I'd like to think she won't pull away, but I've seen others do it and it always makes her laugh so maybe this time she's thinking she'd try it with me.

I open the door and jump in, causing her to laugh. I start laughing, which eases the tension in the car. She pulls out and heads to my parents. The quick drive seems to happen so much faster. I'm dreading the moment I walk in and hope that only my mom is home. When she turns onto my dirt road, I see both my parents out front. This is not good.

I give Dylan a silent goodbye as I slip out of her car. My mom smiles softly at me. Her long blond hair is nothing like Hadley's. Where hers is full, my mom's lays limp upon her back as if there's no life there. Her brown eyes are hidden behind dark, chunky glasses. I've told her many times to get contacts because I think she's beautiful, but she mutters something about being vain and leaves the room.

My dad comes around the front of his truck. His coveralls are stained with grease. He's wringing his hands together with an old towel. His blue eyes bore into me. I have to look away, breaking eye contact and remembering that I'm almost eighteen and I'll be leaving soon. My intention is to stay until graduation but I may not make it.

"Hi," I say meekly. My dad scares the living shit out of me and I don't want to cross him. The way he's looking at me makes me think I'm about to be told to go out back and pick my own stick for an ass beating.

My mom looks over and smiles. I wish she'd smile more. Somehow I think when they started dating she expected a bit more out of their relationship, but no, Joe Stone was destined to stay in Brookfield and follow in his daddy's footsteps. I don't know what my mom wanted to be, but it couldn't be a receptionist at a small construction company. I'm sure she had dreams.

"I'm just going to go shower."

"Hold up," my dad barks out. I stop immediately, afraid to move a muscle. "You have a curfew and you missed it. I know your mom gave you permission to attend the concert, but this other crap you pulled doesn't fly. You're grounded for a week. The list of chores is on the counter."

I knew I'd have some sort of punishment when I got home, but I wasn't expecting this. I nod as I walk into the house and head straight for the bathroom. I take my allotted five minutes and wish they weren't home so maybe I could sneak another three minutes. In and out as fast as I can and into my room before my dad comes down the hall. I slip into clean boxers, shorts and a t-shirt and lie down. I know I have chores to do, but I need a moment to figure out what I'm going to do tonight.

chapter
ten

"Stop pacing."

I turn and glare at Alex. I can't stop. I'm anxious and nervous. More nervous than the first time I went out on stage at twelve. Performing is second nature, almost like sleeping. But this… this decision has so many ramifications – not only for me, but for Ryan – and I can't help but feel my heart in my throat right now.

When he texted and told me he was grounded I wanted to cry. I did cry. I also screamed into my pillow and kicked my feet. Only when he texted back saying he'd do something he had never done before did I start to smile.

And now I'm pacing. My hands are red from the constant pulling that I'm doing on them. I should sit, but I'm afraid I'll wrinkle my dress. All I want is to see him again.

"You really like him, don't you?" Alex asks as she places her hands on my shoulders in an effort to calm me down. I look at Alex and admire how beautiful she is. Tonight she's wearing a light brown mermaid-style dress with a chocolate brown bodice. The contrast with her skin tone is perfect. Her long, dark hair is swept up into a French twist with just minimal make-up highlighting her eyes. I'm in awe of how natural she looks tonight.

"I do. I can't explain it, Alex. It's almost like the sun is shining on me for the first time. Looking at him from across the room the other night was one thing, but talking to him or when we touched for the first time, it's like I burst into flames."

"Are you going to ask him to finish the tour with you?" she asks this jokingly. My face deadpans and hers morphs into nothing less than horror. "What is it?"

I shake my head. "I'm in so much trouble."

"Why? Did you have unprotected sex?"

"No, nothing like that, although with what I'm feeling right now I probably wouldn't have told him no. But we can't do anything like that, at all."

"Does he have a girlfriend or a wife?"

I look at Alex with tears forming in my eyes. She dabs them gently before they spill over and ruin my make-up. "He's only seventeen, Alex."

Alex doesn't need to tell me what she's thinking. I can see it on her face. I imagine that is what my face looked like when Ryan told me, but everything told me to forget that he's not yet of age and still be a part of his life. I can wait. I can be patient.

"Hadley –"

"I know, Alex," I interrupt her. "Believe me, I know, but I can't be away from him. I just can't. He makes me feel…" I cover my face with my hands and fight the tears. Her arms wrap around me. She's soothing me even though she knows I'm making a huge mistake.

"This can become dangerous, sweetie. You're an adult and should know better, but I understand the feelings, sometimes they're so strong you just can't ignore them," she whispers into my ear.

I nod because she's right. If I ignore them not only am I denying myself happiness, but I'll be hurt and sad and can see myself withdrawing from my life. "I have to have him in my life," I mumble from behind my hands.

"How far did you guys go last night?" she asks as she steps around me, pulling my hands away from my face.

If it was anyone but Alex asking, I'd punch them. I know she's asking because she's my best friend and that's what best friends do.

"Nothing at first, just holding hands and I fell asleep on him. I couldn't help it. But in the morning, he kissed me and I wanted it so bad. I didn't stop him, I couldn't." I want to look away from her, but don't want her to think I'm ashamed of what happened with Ryan, because I'm not. If I had to do it all over again, I would. I wouldn't hesitate.

"You need to be careful, Hadley. I'm not going to give you a tongue lashing because you'll end up getting that from Ian when he finds out. Besides, I'm your best friend and I like seeing your face light up when you talk about him."

I pull her into a fierce hug. "Thank you."

She taps me on the shoulder, I look at her and she points. I turn and there he is, dressed head to toe in black with the black bowtie hanging loosely as if we were just returning home after a long night. Alex releases me and walks over to Ryan. His eyes go wide as she reaches for his neck.

"Let me fix this for you," she says so sweetly that I want to hug her again.

We could have a love-in and I'd be happy missing the party just for that. I stifle my laugh as she tugs and straightens the tie for Ryan. He stands there, stock still, probably afraid to move.

"There, now you're perfect." She turns to me and winks. "I'll just be outside the door."

Ryan watches me as I watch Alex leave. Once the door is shut, I move to him, faster than I mean to, but I need to touch him. It's been under ten hours and I've missed him so much. My hand reaches for his, his fingers interlocking with mine. I pull him gently to me. He almost stumbles into me before he catches himself.

"Sorry," he says. He's biting his lower lip, trying not to smile.

"Were you trying to tackle me?"

"Maybe." He shrugs and looks away before I catch the smile. I reach up and pull his face toward me so I can see him.

"I would've caught you."

"You already did."

I want to kiss him, desperately. My eyes go from his eyes to his mouth and back again. This time he does smile, but not the '*I got a puppy*' smile, but the '*Yeah, she's my girl*' smile. And I definitely like being on the receiving end of that one.

"So what did you do?" I've been dying to ask him since earlier. All he said was to keep the plan as we had it.

"I snuck out. My parents, they don't check on me, haven't in years, so I figured why not? You wouldn't happen to know how a car ended up in front of my house, would you? One that just so happened to have this tuxedo and invite?" Ryan pulls the ball invitation out of his coat pocket and shakes it.

"I haven't a clue about the car," I say while trying to fight a grin. "I can't believe you snuck out. I don't want you to get into trouble over me."

Ryan leans in. "Hmm… I heard that you like bad boys so I thought I'd give it a try."

I'm not sure if I should be happy or pissed off that he did this to be with me, but the thought of him being a bad boy is exciting. My heart and brain aren't agreeing once more. The logical part is saying he shouldn't be doing this, but my heart is screaming for me to jump in his arms and show him how thankful I am.

There's a soft knock at the door, I look over his shoulder and move to answer. His hand finds my waist, holding me in place. Before I can say anything his lips are on me, soft and slow. He pulls away too soon, but his expression tells me that he's happy he did that.

"I wanted to do that before we went out there." His head motions toward the door.

"Yeah, we can't do that out there with all those people. Listen, when we're out there, you're with Alex. I don't like it and I don't expect you to either, but we can't be seen together because there will be questions and we can't have that.

I won't be able to do this," I press my lips to his briefly. "Know that I want to."

He nods and grabs my hand pulling me toward the door. He swings it open, startling Alex. Her smile brightens as her eyes take in our handholding. Ryan gives my hand a squeeze before letting it go.

Alex opens the next set of doors and stands aside letting me go through. As soon as I am over the threshold, the music shifts and the master of ceremonies announces my arrival. I plaster my bright *I'm happy to be here* smile and stand there for a few moments allowing people to take my picture. This will be the first time Ryan and I are photographed together even though he'll be standing next to Alex. Only he and I will know the significance of what tonight means.

I turn and look at Ryan. He extends his arm to Alex as if he's done this a hundred times. Alex takes his arm and leads him through the maze of tables, whispering something into his ear. A server signals to my table; I offer him a slight nod. Ryan releases Alex's arm and pulls out her chair first and then mine, effectively dismissing the server. As soon as I'm seated, he pushes me in slightly before taking the seat next to Alex. I try to hide my jealousy. I'm sure it's evident on my face. Alex snickers at me. I roll my eyes and lean over toward Ryan so I can talk to him.

"Where did you learn how to act like that?"

Ryan picks up the glass in front of him and takes a sip of the water. He holds the glass in his hand, as if he's admiring the glasswork. "My grandma made me take an etiquette class once."

"Why?"

"I had to escort her to the opera once and she wanted everything to be proper."

"Just once?"

Ryan looks away and shifts in his seat. I wish he was sitting next to me so I could reach under the table and comfort him or maybe take back the question. He looks down at his place setting and fiddles with the napkin sitting there. A server appears, placing his dinner in front of him. He looks up quickly and says thank you.

He watches the server as he places my dinner in front of me. I look at the server briefly before gazing back at Ryan, waiting for an answer.

He clears his throat. "She died the night of the opera. We went out to dinner, to the opera and out for coffee afterward with some of her lady friends. The next morning she never woke up."

"Oh, Ryan, I'm so sorry." My heart breaks not only for Ryan, but for myself because I can't comfort him. Alex rests her hand on his arm, playing the part just so I can be in the same room with him. The things she does for me.

chapter
eleven

RYAN

I spend a lot of time with Alex as Hadley has to be on stage or meeting with other people. Alex tells me that Hadley is a very private person and that although she can't be with me tonight, she wants to be.

I wish I knew what is going on with Hadley and me – or maybe there isn't anything going on at all. I'm not sure how I'm supposed to act around her, but everything feels natural and exciting. Kissing her tonight was something I had thought about since I left her hotel earlier this morning. I didn't know if she'd want me to, but she did. I haven't a clue where all these feelings are coming from, but I know it's Hadley. She's bringing them out of me. I just don't know how to control them.

I watch as she works the crowd. I've never looked at how women dress before. My mom has the same look all the time. She never varies. Dylan wears a lot of jeans and shorts. I've never seen her in a dress. I guess it's because she's just one of the guys. Hadley, though, looks so beautiful in her pink dress. Her hair is pulled up away from her bare shoulders. When we were together earlier, I saw glitter sparkling off her skin and thought how lucky it is to be the inanimate object that gets to be a part of her for the night.

Her dress isn't bulky like the one Dylan wore to prom last year. I remember shopping with her and having to carry it to her car. I don't know how she moved in it, but when she tried it on, she declared 'this is the one' by spinning in front of the mirror.

Hadley's dress fits her, showing me the perfect spot to place my hands when we are able to head back into her private dressing room. Never have I had the desire to kiss a girl until I kissed her this morning. I wasn't nervous or anxious. Everything felt right and now I want more. So much more of her and her lips pressed against mine.

Alex pulls me away from where we are standing. She sets her arm inside the crook on my elbow. She makes it look as if I'm guiding her when in reality I'm following her, hesitantly. I trust her not to take me too far away from Hadley. We stop at the bar and she orders us two Cokes, handing one to me, before leading us to the terrace.

She sets her coke on the table nearby and looks at me. "We have a problem."

I'm taken aback because I thought the night was going well. "Um... okay."

"It's not what you think, or maybe it is, I don't know, but I can tell by the look on your face that you're scared. Hell, maybe you should be." She shakes her head and takes a deep breath. Hadley and Alex are so different. Where Hadley seems calm, Alex is on edge. "Your age is going to be a problem. Her uncle isn't going to like any of this when he finds out."

I look at her, not knowing what to say. I know I'm only seventeen, but surely Hadley knew this before inviting me.

"Hadley likes you, Ryan, and she has no intentions of letting your age affect a relationship between the two of you."

Hadley and I haven't discussed anything, let alone a relationship. I'm not stupid. I know she can do better than me. I'm just a boy from a small town who has nothing to offer her. I'm here making memories that will last me a lifetime. Ones I'll only be able to share with myself.

"I can tell you're confused."

"Maybe a bit," I reply.

Alex turns me so I'm facing her. Her hands are firm on my biceps. "She likes you a lot. If you think yesterday and tonight is how she is, you're sadly mistaken. The only reason you're with me now is because you're seventeen. She needs to protect herself."

"She's embarrassed?" I ask.

"Hell no," Alex says. "She's breaking the law if she pursues you."

I hadn't thought about the law or how being underage affects her. All I've thought about is how Hadley makes me feel when I'm next to her. Not even next to her, but in the same room. It's like I've never seen the sunshine before until I met her.

I stuff my hands into my pockets and step away from Alex. I don't know how to respond and I'm still confused about something Alex said. "What did you mean by 'how she is'?"

Alex reaches for her Coke and takes a drink, keeping the glass in her hand. "Hadley doesn't pick up fans, ever."

"I'm not a fan." I blurt out.

Alex shakes her head. "Anyway, you're someone special, even I can see the way she looks at you. Hadley likes you and I don't think she's going to let you go."

A group of people approach us, silencing our conversation. Alex turns and leans against the railing, chatting animatedly with the group. She doesn't introduce me and I'm okay with that. I'd rather not know any of these people. Alex is working, I can tell. She pulls out her phone and starts talking about Hadley's appearances. It dawns on me that this could very well be the last time I see her. She has a life away from here, a real one. One that requires her full attention and that's something I can't compete with.

She's not going to have time for a high school senior. I should've told her no when she asked me to attend this party with her. I should've left her on the balcony last night and saved myself from hearing what I'm sure she'll be telling me later tonight.

I step away, Alex doesn't even notice and I walk back into the party. I scan the crowd for Hadley, but don't see her. That's my sign. I know it is. Taking a deep breath, hands in my pockets, I resign myself to accepting that whatever this is, or was, with Hadley is just a dream. With one last look around and a silent goodbye, I head for the door.

"Why is it that every time I go looking for you, you're about to walk out of my life?"

I turn and find Hadley behind me. Her dress is bunched in her hands, as if she's about to start running. She motions toward the room we were in earlier. She looks behind her briefly before walking over there and opening the door. I follow her in and shut the door behind us. She opens the second door, the one leading to her room. She waits for me to enter before shutting and locking it behind me.

"You were going to leave without saying goodbye?" she turns, her brown eyes penetrating mine.

"I was just trying to save myself from the 'it's not you, it's me' speech I've heard about before."

"That's not fair," she says as she moves closer to me. She lets go of her dress, her finger in my face. "I want you here with me. I wish I could show everyone out there that you're *my* date and not Alex's. You don't know what it did to me to see you treat her so well."

My eyes immediately go to her mouth. I can't help it. I'm a guy. She licks her lips and leans toward me. She knows what I'm thinking and maybe she wants me to kiss her again. Her hands rub up the lapels of my jacket, her eyes on me.

"I don't want you to leave, Ryan. In fact, we need to figure this out tonight so I can see you tomorrow and make plans to see you again on my next break."

"You can have anyone—"

She silences me with her lips. My hand finds her waist, holding onto her as if I'm afraid she's going to go away. Her hands leave my jacket, one moving into my hair and the other pressing under my jacket against my white dress shirt.

Her tongue traces my bottom lip, my mouth opening on instinct. When her tongue touches mine, my mind explodes. Heat soars through my body, urging me on. My hand grips her waist tighter, pulling her closer. My free hand cups her face. My thumb gently rubs along her cheekbone until I spread my fingers out behind her head, holding her to my mouth.

She pulls away. I'm not ready. I'm desperate for her. Hadley rests her forehead on my chest. Her hands leave my hair and circle my waist. I hug her back, taking advantage of her exposed skin. I place small kisses on her shoulder, her neck, purposely staying away from her mouth because I know if I return there I'll want more.

"I'm here for one more day," she says, tilting her head, giving me more access to her neck. "I want to see you tomorrow."

I stop and pull back. This is exactly why we can't work. Someone like Hadley Carter shouldn't have to stoop to be with someone like me.

Looking into her eyes, I want to get so lost in the magic they hold. I drop my hand from her cheek, her expression changes immediately and she steps back.

"If you don't want to be here, Ryan, then just go."

"It's not that. Believe me when I say that. I'm just confused."

"About what?"

"This," I say, motioning between us. "It doesn't make sense."

Hadley steps forward and picks up my hand. She places it over her heart, my fingers brush against her breast. I attempt to control my breathing in front of her. I'm having so many firsts in such a short amount of time and each one with her. She makes me feel amazing.

"Do you feel this?" she asks as she taps my hand with her fingers. She smiles when I nod. "You do this to me."

"But –"

"No buts. Just hear me out. I heard what you said the other night and I remember. Material things don't mean anything to me. This..." she rests her hand against my heart. "Means everything to me. It's one thing if you don't feel the same as me – and if you don't, I'll walk away, but I have a feeling that you do."

"You could get into trouble."

"It's a risk I'm willing to take. We'll be careful."

"My parents won't like this, they won't approve."

She steps closer, my hand moving with her body, cupping her neck. "They shouldn't. I'm too old for you, but I'm willing to try and play by the rules for the next few months." Hadley kisses me full on the lips. I wrap my other arm around her, pulling her as close as I can.

"Can I see you tomorrow?" she asks, breaking our kiss.

"I have church."

"I like church."

I can't help but smile and start nodding like a love-struck teenager. Now I know why Dylan acts the way she does when she says she's in love. I'm not sure how it's going to work, but I don't want to fight her. She drags me over to the love seat and we sit and talk about my town and how behind-the-times it is. When I put my arm around her, she snuggles into my side. I rest my head on top of hers and close my eyes, dreaming of what life can be like with Hadley.

chapter
twelve

HADLEY

"How do I look?" I ask Alex as I straighten out my dress. Alex French-braided my hair this morning before we made the two-hour drive to Brookfield. Ryan wasn't lying when he said time had forgotten his town. Half of it's modern and thriving, but the other end is full of dilapidated housing and buildings that look like they're functioning, but barely able to stand.

"You look fine." Alex slams the car door and meets me in the front. She's none too thrilled to be going on four hours of sleep and about to sit through a church service. I can't remember the last time I went to church, maybe for my cousin's wedding. I thought Alex was going to kill me when I told her we were going. I believe her eyes turned red.

"I'm nervous," I say as I adjust the large hat I just put on. The last thing I want is for people to recognize me.

"You should be." She links her arm with mine. We start walking toward the church. People stop and stare as we pass by. I'm not sure what they are looking at. Maybe the fact that we're wearing sunglasses and the sun is still sleeping. Or is it simply because we don't belong here?

"I can't believe we are doing this," she mutters as we step into the church. It's small compared to the church my cousin was married in. This has about twenty pews on each side and there isn't a balcony like the churches I've been to in New York. There is a choir singing. They're all wearing white robes. I didn't even ask Ryan what denomination he is, not that it matters. I just hope we aren't inside some voodoo sect.

After I convinced Ryan that I wanted to attend church, he finally relented. He probably thinks of me as some stalker willing to attend a service just so I can see him. I'm not, at least not yet. I think as long as I figure out a schedule that works, I'll be okay.

What worries me is the rest of my tour. I'm not sure how I'm going to handle the next month. I'll be on the west coast, a place that I used to love and look forward to visiting, until now. Alex asked me on the way here, "why Ryan?" And all I could say was, "why not?" I can't describe how he makes me feel and I'm not talking about when he touches me, but when he looks at me. It's like we were meant to know each other. Maybe not be together, but definitely be part of each other's lives forever.

Although, not being with him isn't an option for me, at least not right now. Last night when he was with Alex, I felt anxious and uncomfortable being in that room full of people. In a matter of twenty-four hours I've become dependent on someone. Someone that society says I can't have.

I spot the back of Ryan and tug on Alex's sleeve as I start moving toward him. This part isn't planned. We didn't talk about what I'd do when I got here. We walk around the back of the church, staying clear of the center aisle. My eyes are trained on Ryan as he sits forward, either mesmerized by the choir or asleep. If it were me I'd be sleeping. I walk in first, my movements catching his eye. His expression is one of shock and quickly changes into the smile I've grown so quickly to love.

I sit next to him and look at his parents, but keep a safe gap between us. This is as close as I can get. His mom wears her blonde hair down, the top pulled back into a barrette. Her dress is gray, solid in color and she holds a Bible in her hands. His father is in an old, brown suit jacket. The color is so faded the elbows look almost white. I look around and see others similarly dressed on this side of the church, but on the other, people are dressed in new, flashy clothes.

I jump slightly when his fingers touch mine. I wasn't expecting a display of affection and I'm a bit sad when he pulls his hand back. He looks at his parents before turning his attention back to the preacher.

There is distance between us during the sermon, which I expected. What I didn't expect was the tingling sensation coursing through my body. When the service ends, his mom looks at me. She doesn't smile, but appraises me. Her eyes travel up and down as if she's never seen another female before.

"Mom, I'd like you to meet my friends, Hadley and Alex." Ryan looks at me and smiles. "This is my mom, Sally Stone."

"Mrs. Stone," she says, without offering her hand. Alex pinches my side briefly.

"It's nice to meet you, Mrs. Stone." I offer her my hand and should've taken her hint that we weren't going to shake hands. She looks down at my hand as if I've dipped it in meat sauce. I drop my hand and smile. I'm a performer, winning her over shouldn't be this hard.

"Are you new in town?"

"No, ma'am, we're just visiting. I met Ryan –"

"You just met Ryan and were already touching him?" The way his mother looks at him makes his head drop. I want to ask her if she believes in love at first sight or that instant connection you feel with someone that makes you do crazy things, but I don't dare.

"Mom?" Ryan's voice is soft, questioning. Nothing like the voice I've been playing over and over in my head since we've met.

"I'll see you downstairs, Ryan." She turns and walks away from us. I watch her retreat to people she must know. A few of them point, but she shakes her head, not even turning around to see if we are watching her as she blatantly talks about us behind our backs.

"I'm sorry about my mom." His words are quiet, meant only for me. I wonder if Alex makes him nervous or if he's just always this shy. I've seen glimpses of someone different underneath, someone that I fully want to explore if given the opportunity. I have a feeling that he's saving that side of him for a rainy day.

"Don't be," I say, placing my hand in his. I need to touch him, especially when he's this close. "She's a mom and protective of her boy. I get that."

Ryan runs his free hand through his hair, creating a mess of waves. I'm curious if he always keep it this shaggy or if he wears it shorter, or maybe even longer. Not that I'd like him any different.

"There's coffee and cookies downstairs if you want to come down." I nod and look over at Alex, who is clearly bored.

"Coffee and cookies downstairs," I say quietly. Her eyebrow rises as if I'm joking. This is so off-the-chart for her. Alex shakes her head and walks away. I can't tell if she's mad or actually going to go downstairs. I didn't ask her to leave. Maybe being here as a third wheel isn't her idea of fun.

I look back at Ryan and smile. He's been watching me this whole time. "Coffee and cookies it is."

Ryan smiles and starts looking around. He pulls me out of the pew, gripping my hand tightly. We walk in the opposite direction, away from the main door we came in. He brings us down a dark hall and into a small room. I follow in behind him; it's dark, with only a tiny window at the top of the wall, near the ceiling, letting in a streak of light.

I turn at the sound of the door closing, at the same time Ryan is pulling me to him, knocking off my hat. His hand cups my face, his lips not hesitant like before, but daring. I weave my hand into his hair and gasp when I feel his tongue touch mine. He lets go of my hand, wrapping his arm around my waist. His grip is firm, bringing us closer to each other. His hand trails down my face, my neck, my shoulder and finally his fingertips brush along the side of my breast.

I pull him closer and shift our bodies, his leg between mine. When he moans I know he feels the same sensation that I do and that makes me stop and pull away from him. I'm thankful that the minimal light casts only shadows in this room, because I don't want him to see the pained look on my face. And I definitely don't want him to think I'm rejecting him, because I don't want to, but I have to.

"You make me want to try things I've never thought about before." His lips ghost on my neck, sending shivers down my spine. I want to pretend that I don't know he's only seventeen and give into his raging hormones. It's like I've woken a sleeping giant and now that he's alert, there's no stopping him. I don't want to imagine him looking at or even thinking about touching another woman, only me. I'm selfish in thinking that I'll be enough for him, especially when all I can allow is kissing and even that is probably taking it too far. Standing here in this darkened room, with a horny sexy boy who makes my skin feel as if it's being burned, all I can think about is showing him how good we can make each other feel.

I step back, putting distance between us. I sense his body go rigid, pained. He lets me take his hand when I reach for it, although I can feel his resistance.

"Have no doubt that I want this between us," I whisper so prying ears beyond this door can't hear what I'm about to tell him. "Have no doubt that I want to feel you pressed against me, to let you explore and learn what your touch does to me. As much as it pains me to not touch you and claim you publicly – to tell the world that I've found someone that I want to spend every conceivable moment with, even after two days – we have to be cautious and act as if we're friends. Trust me, it's killing me. People always say you know when you've found that one person and I *know*, without a doubt, you're the one.

"We just have to be careful. There's going to be a day when we can do this and not have to worry about the consequences."

"I can't help myself, Hadley. I look at you and I imagine *things* that I want to do and try with you. I've never had these types of thoughts about anyone until I met you, until you let me kiss you." Ryan bridges the gap between us and kisses me forcefully. "I don't want to help myself."

"I can't either, but we need to try, for both our sakes. Your mom clearly doesn't appreciate your new friend and once she finds out who I am and how old I am…" I shake my head at the thought. When Ian finds out about Ryan, shit is going to hit the fan. I can't imagine what Ryan's mother is going to do, or his father. "We need to be careful."

"We'll be careful," he says, his lips brushing up against mine as he speaks the three words that will hopefully keep us safe.

chapter
thirteen

RYAN

Having Hadley in this dark room only spurred the thoughts I've been having about her. I've never thought of a girl *that* way before until now. When I close my eyes, I picture what she looks like with me hovering over the top of her, or pressed against the wall with her legs wrapped around me. These visions of lust cloud my mind. Holding her hand simply ignites a fury beneath my skin with anticipation of what could come.

When my fingers brushed against her breast, the thought of knowing I could touch her freely, even if it was behind layers of fabric, sent a thrill right through me. Having her pull away, though, is not my intended plan. I know she's being smart, cautious. That should be me. I should protect us, shy away from her to keep her safe. I know what my mom is going to say when she finds me alone. A conversation I don't want to listen to.

Hadley is right, though. This friendship, or what I want to consider a relationship, needs to be kept quiet. The last thing I want is for Hadley to be in trouble because of me. If kissing her in private is all I'm allowed to do, then so be it. I'll take what I can get until my eighteenth birthday. I'm hoping then that she'll still want me.

"You should go downstairs. I'll follow behind." She says this with confidence while my heart is aching for her to come with me.

Opening the door, I peek out into the hallway, looking for Reverend

Monroe. I saw him and my father walk toward the basement before I brought Hadley in here, but I don't want to take any chances. I need to protect Hadley from the scrutiny she'll face if we get caught.

I give her hand a quick kiss before stepping out into the hallway. There's a soft glow from the nightlights used to illuminate a path. I take a deep breath before entering the church, walking down the aisle and descending the stairs.

People are gathered, as normal. They congregate by their job or financial status. I hate this church. Reverend Monroe preaches about giving back to the community and treating everyone like family, yet the rich are on the right and the poor on the left. We're segregated by status and told, without using the words, to never cross that imaginary line.

Dylan pushes me into the corner, her face full of anger. I've never seen her cheeks so red. Her teeth are clenched, causing her jaw to protrude slightly. Her grip is strong as she squeezes my arm for effect.

"You invited her to church?"

"Not really. She asked if she could come. Besides, what's the big deal? No one can tell who she is or anything. She's wearing that stupid hat."

"That's not what I meant," Dylan says through pursed lips. "What is going on with you and her?"

I shrug. If I'm supposed to be careful, I can't really tell Dylan that I've taken on the newfound hobby of French kissing her idol. "We're friends. I make her laugh." The last part is a lie, I'm not sure that I do and I haven't told her any jokes to find out.

"I think there's more to this story. You spent the night with her."

"I didn't, Dylan. I told you this. We talked and it's all thanks to you. Had we come home like planned we wouldn't be having this conversation and I wouldn't be grounded."

"You're grounded?"

"Of course I am." I don't tell her it's all worth it. I wouldn't trade that first night with Hadley for anything. Nor the second, although my parents don't know about the early sneaking in I did this morning. "It doesn't matter what my mom says, she cowers to my dad and you know that."

"I'm sorry." Dylan sounds remorseful. She knows my home life is anything but stellar. While she and most of my classmates are living the life of luxury – even the same ones in my neighborhood have more than I do – I'm stuck in the sixties where the man rules and the wife does everything he says. And the children – they have no voice.

I spot Alex in the corner. Her eyes are trained on me while she's talking to another parishioner. Her eyes turn to the entry way and I follow. Hadley steps through. She looks calm and reserved. Dylan turns and shakes her head.

"Really?"

"What?"

She looks back at me. "You like her, don't you?"

Like? No, that word does not begin to sum up how I feel about Hadley.

"She's… nice," I mutter, catching Dylan's look all too soon. She steps back as if I've hurt her, stabbed her. She shakes her head, her eyes downcast, examining the white tile floor stained yellow from years of abuse. I don't understand what just happened.

"Did you sleep with her?" she whispers. I look at her, at Hadley and then back at Dylan. I shake my head. We slept, but not in the way Dylan is asking. Her mouth drops open, a small gasp of air escapes. She doesn't believe me. I know this by looking at her. I reach for her as she turns and runs away. I call out her name, but it's too late. She's gone and people are staring, including Hadley.

This small incident catches the attention of my mom. She looks from me to Hadley and frowns. Mom loves Dylan and is probably figuring things out. It was a mistake agreeing to let Hadley come to church.

Hadley excuses herself and walks over to me. I motion for her to follow me back upstairs. If we were going to talk, I'd rather do so without an audience. The soft tap of her shoes echo behind me as we climb the hardwood stairs. I want to reach behind me and hold her hand, but I don't. I push open the door leading to our small courtyard and walk to the bench that sits under the large oak tree that my dad and I made a few years ago and donated to the church.

I reach for Hadley's hand as I sit down. I don't know what we're doing out here. I just wanted to get away from the stares I was getting downstairs. Hadley stands in front of me, her dress blowing lightly in the breeze. I look up at her and smile. I already feel at ease with her away from everyone.

"What are we doing out here?"

I shrug. "I wanted to get away from people staring. And I wanted to spend a few more minutes with you alone before it's time to leave."

Hadley sits down next to me, she's brings her knee up under her, resting it against my thigh. I want more than anything to touch her, to find out how soft her skin is there.

"I leave tonight," she says. I try not to let her words affect me, but they do. I knew this was going to happen, but wanted to stretch these days as far as I could. "I have to head out west for a few weeks before I have another break. Then I thought I could come see you."

"Okay."

She smiles. "I also thought we could text and talk as much as possible. I'm not sure I can go a day without hearing your voice."

"I can't," I say.

"Why not?" The look on her face kills me. I sit forward and put my head in my hands. I can never be what she needs.

"I shouldn't tell you this. You might think differently and that's the last thing I want, but I work part-time to help out at home and sometimes I have extra money to buy minutes for my cell phone. I don't always have minutes to use," I mumble quickly into my hands.

She shifts, but not away, closer. Her fingers thread through my hair at the nape of my neck. Her touch is soft. I lean into her, wanting to be enveloped by her.

"I can help."

I shake my head. I'm not going to allow her to take care of me. That is embarrassing and degrading. A man should take care of his girl, not the other way around.

Hadley kneels in front of me, pulling my hands away from my face. "If I get you a phone, it's all for me. I'd be doing it for me so that I can talk to you. I'm going to need to talk to you every day. Knowing me, it's going to be multiple times a day."

Her fingers lift my chin, so we're eye to eye. I can tell she's serious in this request, but my pride is on the line. She shouldn't have to buy me anything. It should be me spending money on her.

"You can let me buy you a phone, or I'll leave mine sitting on this bench and you'll be stuck with it and I'll just use that to talk to you."

I turn away and try not to smile. "You're pushy." I lean back, putting some distance between us. She stands, placing her hands on her hips. I laugh at her when her foot starts tapping. I shake my head and rub my hands over my face.

"Ugh." I groan. I can't keep looking at her. If I do, I know I'll say yes to whatever she asks of me. Hadley steps in between my legs and threads her fingers through my hair. My eyes close on their own volition. I can't believe that with just a simple touch from her, I'm about to buckle. I lean forward, placing my head against her stomach.

"I know it's not conventional."

"I have a feeling we won't be conventional," I mumble against her.

"Why be normal? Normal is so over-rated and boring. I don't want to be boring. I want to be adventurous and daring."

I shake my head and laugh. I place my hands on the back of her thighs, pulling her a bit closer as I kiss her stomach. She kneels in front of me again, her lips finding mine.

"Okay," I say. She steps back and pulls the back of my hair to lift my head. The smile spreading across her face is enough for me to forget about what we just talked about, even though my decision is weighing heavily on me.

chapter
fourteen

HADLEY

*A*nal Anna pulls my hair. Not sure what hairstyle she's going for, but she says it's something she learned while I was gallivanting all over Jackson for three days. My head rears back, my mouth drops in a silent ouch as she tugs. This is pure torture, plain and simple. I want to turn around and pull her hair, just like I would've done in kindergarten. I bite the inside of my cheek to avoid a verbal confrontation with her.

I haven't seen Ryan in almost a week and it's been nothing but agony. Facetime isn't cutting it. I've been trying to find a way to sneak to Brookfield, even if it's only for a few hours, but to no avail. I'm booked solid and the slightest gap in my schedule is being filled by last-minute appearances or interviews.

Each time someone asks about my personal life I want to tell them about Ryan and how I might be in love. Definitely falling in love, but not sure if I'm there yet. Although, I know I'm lying to myself, I'm there, just not willing to admit it to myself for fear he doesn't feel the same way.

Ryan tells me that the guys in his school have my picture hanging from their lockers and that it pisses him off how they talk about me. He says they act like they know me and I have to remind him that they only know the performer – the one they read about in the countless interviews and articles – that he is the only one who truly *knows* me.

Alex walks in, her face grim. I try to ask her with my eyes what her problem is, but she just shakes her head and eyes *Anal Anna*. I'm not sure I like the look on Alex's face. It usually means something is up and that probably means I won't like it. Who knows what my uncle has done now.

The thought of my uncle brings him into my dressing room. The door flies open, slamming against the wall, causing Anna to jump and poke me in the scalp with a bobby pin. I rub the spot, only for her to slap my hand away.

"Anna, I need to speak with Hadley in private."

Anna nods, stops what she's doing and leaves. Through the mirror I notice dissension between them. My eyes look to Ian. He's showing no emotion as she walks by. Maybe they're having a super-secret lovers quarrel and trying to maintain professionalism.

Who am I kidding? Those two are anything but professional.

I spin my chair around just as Anna shuts my dressing room door. Ian looks at Alex and I shake my head. He knows better than to ask her to leave. I tell her everything and I hate repeating myself, so this saves me time. Plus she helps me figure out Ian and his erratic attitudes.

"Is there anything you need to tell me?" he sighs when he asks this question. He moves, slowly, toward the stool in the corner. He's acting as if I've committed a crime. Maybe I have. Is kissing an underage boy a crime? Probably is, knowing my luck.

"No."

Alex shifts closer, her elbows resting on her knees. She's watching Ian, waiting for him to do or say something.

He clears his throat. It's rough, like he's getting sick or had too much to drink last night. I'm thinking it's probably the latter. He pulls the stool into the center of the small room. He sits down, resting his feet on the pegs.

I cross my legs, staring at him, waiting.

"Are you sure?"

What kind of question is that? My parents used to do that to me when I'd bring home a bad grade or forget to turn in an assignment. Am I sure? Of course I am. If I was in trouble I'd think I'd know. Or at least have some sort of idea that I've done something wrong.

Ian looks at me as if he's my father. His brows are furrowed, his eyes slanted. Really? If I weren't trying to be respectful of his "managerial duties" I'd start swinging my feet just to piss him off. He pulls out a newspaper, one that he's had tucked inside his coat. His antics are starting to bore me. I roll my eyes at Alex, who shakes her head.

I sit up a bit straighter and look at her. Her eyes, boring into mine, are telling me to behave and that this is serious. All I can think about is Ryan and that maybe he told the wrong person about us and I'm about to be sent to the county jail for child endangerment or something harsher.

Ian shakes the paper. The only thing missing is his orange juice and toast and I'd think this is a common morning at my parents' house. By the look on his face, I know this is anything but. Something is in that paper, causing him more stress than usual.

"What's going on, Ian?" I'm tired of waiting and of this beating-around-the-bush.

Ian stands and paces, one hand stuffed deep into his coat pocket, the other clutching the newspaper. He stops in front of me, hovering over me. "You made the paper the other day."

"Okay." I draw out the word. "I'm in the paper all the time."

Ian shakes his head. He looks at Alex, who I swear slinks back into the sofa. What the hell? I stand up, my hands planted firmly on my hips.

"What is going on with you two? I'm starting to get pissed."

Ian hands me the paper, his eyebrow cocked in defiance. He's testing me. I know this. I open the paper carefully, my eyes slowly traveling up the page. I want to cry out when I see not only my shoes, but the shoes of the boy I was with when this picture was taken. My legs are pressing against his bent legs, his hands resting on my hips – that is what I'm looking at. Except I know in this moment that his fingers are digging into my flesh as his lips work against mine in nothing but pure temptation.

The memory of his tongue moving against mine overcomes my senses. I can feel every touch, every movement of his hands on my back, as if he's holding me now.

"Explain yourself."

Ian's voice knocks me for six. Someone caught me... us. This wasn't supposed to happen. We're a secret, a dirty, forbidden tryst. Alex pulls the paper from my hands. Her hand rubs circles on my back as she directs me back to the chair. Ian huffs, shuffling back to the stool. His throat clears again as he prepares to lecture me on the do's and don'ts of a public relationship. The problem isn't that there's a public picture, but his age.

"The last time you had a relationship that the public was aware of, it ended badly."

Alex scoffs. "If a relationship is ending, obviously it's bad, Ian. People don't break-up when they're happy."

I want to hug her for standing up to him, but he's right. My last relationship, the break-up was very public and nasty. I thought he, Coleman Hollister, was the one. I took the break-up hard and the press had a field day. We were two famous kids in love, destined for greatness.

"Please tell me this isn't what it looks like?"

That would be the easy thing to do. Just brush it off as some Photoshopped image, but that would be as if I'm denying Ryan and I can't... I won't do that. I don't care if it saves my image or keeps my face out of the press. I'll just have to be more careful.

I shake my head. "It's exactly what it looks like." I want my voice to be confident, but it's not. It falls flat, weak.

"Who is he?"

This time I clear my throat. I have to tell Ian everything; if I don't, he won't be able to protect Ryan and me. "His name is Ryan Stone and I met him in Jackson."

"And?"

I look up at Ian. He's leaning forward as if I'm about to tell him a story, like one he hasn't heard in years, the type my grandma used to tell me when I was little.

"And what?" I play stupid.

He stands up, tossing his hands in the air. "I hate it when you play stupid, Hadley. That photo was not taken in Jackson." He paces, stopping every two steps to shake his head. I know he's trying to keep his temper in check. My image is everything, not only to me, but to my brand. I've worked hard – and he's worked hard – to create this persona that America loves and I know I can't afford to screw it up.

"I went to his town… for church," I add, hoping to ease the tension.

"I went with her."

"Yet you let her sneak off with some random guy so she can make out under a fucking oak tree?"

Alex steps forward. I grab her arm, holding her next to me. She doesn't need to fight my battles, especially this one.

"Alex didn't let me do anything. I went with Ryan, willingly. It was my idea. I took Alex along so that I wouldn't be alone on the drive out there."

Ian nods. "Are you done with this guy?"

"No," I say, strongly.

He leans his head back and laughs. "Perfect. So I can expect him on tour."

I shake my head. "No, he's in school." Alex sets her hand down on top of my arm. I look at her. She's shaking her head, telling me to keep quiet. I look back at Ian as he watches our silent exchange. I know he doesn't like Alex, never has, but I don't care. She's not here to appease him, but to accompany me. "Ryan won't be joining us on tour, Ian."

He looks at his watch and walks over to the door. He opens it and I half expect *Anal Anna* to fall through from pressing her ear against the door. Ian looks back at me and shakes his head. I know what he's thinking; he's worried. Worried that I'm going to screw up again and he'll have to do damage control. The only problem is if I screw up, I'm pretty much done. Damage control or not, I'll never sing again if we get caught.

Ian pulls the door shut, loudly. I jump as the metal door bangs against the door casing. I look at Alex, the realization that I'm in deep shit evident in her eyes. "What are you going to do?" she asks. It's the million-dollar question, isn't it? I've done this to myself, created this mess. Ryan was an innocent party until I needed to talk to him. He's going to be dragged through the mud, any and all skeletons exposed. He's going to hate me.

"I don't know." I move away from her, needing space to think. There's a knock on the door before Anna is back in, ready to finish my hair. I go on in thirty minutes and for the first time in a long time, I don't want to. Right now, all I want to do is pick up the phone and apologize to Ryan for this mess I've put him in.

Anna motions for me to sit down. I sulk over to my chair and sit. Her hair-pulling begins immediately. Alex hands me a tissue for my tears and I can't help but wonder if she knows they're for Ryan or because she sees Anna destroying my hair.

chapter
fifteen

RYAN

School sucks.

It's always sucked, but now all I do is watch the clock for the bell to ring so I can text Hadley. This newly-formed habit makes my day drag out longer. The one, maybe two, texts in between classes do nothing to curb my desire to speak with her.

It's been over a week now since I've seen her and probably one of the longest weeks of my life. Although, I've never counted time that way until now. I've been caught daydreaming a few times. A few slaps on my back from classmates to get my attention while a teacher stands at the front of the room, glaring. I've always answered when called upon, but that was before.

In a matter of one week I've gone from that dependent student – the one who turns in all his work, stays for extra credit and never says a word without raising his hand – to a zombie teen who isn't sleeping at night and is forgetting simple things, like putting my name on the top of my paper.

It's Hadley's fault. I'm not strong enough to tell her that with the time difference, I should be sleeping instead of waiting for her to call after her show. I wouldn't tell her anyway, I need to hear her voice. It doesn't matter what time it is or if I'm asleep. She's all that matters.

And it scares me.

Everything about being in her life scares the shit out of me. I don't know what to do about the emotions I'm feeling. I can't talk to my dad and talking to Dylan is out of the question. There's no way I can talk to Hadley about what I'm feeling. What if she doesn't feel the same? Then I'd look like some lovesick teenager. I already feel weak around her. Never in a million years did I think I'd fall for someone famous, yet I did and she's interested in me. But the feeling of inadequacy nags at me. What if I'm not enough for her?

When the bell rings, I'm up and out of my seat before the rest of the class puts away their binders. My phone is out of my pocket just as I step over the imaginary line separating the classroom from the hallway. I have thirty minutes to talk to Hadley and I don't want to waste a single second.

I push open the door leading to the courtyard. I've eaten lunch out here every day so I can be on the phone. I'd never be able to talk to her and sit in the cafeteria, especially with Dylan glaring at me.

"Hi." The way she says hi makes me weak. Who knew a simple one-syllable word could bring me to my knees.

"Hi," I say back to her, probably not as eloquent as her, but I try. I sit down and lean up against the tree. The ground is uncomfortable because of the overgrown roots, but this little privacy is enough for me.

"How's school?"

"It's dragging. I'm ready for winter vacation."

Hadley starts laughing. "School just started and you're ready for vacation?"

Of course I am. "I'll be eighteen then."

There's a long silence. I can hear her shuffling around her room. "How many days?"

"I don't know, but I could count them and let you know."

"I'd like that."

I'd like it too. I want to know how many days until I can start making my own decisions. Until my parents don't have any control over me. I want to leave, but I'm not stupid enough to quit school. I need my diploma.

"Are you ready for your show tonight?"

Hadley sighs. "Not really. Ian, my manager, is on my case about some shit."

"Like what?"

"You."

"Me?" My voice cracks when I ask her.

"It's stupid, a mistake because I wasn't paying attention."

I don't know what to say. I always knew the day would come when she'd realize we're a mistake. That nothing about us makes sense. I guess it just took her manager to say something to her about it. Help her see the error of her ways, as they say.

"Ryan?"

"Yeah?"

"I know you're thinking I mean you and I don't. We've been through this. I want to be with you. Thing is, someone took a picture of us when we were sitting outside and it's suggestive. They know it's me, but they don't know who you are, so for right now we're safe. We just can't do something like that in public again."

I'm relieved when she tells me that my name isn't mentioned, although I feel bad for her not having any privacy. Another reason I can't wait until my birthday. I want to be able to hold her hand and walk down the street.

"The bell is going to ring." I hate saying this to her. It makes me feel like a child.

"I'll call you after my show, but I did want to tell you this – I'll be there next weekend."

"Yeah?"

"Yeah. It will only be two days, but I need to see you. We'll figure out the rest later, you better get to class."

"Bye, Hadley." She says bye and ends our conversation. I hold my phone, the one she made sure I would take, pressed against my mouth in deep thought. I'll be seeing her next weekend, which cannot come fast enough.

"You're talking to her on the phone?"

I jump at the sound of Dylan's voice. I look up to find her standing there, in front of me. I never saw her come in the courtyard. Her hands are on her hips and she's scowling. We haven't spoken much since church. She still picks me up in the morning, but our conversation is very minimal.

I stand and brush off my pants, pocketing my phone. I know she saw the iPhone. Her eyes are trained on me. She looks different. Not the same Dylan I've known for the past few years. Her expression is hardened, almost as if she's upset.

I know I have to answer her. I also know she's not going to like it. That day driving back from Hadley's Dylan made it very clear how she felt. Those feelings don't change overnight.

"We talk." I shrug and step forward. Her hand comes out and stops me. We're standing shoulder to shoulder, facing in opposite directions. The air is thick with tension. My relationship with Hadley has caused this hiccup in our lives.

"You talk?" she asks in barely a whisper. I nod and step back to look at her. To really look at the girl I've called my best friend, my only real friend. Her eyes are swimming with tears and I don't know why. Is it so bad that I'm talking to Hadley?

"Why are you crying?"

Dylan shakes her head. "It's nothing. I just miss my friend." Her head falls forward to my chest. I wrap my arms around her, pulling her into a hug. We've done this before, but it feels awkward now. Her arms hold me tight, as if she's trying to hold on for dear life.

"Do you want to hang out after school?" No, I don't, but I can't say that to her. Things shouldn't have to change for us, even though I know they have. I'm not sure if I want things to change because I, too, miss my friend. I miss having someone to talk to. Maybe I can discuss my feelings about Hadley with Dylan.

"Sure," I say, knowing this makes her happy. I should want to hang out. It's not like Hadley will be calling after school anyway. She has work.

Dylan pulls away, looks up at smiles, her gray eyes shining. By saying yes, I've made her happy. When she tries to hold my hand, I pull away. I know Hadley and I aren't defined, but I like Hadley and don't really want to jeopardize whatever it is that we have. The look on Dylan's face tells me nothing. Her eyes drop, but she stands next me. She keeps in step with me as we walk to our side-by-side lockers and pull out our textbooks for our next class.

She waits for me to shut my locker before turning into the hallway traffic. We have only two classes left before we can leave, both of us having a free period at the end of the day. From looking at her though, I have to wonder if she still wants to hang out after school. Who knew that not holding hands would get this reaction?

I sit down behind her. The same seat I'm always in when we share a class together. I lean forward, moving her hair out of my way and whisper to her. "Are you mad at me?"

She shakes her head and hands me a note. I stay where I am, allowing her long, dark hair to be a curtain from the teacher's prying eyes.

We have the homecoming dance in a few weeks and I was wondering if you'd like to be my date?

We've never done the dance thing before; she's always had a date. I'm surprised she's asking when I know there will be a line of guys waiting to take her. I'm not sure how to answer her. I know I can't take Hadley, but would hate to say yes to Dylan and find out Hadley will be in town that weekend. I'd miss time with Hadley and I don't want that. There is also the possibility that Hadley and I are no longer together, or whatever it is we are, and I'd miss the opportunity to take my best friend to homecoming. Not that I can afford homecoming.

Don't you want to go with someone who can afford to take you out?

I hate writing those words, but it's the truth. Dylan deserves to be treated like a princess, not a second-rate citizen from the slums. I have nothing to offer her except my discount at *Stan's Burger World*. I fold the paper and slide it under her arm. The teacher is lost in a lecture and I'm not paying attention.

The note is back under my hand within seconds. I've never understood how girls can be so stealthy.

I don't need those things to have fun. Just you ;)

I read the words over and over. I'm caught on the 'just you' part. Dylan has never said things like this to me before. It's all new. I'm not sure what to make of it and, once again, wish I had a guy I could talk to.

OK.

I slide the paper back to her and wait. I'm staring at the back of her head, wondering what I just agreed to. She doesn't write back, nor does she turn around, so I have no idea if she's happy. I mean, she should be happy, right? She asked me to the dance and I said yes.

I should be happy too, right?

Except I'm not, because all I can think about is telling Hadley what I've done and what her reaction might be. Maybe she won't even react because I'm reading too much into what we have going on.

I don't know.

The only thing I do know is that I'm confused about her and now Dylan. Being with Hadley, my thoughts are places they've never been before. My body is directing me to do things I haven't even dreamed about with her. With Dylan, I look at her as if she's just one of the guys, yet we are going to a dance together.

chapter
sixteen

HADLEY

"What's this?" I ask as Alex tosses a newspaper in front of me. "Am I front and center again?"

She sits down, falling into the white overstuffed chair. She kicks her legs over the side and smiles. I know something's up. Picking up the paper, I open it. There are red circles in the classified section highlighting houses for sale. I look up at her. Her smile is devious.

"I have an apartment. I don't need to buy a house."

"I don't think you looked at where those houses are located." She pulls up her hand and starts looking at her freshly manicured nails.

I turn to the front page and stare at the name that has been a part of my life for the past two weeks, *Jackson*. Alex wants me to buy a house in Jackson. Doing this would give us a place where we can be together without having prying eyes around us or having to pretend. It's still not being public, but it's better than nothing.

"I don't know, Alex. Don't you think this is sort of presumptuous? I mean, what if he doesn't want to be with me like I want him. He has his whole life ahead of him to pick someone. I'd look like an idiot if I bought a house and he didn't want me there.

"He has a life away from me. I'm this weekend thing, occasionally. He probably has another girlfriend that he's keeping from me."

"You're impossible." Alex gets up and moves to the window, throwing open the curtains. The sun is shining. Misleading the people of Chicago in thinking it's a gorgeous day. That is, until you step outside and get whipped by a gust of wind, which is the main reason, I'm holed up in my hotel. I wanted to shop today, but am not in the mood to deal with the weather.

"I'm not. I'm being realistic." I set down the paper and pull my knees to my chest. "What if I'm just passing his time? He's said so himself that he plans to leave when he's eighteen. What if I don't factor after that?"

Alex turns with her hands on her hips. She's glaring at me. "Like I said, you're impossible. That boy let you come to church, where his parents were, just so he could have a few hours with you before you left. He snuck out of his house to attend a charity ball with you. That boy is smitten with you, probably just as much as you are with him."

I roll my eyes at her. She walks away, leaving me to contemplate what she's said. I've been so scared to love since my last boyfriend.

I swore off relationships. Then I met Ryan.

I wipe the errant tear from my face and go to look for Alex. I find her, reading on her bed. I crawl up beside her and snuggle into her. I love her. She always knows what's best for me.

"I'm sorry."

"You have nothing to be sorry for. I'm just seeing things with clearer eyes."

"I'm scared to open up to him. I'm going to get hurt."

Alex rolls on her side, moving me in the process. "I don't think you have to worry about that with Ryan. Hadley, he didn't even know who you were. This is a guy who sat in the corner of a meet and greet with you and almost left the after-party. Clearly if he wanted you for your fame or money, he would've been all over you the first chance he had."

I nod, knowing she's right. I close my eyes and think about Ryan. I've been counting the days, only a few more until I can see him. Even if it's for minutes each day, seeing him will be enough to hold me over for the next time.

If I buy a house in Jackson, I could be there more often instead of being in New York. Nothing is holding me there, especially when I'm not touring.

We could be together.

The loud chanting reverberates though my body. I get chills when they yell my name. My foot taps to the sounds coming from the crowd. They're here to see me, which still amazes me. Tonight, for the first time in a long time, I'm leaving right after the show. Alex and I are flying into Jackson. There will be no meet and greet, no radio show winners hanging out with me after the show. I'm taking time for me, something I've never done.

I take the stage and the crowd gets louder. The songs flow, the clothing and hair changes work, and the fans – they're happy. When the lighting allows, I can see some of their faces. They're smiling, laughing and some have tears in their eyes. I know for some of them this is a dream come true. They've been waiting years, saving pennies and traveling far distances to see me on this stage. For that, I'm thankful.

Alex meets me at the side, handing me my bottle of water. She's packed our luggage and ordered a car to wait for us. She takes my hand and guides me down the hall, opposite of where I need to go. Ian is expecting me in the pressroom. He'll be pissed when I don't show, but telling him what I'm about to do will only set him off. It's not that he doesn't want me in a relationship, it just needs to be on his terms and with someone he designates the 'proper' person.

Sadly, for me, Ian's idea of a 'proper' person is not mine. He's brought guys around before, but none that I've ever wanted to stay. The one Ian wants, the one that he deems good for my image, is my ex and that's not about to happen.

The driver is waiting by the car when we push open the side door. Alex follows me into the car, and the door slams behind us. Once the driver is in, we're off.

"Excuse me, where is our luggage?"

"Already in the trunk, Ms. Carter," the driver says before putting up the partition. I relax as soon as we hit the road away from the venue. Alex holds my hand, a grin spread across her face. She loves it every time we do something that undermines Ian. They're not fans of each other.

The drive to the airport is quick. I'm pleasantly surprised to find there are no lines at security. With our bags in hand, we run to our gate. We get there with a few minutes to spare. I'm asked for a few autographs, mostly from young girls. Alex declines requests for photos.

We board before everyone else, which I never understood. Being in First Class, people walk by and recognize us, each one staring as they pass by. It would make sense for us to board last. I know people get tired of waiting though, so I get it.

I'm surprised to see how booked our flight is. Who knew Jackson was a travel destination? The flight attendant hands both of us a drink while we wait for everyone to board.

"Would you like something to eat?" she hands me a menu just as my stomach growls. Alex starts laughing and asks the flight attendant to come back. I look over the menu and even though I'm hungry, airplane food is so unappealing.

"It looks gross."

"Not in first class."

I tell Alex what I want and she orders it for me. The flight attendant tells us that we'll get it as soon as the captain gives the okay.

Alex hands me the paper, the same one I thought I left in the hotel. "I called a few that I liked since you didn't bother to tell me which ones you liked."

"Alex—"

She shakes her head. "It doesn't hurt to look."

She's right. I look over the list and see that I like them all. Alex knew that though. I look over at her, her eyes closed, but she's trying not to smile. I bump her arm with mine and she breaks out in giggles.

"So, are we taking up residence in Jackson for a bit?"

I want to say no, I do, but I can't get over how convenient it would be for me to carry on with Ryan and I hope that he'd want me close, at least until he turns eighteen.

Once in the air, Alex and I eat and make small talk with the people next to us. They're from Jackson and overheard us talking about buying a house. The man is a real estate agent and offers to help me find a house. I take his card and promise to call him. The woman is an interior decorator and Alex snags her card right away.

"You know, that's the business we should go into."

"What's that?" I ask her.

"You buy houses and I'll decorate and we'll sell them for profit."

"Defeats the idea, don't you think?"

Alex shrugs and picks up her book and starts reading. I lean back, closing my eyes. I conjure up an image of Ryan and I sitting on my couch, enjoying the privacy of a home. Thinking about him makes me realize that I won't be able to see Ryan tonight, but tomorrow is a different story.

I startle when the captain comes on to tell us we're about to land. I must've fallen asleep. Moments later, our plane touches down. The only thing I can think about is Ryan. I pull out my cell phone and text him.

I'm in town

I barely put my phone away before it vibrates. I pull it back out and smile.

I can't wait to see you. Tell me where and I will be there

I can't hide the elation and show Alex the text message.

"I told you so."

chapter
seventeen

RYAN

I think telling Dylan I'd go to Homecoming with her is a mistake, but I can't change my mind now. She's told my mom. If I knew she was going to do that I would've said no. I've always known Dylan to be sneaky, especially with her parents, but I didn't expect her to burst in after dinner with magazines to show my mom the dresses she's thinking about.

I wanted to run into my room and hide under the bed. Instead, I was forced to sit at the table while they gushed over things I have no interest in. I think I took up the art of eye-rolling every time I heard 'this is perfect'. My mom should've had a girl.

Dylan finally left, leaving me to deal with my mom all by myself. I want to tell her that I really don't want to take Dylan to the dance and that I only said yes because she's my friend and I knew it would make her happy.

But the look on my mom's face, when she put her hand on my cheek and smiled, I knew I couldn't say those words to her. I said goodnight and went to my room to wait for Hadley's call.

Only Hadley doesn't call, she texts telling me she is in town. The moment I received her text I wanted to jump out my window and run to her. Unrealistic, I know, but I need to see her. I need to know she's real and that what I was feeling when she was here is still the same. That the simple touch of her turns my skin into flames. I want to remember the burn.

I hate waiting. I hate knowing that she's two hours away and that I can't be with her. I pace my room, listening for my parents. I've grown weary of them since the incident at church. They didn't ask me about Hadley, I wish they did. I wanted to be able to say I've met someone that I want to get to know better.

But they don't ask.

They just stare.

They walk around and look at me out of the corner of their eyes. My dad will shake his head or mumble something under his breath as he walks by, but nothing else. Don't they care? I held a girl's - no, a woman's - hand in church. Someone they don't know and have never seen and they can't be bothered to ask me who she is.

My mom, aside from Dylan coming over, hasn't said anything to me. She hasn't asked about my homework or my work schedule. She hasn't even asked me how school is going. It's like I don't exist. I'm afraid to interrupt her. If she's not cooking, her nose is buried in her Bible and I know not to bug her while she's reading. Yet, she's always reading and probably praying for my salvation.

I look at my phone; she hasn't texted back. I wish I knew where she was staying because I would go there. I don't care how long it takes me to walk. Knowing Hadley is at the end of the road waiting for me makes it all worth it.

But is she waiting? I second-guess her and myself. What if she's here to tell me we can't be anything but friends, especially after her manager saw the pictures of us? Pictures I still haven't seen and would like to. I'd like to have at least one picture of us together. A memory.

The thought of her not wanting to be with me eats away at me, like a thousand fire ants biting and pinching into my skin. The itch is there, the desire to be something to her, yet I'm afraid to scratch because of who she is.

Guys at school talk about her. I hear all about the things they want to do to her. I don't know if this is normal, I've never liked a celebrity before. The only person I can ask is Dylan, but I'm afraid of what she might say. I know she doesn't like me talking to Hadley. The look Dylan gave me in the courtyard was evidence enough. I wonder if Dylan feels like this is her fault. Does she not want me to be happy?

Hadley can make me happy. I know this deep down in my heart. I don't care about the girl all the guys are fawning over. They don't know the *real* Hadley. They only think they know the one who stands on stage night after night singing her heart out.

They don't know that she likes to be held or how soft her hair is. They don't know what her lips taste like or how they mold and fit perfectly against mine. These are secrets that I know about her and intend to keep.

When my parents' door shuts, I know this is my cue. I have to text her. I can't wait any longer. Tomorrow is too far away. I need to see her now.

I need to see you.

I pace back and forth, no doubt wearing a hole into the carpet with my hand in my hair, tugging at the ends. I keep looking at my phone, counting the seconds, minutes, until I see her name appear on my screen.

What's taking her so long?

She doesn't drive. Or maybe she does. I've only ever seen her get into a car and Alex was driving, but maybe Alex isn't with her this trip. No, I'm sure she is. They are inseparable. Why isn't she texting me back?

I look at my message, it says *delivered*. I know she got it. Unless her phone is off. No, her phone is never off. Maybe her manager came with her and is keeping her busy.

I don't know. I don't know anything right now.

My parents' door opens and closes again. There are faint footsteps. They stop in front of my door. I step carefully to my bed and sit on the edge. I slide as quietly as I can onto my mattress, cautious of alerting whoever is standing at my door that I'm awake.

They've never done this. At least, that I'm aware of. I can't tell if someone is still at my door or not. My phone vibrates in my hand. Hadley is calling me, her gorgeous face lighting up my screen. I can't answer it, not now.

I hit ignore and immediately feel my stomach drop. She's going to think I don't want to talk to her and that's not true. I need to tell her before she has these thoughts.

Parents are up and standing at my door.

She's going to run for the hills. I would if I received a text like that. There are more footsteps and another door opens and closes. I can make out some movement. A light comes on, illuminating the hallway. Shadows pass in front of my door, but they don't stop. Maybe they were just checking to make sure I'm asleep.

Call me soon. I'm at the church ;)

I look down at my phone and re-read the words that she sent. Relief washes over me. She does want to see me and couldn't wait, but does that mean she's here to break-up? I won't let her, I can't. She makes me feel alive. She makes me feel things I've never felt and I want to explore those feelings with her.

I have to sneak out. That is the only answer.

I'm on my way.

She's worth getting in trouble for. That is what I tell myself. She'd do the same thing for me. I get up, not worrying about the noise. I pull up my blinds and slide my window open. Getting out is the easy part. I hoist myself up and onto the windowsill and jump. I look back, half expecting my bedroom light to be on. I slide my window shut, leaving just enough of a gap so I can open it later.

I walk along the house, peering around the corner. I don't see any movement. Nothing to alert me that someone is out there lurking around like me. I duck under the kitchen window and turn the corner, hurrying along the side of the house. My shoes squeak in the wet grass, likely leaving footprints marking my escape.

When I get to the front, I look at the picture window. I notice there are candles burning in the living room. They're red, casting an eerie glow. Never have I seen my mom burn a candle. I didn't even know we owned any. I look harder, stepping closer. My mom is sitting on the floor, a book in her lap, probably her Bible.

I turn away and run as fast as I can until I'm at the end of the street. I don't know what I just witnessed, but I definitely don't want to see it again. I slow down and jog the rest of the way to the church. I wonder if my mom will check on me. I sort of hope she does so that she'll at least talk to me.

When I get to the church, I run to the tree where we last sat. She's not there. I hear the creak of metal against metal and realize someone, I hope her, is on the swings. I walk fast, trying not to be so eager until I see her. My stride is wide, covering as much ground as possible.

She stands. I walk faster. Her arms are down at her sides, her face beaming. I don't care how dark it is, I know she's smiling. I'm in a dead sprint, scooping her up into my arms when I reach her.

I bury my nose into the crook of her neck and inhale. I need to bottle her up so I never miss the way she smells when I'm not with her. Her arms wrap tightly around me as she giggles. I feel her lips, pressing tiny kisses against my neck. This is what I want. What I need. She's answering my questions without me having to find the words to ask.

I can't wait any longer. I set her down and pull back so I can see her, take her in. She's in jeans and a sweatshirt, looking nothing like the other girls in my school. My hands cup her face. She holds my wrists, anchoring us together.

I lean in. She lifts her face, her eyes looking from mine to my lips. She steps closer, as if that was even possible. Her hand finds my hair, allowing mine to spread out, my fingers working into her hair. My heart beats faster. It's in my throat. I swallow hard and wet my lips.

"I want to kiss you so bad."

"I want that, too."

chapter
eighteen

HADLEY

I can't stand it. I pull up on my tippy toes and press my lips to his. I know I shouldn't. This is so wrong. I try to pull away, to stop myself, but he doesn't allow it. He holds me to him, his hand cupping the back of my head firmly. His tongue traces my lip, I sigh, melting into his embrace.

I'm an adult, I know better. But he doesn't allow me to pull away. He holds me, pressing us together. Our lips dance against each other creating the rhythm only they can keep up with. My hands roam over his sweatshirt, sneaking under his shirt, fingertips brushing against his skin. He pauses. I've caught him off guard.

Now is the time to stop. To pull away and put some space between us. We can't act like this, like common teenagers making out in the park. I'm not that person. I can't be and neither can he if he's with me.

"Ryan." I'm breathless as I speak against his lips.

"Do you want to go inside the church? I know how to get in."

I should tell him no. The words should flow easily from my mouth. My head should be shaking and my legs stepping away, but that is not the case. I'm not in control and I need to be. My problem is that my heart and mind are connected and they both want Ryan, so I nod and follow behind him as he pulls us toward the dark and empty church.

"Wait right here," he says with a kiss. I watch as he disappears down a set of steps. I jump when I hear something slam. I look around, weary of my surroundings. An owl hoots from somewhere in the trees sending shivers, not the good kind, down my spine.

"Hey." His voice startles me, I scream. My hands quickly cover my mouth. Ryan pulls me to him, kissing me on the top of my head. "You're shaking."

"You scared me."

"I'm sorry." He bends and kisses me, increasing my heart rate, but for the better.

I pull away, still shivering, but in a good way this time. He smiles and takes my hand. He leads us down the stairs, closing the door behind us. I'm confused as to why I didn't just come with him earlier. He pulls us through the dark room, navigating like he's done this many times. Maybe he has. Maybe I'm not his first.

We walk through a doorway, the area lightened by a few candles. There is a blanket spread out on the floor, catching my attention. This is why he didn't bring me down with him and made me wait outside.

"I really don't know what I'm doing, I've never..." Ryan looks away, embarrassed.

"It's perfect and well worth getting the crap scared out of me."

Ryan shakes his head, turning to me. "I'm sorry. I didn't mean-"

"It's okay," I say, stepping closer. His arms come around me. The soft glow of the candlelight gives me just enough to catch the glint of happiness in his eyes. I can't help it. I lean up and kiss him. His reaction is instant and mirrors mine. There's no doubt in my mind that I'm not pressuring him to do anything he doesn't want to. The problem is that I need to stop this. It can't go further than it already has. Even that is too much and very dangerous.

I step back, ending the connection between us. Ryan frowns. My finger trails over the sad lines appearing on his face.

"We have to be careful, Ryan."

"I'm not sure I can."

I shake my head, wrapping my hand around the back of his neck. My fingers play with his hair. He closes his eyes, clearly enjoying the sensation.

"Believe me when I say this." I lean forward, pressing my lips against his. "If you were eighteen, I wouldn't be saying no."

He opens his eyes wide. I bite my bottom lip. I think I've gone too far. That was more than he needed to know. I'm so stupid. He has no intentions of doing anything other than kissing. I read too much into this.

"What can we do?"

I raise my eyebrow at his question. He tries not to smile. "What do you want to do?" I ask, not afraid of what his answer will be. This will help us take care of the elephant in the room. We'll know where both of us stand. Well, at least, where he stands. I know what I want.

Ryan leads me to the blanket. We sit down, knees touching each other. We hold hands. Ryan plays with the ring on my index finger, his finger running over the top, back and forth.

"I'm not sure how to answer because everything that I'm doing with you, it's all new, but I feel so good when I'm with you and when I'm not…" his head shakes, "I feel like I'm going crazy."

"I feel the same way."

"You do?"

I nod. "I do. I needed to see you. I know it's only been a couple of weeks, but it's been the longest weeks of my life. Everything has changed for me."

"Me too."

"So tell me, what do you want to do?"

Ryan leans forward. "All of it," he whispers into my ear. He lingers there, buried in my hair. I lean into him, fighting the urge to kiss him.

"We need to talk." I don't know what possessed me to say those words. He pulls away, his face marred with sadness. I shake my head and smile, hoping to convey anything but sadness. I need to diffuse the situation. "About us and what we are to each other."

"Okay," he says. His response is hesitant. Maybe he's not ready to define us. I could be jumping the gun, but I have to know. I can't imagine him with anyone else and I don't want to be with anyone but him.

"Can I say something first?"

"Of course," I answer immediately, interested in what he has to say.

"I know this might seem stupid, but I'd like to call you my girlfriend." I look at him questioningly. "I mean, not that I'm going to tell anyone, but I'd at least like to think of you as my girlfriend and you think of me as your boyfriend."

I start laughing. I can't help it. We think so much alike it's scary. He tries to pull back, but I don't let him. I move into his arms, whether he wanted me there or not. I sit on his lap, facing him. His arms wrap around my waist, pulling me closer.

"I want to call you my boyfriend. Hell, I want to walk down the busiest street holding your hand and sharing a cookie, but we have to wait for that to happen. I'm telling you, Ryan, the day you turn eighteen, everyone is going to know you've got me."

"My birthday is still months away. Who says we're still going to be together?"

"I say."

For the next hour or so we make-out. Clothes stay on and hands stay on the outside. We both had to stop a few times, especially when his hand brushed against my breast. I had to fight every urge I had to lean in and remove my shirt so he could touch me properly. Or when I pushed myself into his hard-on and he hissed, I knew I had gone too far.

Being held by him, though, that makes all of this worth it. We fit together.

"I have something to ask you."

Ryan leans up on his elbow, hovering over me. "I think I'm supposed to ask you to prom, since it's my school."

I push him lightly. He falls back, taking me with him. He holds me tight to his chest. I rest my head there, listening to his heartbeat. "Prom would be fun. I didn't go to mine."

"Will you go to prom with me, Hadley Carter?"

I sit up enough to look at him. He's smiling. "I'd be honored. And now I have something to ask."

Ryan folds his arms behind his back and gives me the go ahead look.

"I'm thinking about buying a house in Jackson."

Ryan sits up, moving me in the process. He rests on his elbows, me on my knees. I can't tell if he's upset or confused.

"You want to live in Jackson?"

I nod.

"Because of me?"

I nod.

"Will I be able to come over?"

I nod.

"I think I like the idea."

"You do?"

"Yeah, I mean, I still won't have a car, but I'll walk if I have to just to see you."

I run my fingers through his hair, moving his bangs away from his face. "You'll never have to walk to see me. I'll send a car or meet you someplace. Or hell, maybe pick you up at your house because I'm determined to win over your parents."

"I don't want to talk about my parents, but I do want to talk about you buying a house here. I like this idea a lot."

"It was Alex's."

"I think she's going to be my best friend."

Ryan's lips find mine and this is how we spend the rest of our night, into the morning. We don't sleep, sharing kisses and covert touches. When he holds me, whispering into my ear how he feels so different with me, I want to wrap us up in a bubble and take him with me. I don't want to leave this moment.

When the sky turns light, we break apart. I help him clean up the used candles and put the blanket back. We walk hand in hand to my car. He kisses me quickly before he runs off down the road without looking back.

The only reason I get behind the wheel is because in six hours I'll be seeing him again.

chapter
nineteen

Leaving Hadley at her car wasn't my idea of fun, but I stayed out later than I had planned. My dad wakes up early on Saturdays. I intended to only be out for a little while. Oh who am I kidding? I'd still be with Hadley if I knew I'd get away with it.

I'm trying to pace myself, but the longer I take, there's more of a chance that my dad will be awake and looking for me.

When I hit my street, my biggest fear comes to life. The garage door is open, he's awake, but his truck is gone. There's a chance he knows I'm not home or he left earlier and didn't look in to wake me up. I have no way of knowing. I have only one decision to make. Sneak in or walk in through the front door like nothing is amiss.

I do the latter. Better to face the music. Walking up the path, my mom is sitting in the living room. A vision from last night flashes before me. She's dressed in her casual Saturday clothes of gray slacks and a white dress shirt. She's doing a puzzle. Her table is set-up in the living room. Her hand moves slowly as she looks for a place to set the next piece. When she finds its destination, she picks up her coffee cup and takes a drink, her eyes never leaving the puzzle board.

I wonder if she's happy. When I look at Hadley, she's always smiling. Her eyes are so full of life that you can't help but be curious about what goes on in her life. Her laugh, it makes you want to tell her jokes just so you can hear the sounds she makes. My mom, she doesn't smile or laugh. I can't remember a time when she did. That thought alone makes me sad. Shouldn't my dad want her to be happy? Isn't it his job to make sure his wife, the woman he took vows to love forever, is always smiling?

I take the last few steps and enter the house. It's quiet, the clank of the door shutting echoes throughout the house. She shifts, her eyes only looking up briefly before she looks back at her puzzle. I thought for sure she'd smile at me. I'm her son, is she not happy that I'm home?

I don't know what to do. It seems that since Hadley came to church, my mom has been more withdrawn than usual. I wish she were more like Dylan's mom, active and vibrant. Mrs. Ross is always peppy, sometimes too much according to Dylan, but at least she smiles.

I sit down on the couch, rubbing my hands on my jeans. I stop quickly when she turns and looks at me.

"Mom?" my voice cracks. She looks up briefly, before picking up her next piece.

"Go change your clothes, Ryan."

I look down and realize that I'm in the same clothes from yesterday. I get up without hesitating and head to the bathroom and take my five-minute shower. I put on a pair of shorts and a t-shirt before making my way back into the living room.

She hasn't moved. Or maybe she did get up to re-fill her cup, but I doubt it. Her legs are crossed, just as they were when I came in. It's as if she's a statue. Maybe she thinks if she moves, she'll crack and fall to pieces.

I pull a chair from the dining room and sit across from her. Doing a puzzle upside down doesn't really have any advantages, but it is quality time with my mom. I see a slight hint of a smile when I pick up a piece. I try not to stare, but seeing her cheeks rise, even for a brief moment, is nice to see.

"Who's the girl?" She doesn't look at me when she asks. Her voice is soft and caring.

I take a deep breath and place my puzzle piece in the proper location. "Her name is Hadley Carter."

"Yes, I remember that much, but who is she… to you?" Her eyes meet mine and I can't tell if she's upset or not. There is no emotion coming from her.

I clear my throat. My fingers fiddle with the puzzle piece I've just picked up. "She's my girlfriend."

Mom leans back in her chair. Her hands leave the table and rest in her lap. Her eyes, they move from me to the table and to the window. Maybe she's watching for my dad, knowing I'd never say things if he was around.

"She's very pretty."

"She's beautiful, inside and out. And I like her a lot."

She nods and picks up her coffee cup, but doesn't take a drink. "You know you're not allowed to date."

I sigh. "Why's it okay if I go out with Dylan?"

This has been something weighing on my mind. They are always so eager and willing to let me hang out with Dylan. Hell, she even let me spend the night in a hotel room with her without even questioning our motives. For all she knows we were having crazy animal sex all night long.

"Dylan…" Mom smiles when she looks at me. A real smile, one that makes her face light up. She loves Dylan. I know this. "She's a good girl and treats you well."

"So does Hadley."

She shakes her head. "A good girl would never ask you to sneak out at night to meet her."

"You…" my voice catches in my throat. "You know?"

She nods.

"It's not what you think." I look away to gather my thoughts. How am I going to sell Hadley to my mom when she's so smitten with Dylan? "I like Hadley, Mom. A lot and want to see her as much as I can. She doesn't live around here, so it's not like I can see her at school or hang out after. She works a lot –"

"What does she do?" she interrupts me. At least she's asking questions. That could mean she's interested.

"She's a musician."

"Devil's music?"

"Mom, she's not the devil. She's a musician. You'd like music if you'd listen. Hadley tells stories with her songs."

"It's not allowed, Ryan."

"Why not?" I ask, leaning forward. I want her to look me in the eyes and tell me why we don't watch television or even have a radio, but she doesn't. She just sits there with her coffee cup in her hand, holding it tight as if it's her lifeline.

"Mom, please talk to me." I plead. "I saw you last night in here and things looked weird. What was that?"

She looks at me, her eyes cold. "It's called praying. You should do more of it. It will help you guide your decisions so that you are making the best one for yourself."

"Mom, I like Hadley and she likes me. I'm not asking for permission to see her. I'm almost eighteen and am willing to take the risk of sneaking out at night to be with her, but I'd like for you to see things from my side. For the first time, I've found someone that likes me for who I am and isn't turned off by my second-hand clothes. She doesn't care that I don't have money, drive a fancy car, or live in a mansion. None of that matters to her because she likes me, your son, the one you've been raising."

I can't sit anymore. My hands are shaking. I want to throw her puzzle across the room and demand that she show me one ounce of support, to be there for me instead of hiding inside herself all the time. I get up and pace, chewing on my bottom lip. When I turn and look at her, she's crying. I've made her cry.

I go to her, bending down in front of her. "Mom," I say as I move her chair away from the table and take her cup out of her hand. "I want a chance at a life different from here. This life isn't for me. The walls are closing in and I feel like I'm being squeezed of everything I know. Please, Mom, I know you're not happy here. You never smile and it kills me to see you like this."

"I'm happy," she says quietly.

I shake my head. "Well, I'm not. I don't want to work at the mill. I don't even want to live in Brookfield anymore. I hate it here."

"Ryan –"

"No, Mom, listen to me. I need something different. I want to be in a place that is alive, where people talk to each other every day, not just on Sundays."

"And this girl plans to take you away?"

"No, she doesn't, she's not like that." I get up and move back to my chair. "Hadley is different and the way she makes me feel – I didn't know what I was missing until I met her."

"You sound like you're in love with a girl you just met."

I shrug. Maybe I am. I just don't know what love is or what it's supposed to feel like. If love is what my parents have, I don't want any part of it.

"I like her, mom. She makes me happy."

"You just met her."

"I know, but haven't you ever felt a connection with someone so strongly that you'd do whatever it takes to see them?" I lean forward, waiting for her answer. She must've felt something for my dad at one time. He couldn't have always been like this.

She shakes her head. I wonder why she married a man she doesn't love.

"Do you love Dad?"

"Of course."

"But he doesn't make you smile."

"Things…" she takes a deep breath. "Things change after a while."

"If you love someone, your love should only grow stronger. Isn't that what you used to whisper to me at night?"

Mom looks out the window and back at me. "Love is foolish, but I have a feeling you aren't going to listen to me, so you need to be careful, Ryan. You can't let your father find out about this girl or what you've been doing at night."

I sit back, shocked at what she just said. "You'll let me see Hadley?"

She nods, biting her lower lip. "Please don't do anything stupid. I can't protect you."

"I won't, I promise. Would you like to meet her? Again, I mean." I hope that she says yes. I don't want to keep Hadley shut out of my life. I'd like for us to have a normal relationship. Well, as much as one is allowed.

"Your dad isn't going to church tomorrow. I'll meet her then." Mom gets up and walks away, leaving me to think about what she just said. She's willing to meet Hadley and invited her back to church.

I hear the pots and pans clinking together and figure I should help. I roll up her puzzle and put it away, along with her folding table. I have a few minutes before I'm due to leave for work and there's only one thing I want to do.

I walk into the kitchen and wrap my arms around my mom, hugging her tightly. "I love you, Mom." I kiss her cheek quickly, but it was enough to know she's been crying.

chapter
twenty

HADLEY

"We should get up and do something. We could go shopping." I say this with no intention of moving. I'm comfortable. My head is resting on his chest as he plays with my hair. I picked him up at work and we came back to my hotel. When he suggested we go to bed, I admit that I froze. I'm walking a fine line between right and wrong and one slip up and I'm in deep. I have to be careful. When I said we could sit on the couch, he whispered that he'd keep his hands to himself. Something I wanted to tell him wasn't necessary, but knew it was.

Now the sun is shining through the large picture window of my hotel, warming the room. I could stay here all day, locked in his arms. We slept, but not very much. Once I got over the shock of him actually being here, I couldn't keep my lips off of him. He held true to his word though and his hands didn't roam, even if I wanted them to.

Ryan sits up on his elbow, effectively pushing my back onto the bed. His hand trails down the curve of my face. His fingers ghost over my lips. His eyes roam over my face, before his lips touch mine briefly.

I reach for him instinctively when he pulls away, but he shakes his head. He's toying with me and it makes me wonder how he learned to act like this or if this is just natural.

"Would you like to meet my mom?"

I move away slightly, staring at him with shock. I know I heard him correctly, but for some reason I'm having a bit of trouble comprehending what exactly he just said.

"Say what?"

"You heard me." He pulls me back into his arms, nestling against my neck. His lips press against my skin ever so lightly, sending chills down my arms.

"You want me to meet your mom?"

He nods against my neck.

"Does she want to meet me?"

"Yes," he whispers against my skin.

This time I sit up, breaking the connection between us. I can't take him seriously when all I want to do his rip off his clothes. I sit cross-legged in front of him. His hand immediately finds mine. He, too, needs to touch me. It's like we need each other to breathe and that's something I haven't felt for a very long time.

"What's going on, Ryan?"

He sits back up on his elbow. "We talked yesterday before I went to work. I told her that you're important to me."

"Does she know you're here?"

"Yes, she does. I guess she's helping me in a way. She doesn't approve of me sneaking around, but she's not going to tell my dad."

"That's a good thing, right?"

Ryan chuckles. "Very good."

"Where am I supposed to meet her?"

"Church," he says as he looks at the bedside clock. "That gives you two hours to do whatever girls do before we have to leave."

I punch him lightly with my free hand.

"How long does it take you to get ready?"

"I can be ready in forty-five minutes. Why?"

"Because I want to kiss you some more."

"You do?"

"Come here, let me show you."

I fall into Ryan's arms. His hands don't leave my hair, my neck, or my face. They never roam past my shoulders. This PG relationship is not what I had in mind when I thought about having a boyfriend, but I'll take it. I'll take whatever I can get with him.

Pulling away from him is torture. It's like pulling two magnets away from each other. The pull is there and sometimes you aren't strong enough to keep them from reattaching. That's how I feel. He makes me want to be better, to write more, to smile at every little moment that happens to me, whether it's a good thing or not.

I slip on a dress, one more appropriate for church, and stare at myself in the mirror. I'm twenty-two years old and in love with a boy. I mouth the words over and over again, *I love him*. I watch in fascination, as my face breaks out into the biggest grin I've seen in a long time. Nothing can even come close to what I'm feeling for Ryan and he's about to introduce me to his mom. If he had told me this when we first met, I'd call bullshit.

Coming out of the bathroom, he's sitting on the edge of the bed. He's changed into slacks and a dress shirt. If I didn't know better, I'd say we are an old couple following a daily routine. I like the idea of growing old with him.

He stands, taking the few steps that separate us. He pulls my hand into his. He's happy – it's written all over his face.

"I have a beautiful girlfriend."

I shy away at him calling me beautiful. He doesn't realize how much of a compliment that is. How much that word means to me. Sure, I hear that I'm hot or sexy, but never beautiful.

"Thank you."

"I mean it." He steps closer. I want to kiss him. Throw him back onto the bed and rip off his shirt. The desire to feel his skin against mine is there, testing my resolve.

"I know," I say, nodding. "You make me feel beautiful." He does. It's in the way that he looks at me. The way that he holds my hand or caresses my face, his fingers stop against my skin.

A knock on the door causes him to step back; even though Alex knows he's here and knows about us, he's cautious. I can't blame him, but would like him to feel at ease when we're together like this. Alex isn't going to tell anyone.

"Come in," I holler. Ryan lets go of my hand. He turns away and stares out the window, stuffing his hands into his pockets when Alex walks in.

"Your car is here."

"Great, thank you. Do you want to come with us?"

"To church?"

I nod.

"I'll pass. I have a date with my American Express." The thought of going shopping appeals to me, but this is important to Ryan. It's important to me. I want his parents to like me and if his mom is offering an olive branch, I'm not going to turn my back.

Alex turns and leaves. I know she's waiting for a heart-to-heart, the one where I tell her that I've fallen completely in love with him even though we've just met. If I believed in love at first sight, I'd say I had it for Ryan, but I don't. Not after last time.

I walk over to Ryan and slide my arms through his. My head rests between his shoulder blades. He leans back, gently, adding just enough pressure to let me know he's aware of me. My lips press to his cloth-covered back. He turns in my arms, wrapping his arms around me, pulling me close.

"I hate thinking about leaving this room."

"I know. I'll have a house soon, not that it makes much difference, but we'll have more freedom. We'd be able to go outside and walk around."

"I can't wait."

Ryan smiles down on me, giving me a light kiss on my nose. "We need to go."

I reluctantly let him go and we walk side by side out of my hotel room. Our arms brush lightly as we walk. I want to hold his hand, but with the security cameras, I can't risk it. I hate feeling this way – hate it. It makes me feel as if I'm ashamed that he's with me. Of all things, why does he have to be only seventeen?

When we reach the lobby, Ryan slips his jacket over his head. This is something we discussed and as much as I hate it, it's for the best. I need to protect Ryan and this is the only way to do it. The last thing I need is for Ian to have to do damage control. He has already been leaving me angry voicemails and once he figures out I'm in Jackson, he's going to become even more irate. Not that I can blame him. I did leave right after a show without any word to him.

Ryan follows me through the lobby. As soon as the door opens, I look to my left and then right. I don't see any cameras, but that doesn't mean they aren't there, lurking in the shadows and behind brick walls. I slide into the car, followed by Ryan. Once the driver has shut the door, I let out the breath I didn't realize I was holding.

I search for Ryan's hand while watching out the windows as the driver takes off. We're sitting too far apart due to the lack of privacy glass. At least the windows are tinted. Alex will have to be more specific when she orders cars, especially when I'm with Ryan. I don't want to hold back if I don't have to.

Our conversation stills and, believe it or not, we discuss the weather. I never thought I'd be that type of person, apparently I am. Ryan tells me that the temperature here stays fairly warm through the winter, but they do get a lot of rain. He asks me about Christmas in New York City, so I tell him. I watch as his features change, much like you'd assume a little boy on Christmas morning would look. I may have to kidnap him and take him to New York. There is no way I'm not going to try and recreate this image again.

When we pull into the church parking lot, people stop and stare. I wasn't thinking. I should've rented a car and drove us. This black town car is a sore thumb, a blinking light screaming 'look at me'! I lean my head back and close my eyes, wanting it all to go away just for two hours so I can meet my boyfriend's mother without any disruptions. Somehow I doubt that's going to happen.

I slip on my dark glasses and large hat just as my door opens. I'm being treated like the celebrity that I am. I should've asked for no special treatment. I seem to stop thinking rationally when I'm with Ryan. He clouds my judgment. This isn't what his mom needs to see. I look like some rich snob, too lazy to open my own door.

Ryan nudges me. I look at him briefly and smile before sliding out of the car. He follows, reaching for my hand once the car door shuts. I try to pull away, to save him from the onslaught of what's about to happen, but he holds on tighter.

The last time I was here, we snuck in. That was the smart thing to do. This time, I'm out in the wide open and people staring. Funny enough, these are the same people that saw me in the basement and paid no attention to me, but now, they can't get enough of an eyeful.

Ryan walks us by a small group of people. A few of them whisper, one of them points. I should be used to this, but I feel like I'm under a microscope. I'm being scrutinized and I hate it.

His mom walks up to us. Her dress is green and looks new. She beams when she looks at her son. The expression on her face is infectious and I can't help but grin.

"Mom, I'd like you to meet my girlfriend, Hadley. Hadley, this is my mom, Sally Stone." Ryan repeats the same words he said last time he introduced us, only adding *girlfriend* this time. I extend my hand and am warmly met by Sally Stone's hand.

"It's a pleasure to meet you, Hadley." Her hand is cold in mine. She doesn't have a strong grip.

"Believe me, Mrs. Stone, the pleasure's all mine."

"Please, call me Sally."

I look at Ryan, who looks pleased, if not sitting on the edge of excited. "Thank you for inviting me today."

"Well, I know you're busy so I'm glad you could join us."

Ryan leans in and gives his mom a kiss on the cheek. Her face lights up, like this is the first time he's done something so sweet. Somehow I doubt that.

We follow his mom into church. I try to ignore the stares and whispers and wonder if Ryan is listening. If he is, does he care? I pray that he doesn't, because this is peanuts compared to what things will be like if we were to be seen in someplace like New York.

We stop short when his friend, Dylan, steps in front of us. She looks upset. Her hands are resting on her hips and her eyes are red. It looks as if she's been crying.

"I can't believe you brought her here after you told me yes."

chapter
twenty-one

RYAN

I freeze when Dylan stops in front of us. I never got a chance to tell Hadley about the stupid dance. No, that's not right. I had many chances, but couldn't bring myself to say the words. Deep down I have a feeling I've done something wrong. Every time the words were ready to come out, my heart feels as if it's squeezing, cutting off my circulation. I don't know what's going to happen when I tell Hadley, but my gut is telling me that she's going to be hurt.

Dylan stands in front of us. She looks stiff, nothing like the Dylan I'm used to. Her eyes are dark, heavy with make-up. She tried this look once before and I told her it made her look scary, only I can tell she's been crying. She looks at Hadley and back to me, her eyes becoming wet.

I look at Hadley as she pulls away, joining my mom in a pew. My mom nods to Dylan and looks at the side door. I suppose that means I need to talk to Dylan, but what do I say? I'd rather sit with Hadley through the sermon and deal with Dylan later. I turn around and walk back down the aisle toward the side door with Dylan following.

She slams the door and pushes me, her fists clenched. "What is she doing here?"

I step away from her and her flying fists, waiting for her to calm down. I've never seen her like this. Dylan crosses her arms and stares out the window. I wait, but hope that she gets on with whatever her issue is because I want to get back to Hadley.

"Ryan?"

"Yeah?"

"You said you'd take me to Homecoming."

"And I will."

"But you're still going to see her?"

I run my hand through my hair and sigh. Maybe this is why I've never had a girlfriend, because this is all complicated. Did agreeing to take Dylan to a dance mean we were now a couple? Because if that's the case it's not what I meant.

"Why would I stop seeing her? I like her."

Dylan turns and shakes her head. She presses her face into her hands. I don't know if I should reach out and touch her shoulder or what, so I just stand here with my hands stuffed into my pockets.

She walks to the door and opens it, leaving me rooted in my spot. She turns and looks at me and doesn't say anything before walking back into the church. I scratch my head, wondering why I had to come back here if she wasn't going to talk.

I also wonder what is going on with her.

I quietly close the door behind me and walk to the pew where my mom and Hadley are sitting. They are right next to each other, sharing a Bible. I can't help but smile. I sit down next to Hadley and pull her hand into mine. She looks over at me briefly and smiles before giving her attention to my mom. I think this one time I'm okay with not being the focus of her attention because when I lean forward I see my mom smile – and that is a sight I want to see every day.

Sitting through this sermon is torture. I think this is why mom suggested Hadley come, to teach us a lesson. I think about plugging my ears, but I'm not sure that would go over too well. Instead I listen to Reverend Monroe talk about the sins of sex before marriage and I start thinking that while this may put my mom's mind at ease, it only spurs mine.

I don't think Sally Stone would be too happy to find out her son now wants to test the waters after listening to Reverend Monroe go on and on about the pleasures of sex between a man and a woman, even if he's telling the young members of the congregation that we should wait.

When he finishes speaking there are snickers from the younger members. I have a feeling his message of abstinence didn't hit home like he thought it would. I look around and spot Dylan, who is glaring at me. I try to grin, but clearly that is the wrong thing to do. She stands and walks out of the church. A few people turn and look when the door slams. This, of course, catches my mom's attention. She looks down and shakes her head before standing and greeting other parishioners like she's never met them before.

I pull Hadley up, leading her out of the aisle toward the basement door. I can't sneak her into the utility closet this time, even though all these thoughts are running through my head, courtesy of Reverend Monroe. I'm tempted to find out just what her skin feels like against mine. If it's as pleasurable and sinful as he described. This is a sin I'm willing to commit, but I doubt she'll let me.

When I look back, she's staring at me. For a moment I think her eyes sparkle, but I know that's ridiculous – it's the light from the stained glass window shining just right against her, making her beauty stand out. I've never seen someone so pretty, at least not like her. I've never thought of Dylan as pretty, I guess maybe she is. I know guys at school think she is, but to me she's just Dylan. But when I look at Hadley, I want to get lost in her as if she's my salvation.

She pushes me forward, shaking her head and laughing. I'm not sure I'll ever get used to the way I feel when I look at her, or the way she makes me feel. I suppose if I don't, it's something I can look forward to each time I see her or am in a room with her. This feeling, it's not something I want to go away.

Hadley wraps her hand around my forearm and leans into me. I like this. I like the way she's being with me here. But I know this is only because we're away from others and somewhat secluded. No one has headed toward the social gathering in the basement, but they will soon.

I'm surprised to find Dylan downstairs when we get there. She looks at me briefly before turning away. She's putting out the cookies, which is something I usually help her with. Hadley grabs my hand and drags us over to the table.

"Hi, Dylan."

Dylan stills, her hand lingering over the tray. She sets down the package of cookies and turns toward Hadley. I can't tell if her smile is genuine or not, but her eyes definitely look cold.

"Hadley, it's so nice for you to join us."

"Thanks. I like your church."

"Of course you do," Dylan mumbles as she turns back to the cookies.

Hadley lets go of my hand and starts unwrapping a pack of cookies. Dylan looks at her out of the corner of her eye, but doesn't stop her. Maybe if I leave them, they can talk and Dylan can go back to being Hadley's number one fan.

I step away and go set up the coffee. As much as I'd like to stay and listen to what they're talking about, I'd like Dylan to go back to liking Hadley. I'm still not sure what Dylan's problem is. I wish someone would tell me though, because I miss my friend and don't really like being on the receiving end of her dirty looks and angry outbursts.

I sneak glances at Dylan and Hadley every few moments. They seem to be chatting and Dylan smiles a few times. My mom joins them and laughter ensues. I'm a bit jealous that I'm missing what's so funny, but I have feeling I'm the cause of Dylan's anger so it's probably best that I stay away. Even if that means I'm missing Hadley.

Reverend Monroe comes over, slapping me on the shoulder.

"Coffee, sir?"

"If you're offering, I wouldn't mind a cup."

I press down on the pump, watching the hot liquid fill the Styrofoam cup. I can't stand the smell of coffee and don't know how people stomach it. Dylan loads hers full of sugar, not sure why she just doesn't eat a candy bar. I hand the Reverend his cup and pretend to be interested in the packets of sugar. I don't know why he's lingering, I hope that mom didn't ask him to talk to me. I mean, if she's worried about me doing something with Hadley, she shouldn't be. Hadley won't let me even touch her like I want to.

Never have I thought about being with a girl before until Hadley and now I can't stop thinking about it.

"Did you learn anything from today's sermon?" he asks.

Yes. I learned that I want to find out what my girl tastes like thanks to your sermon about sweet and sinful desire, I want to say, but I don't.

"Yes, sir," I reply without making eye contact. If I look at him, he'll see right through me. I peek over his shoulder, looking for Hadley. She's with my mom, talking with others. Reverend Monroe looks behind him and smirks.

"That's exactly what I was talking about. Young men like yourself getting involved with the poisoned apple."

I look at him, confused. What's he talking about, poisoned apple?

"I'm sorry?" I ask, this time making eye contact. I want to see him when he tells me that Hadley is poison and that I have to stay away from her.

"Just saying that girls like her, they are poison. They lure you to their wells only to drown you when they're done with you."

I scratch the back of head, wondering what the hell he's talking about. I don't remember him saying any of this stuff. Maybe I zoned out more than I thought I did. I don't know, but he isn't making any sense. Hadley isn't poison. She's far from it.

"Um… I think I'm going to go –"

He steps closer, leaning in. "Your father knows about your little friend. It might be best for both of you if you cut your ties before things become too complicated."

I step back and look at him. He raises his eyebrow before he turns, walking away. I'm left standing, rooted as if my feet were buried in cement. I don't like the idea of my dad knowing about Hadley. Nor do I care much for the subtle message that Reverend Monroe just gave me.

I need to talk to my mom, find out what she knows. I don't want my father talking to Hadley or knowing anything about her. I'm not ashamed of Hadley, just afraid of my father and what he might do.

I look over to where mom and Hadley are standing, only to see Hadley stalking toward me. Her eyes are pinched, her mouth in a straight line. I've never seen an angry Hadley, but I have a feeling this might be it.

"We need to talk," she says as she walks by me. I have no option but to follow. I'm a few steps behind her as she stomps up the steps. She pushes the door, hard. It hits against the outside wall and bounces back in time for me to stop it with my hand before it hits me in the face.

I follow her to her car. The driver is resting against the side, trying to look nonchalant against this blacked-out car. He looks up when he sees us coming and opens the back door. She slides in. I hesitate until I hear her sigh loudly. The door slams just as I sit down. Good thing I moved my leg in time. I reach for her hand, only to have her pull away. I knew a relationship like this wasn't going to last. She realized today, being with my mother and meeting the parishioners that she can do so much better.

"Do you have something to tell me?"

I look at her, confused, and shake my head.

She turns her head slowly, her eyes penetrating. Whatever it is that I *should* be telling her and I'm not is pissing her off. I slowly inch away from her gaze. For the first time since I've met Hadley Carter, I'm completely uncomfortable. She turns and looks out the window, shaking her head.

"I should've known a long-distance relationship wouldn't work." She says this so quietly I almost didn't hear her.

"Why won't this work? I mean, I know I can't drive or fly to see you, but soon –"

"It's not about you being able to drive or fly to be with me. I'd do that if you asked." She turns her body, resting against the door, bringing her knee up and hooking it behind her leg. I so want to run my finger along the curve of her knee to the hem of her dress, but don't know if I can take her shying away from me again.

I don't know what to say so I stay quiet, just like I do at home when my dad is harping on me.

"Are you in love with Dylan?"

"What?" I squeak out like a girl. I clear my throat and ask her again.

"You heard me."

"I did, but not sure why you'd ask me that question."

"Because Dylan said that you asked her to the homecoming dance the other day and I'm trying to figure out why you'd ask her if you have a girlfriend."

"I didn't ask her."

Hadley shakes her head. "So you're not going to homecoming with her?"

"No, I didn't say that. She asked me. She said she couldn't find another date and didn't want to go alone or something like that. I'm so used to saying yes to her that I didn't really understand what I was agreeing to.

"She told my mom before I had a chance to tell her that I really didn't think you'd like the idea of me going with her and I'm gathering from the way we're talking, I was right."

Hadley bangs her head against the car window. Her hands cover her face. When she pulls away, her eyes are glistening.

"I'm sorry I didn't tell you. I didn't tell you because I didn't know how."

"Do you want to go to homecoming with her?"

I shake my head.

Hadley comes over, straddling my lap. "You can't ever lie to me, Ryan. If you don't want to be with me or want to date other people, just tell me. Don't worry about my feelings or breaking my heart. I'm falling in love with you, but if you don't want me, just tell me and I'll go away. I promise."

I look around for the driver and notice that he's no longer standing near the car. I drag my hands up her legs, under her dress. I'm waiting for her to stop me, but she doesn't. My hands rest on her ass, pulling her closer to me. I lean my head back, my eyes rolling, when she pushes down on me. The feeling of her against me, it's something I want to explore. Her hand trails up my chest, around my neck and into my hair. Soft lips press against mine and as much as I'm enjoying the feel of her in my hand, I need her closer.

My hand finds her hair as her tongue touches mine. I hold her face softly in my hand. My other hand grazes over the side of her breast. She pushes into me more, urging me. Leaning forward, I take a chance. Moving my hand to the top of her dress, my fingers trail over the swell of her breast. She bites down on my tongue, lightly, but enough to keep me going. I want to tear away from her so I can see what I'm doing, but I don't dare stop. I move one strap, then the other and finally move away from her lips to her neck until I reach her breast. Her hand pulls at my hair. It should hurt, but it feels good and I want her to pull harder.

I move the top of her dress, exposing her pink bra. I kiss along the lace, moving it a little each time until her hand stops me and her face is buried in my neck.

"I want you, Hadley," I say into her ear, taking a chance with my words. "I know I'm not experienced, but I know everything in my body is telling me that you can help get rid of this ache I'm feeling."

"I can't, but I want to."

"Can you look at me?"

She lifts her head, kissing along my chin to my lips before she's upright. She moves my hair away from my eyes; her touch is tender and loving.

"I'm falling in love with you, too."

"Yeah?" she asks, her eyes beaming.

"Yeah," I say, matching her expression.

"I can't wait to be with you." Her lips find mine again and all I know is that my birthday can't come soon enough.

chapter
twenty-two

HADLEY

It's been a month since I've seen Ryan. Actually, it's been thirty-seven days, eight hours and forty-two minutes and I hate every second of it. The last day that I saw him, I was angry at him. I thought he was a no good two-timer, but he isn't and I have to remember that. Just because Cole cheated on me, doesn't mean Ryan is going to.

We've officially begun the countdown until his birthday. I don't have anything planned, other than to see him. It will, however, be a welcome relief to kiss him in public without the threat of being arrested. Right now all we can do is video chat or text. By the time we can actually meet up on the phone, he's either tired or doing homework or I'm exhausted. The time difference doesn't help, either. All of this has made me crabby or a *royal bitch*, as Ian says.

I knew my occupation was going to be a problem, I just didn't expect it to be something like this. When I came back from my impromptu trip, Ian was pissed and completely unhinged. Apparently, my escape from my life cost me dearly. I missed an important interview with a high profile magazine and they aren't willing to reschedule. In fact, they ran with an expose and went as far as saying that I was shipped off to rehab, causing a total uproar.

This prompted Ian to call my parents. I could've asserted myself and reminded him that I'm an adult and his employer, but he was right. My decision to just up and leave had a repercussion on my career and I can't afford bad press, which brings me to my latest dilemma, Ryan. He's angry, hurt and anxious for me to visit. I can't blame him and I feel the same, but there isn't anything I can do. Ian has me on a short leash and each time I tug, he tightens the collar a little bit more. The last thing I want is Ryan's mom thinking I'm some junkie.

Alex is another story. Her mom fell ill so she has stayed back in New York while I've been in Los Angeles working. It kills me that I want to be in three different places and can't be. I should be with Alex and her mom, but I also want to be with Ryan. Work calls though and with Ian watching me like a hawk there's no way I can sneak off for a weekend.

"Hello?"

"Good morning, sunshine." I pull my phone away, look at the screen and roll my eyes. With the invention of caller ID I should never have to talk to someone I don't want to and yet, here I am, doing just that.

"What do you want, Ian?"

"You have a meeting today."

"No, I don't."

"You do. I just scheduled it and you won't miss it."

I sit up and adjust my pillow. I know I pissed him off, but I think he's being a bit extreme. "It was one interview Ian, that's it. I don't understand why you're being like this."

"You have no idea what it is I do for you on a daily basis, do you?"

"I guess you're about to tell me, aren't you?"

"You're right, I am. When you took off to do God knows what with that underage boy, I was left to pick up the pieces. This isn't the first interview you've missed. Remember last year when you blew off the talk show because they had Coleman on the hour before and you didn't want to run into him? How about the day you showed up to your photo shoot and looked so doped up because you hadn't slept in two days? Is any of this ringing a bell, Hadley? Each and every time I'm there to fix your mistakes. The pregnancy rumors, the drinking, the drugs, over and over again I'm putting out fires that you've started because you're too stubborn to think before you act.

"This time, you blew off the same reporter from the TV show so she instantly ran with how unstable you are. You can't afford this. You can't have mothers telling their daughters that they can't listen to your music. You can't have movie directors wanting to take a chance on you, only for them to think you're some high-society socialite who doesn't give a rat's ass about anyone but herself."

"None of this happened."

"Why, because you didn't hear about it? There's a reason for that, Hadley. You and Alex have your heads so far up your asses you don't know what the hell is going on around you. You go around doing whatever it is you want without any repercussions, leaving me to pick up the pieces."

"Well I guess that's why I pay you the big money, isn't it?"

"See, that's what I'm talking about. You don't care. Maybe I'll stop caring, especially when reporters are sniffing around you and this boy toy. Maybe I'll let it drop that he's only seventeen and you aren't exactly keeping things PG."

"You wouldn't."

"I would. Now get your ass over here, pronto."

"Fine! Who is the meeting with?"

"Another musician. It's for a small tour, starting immediately. You need this tour to fix your reputation before it tanks. Hadley, don't be late. I'm getting sick of your games."

I sigh heavily as I roll out of bed, throwing my phone into the chair. My neck is sore and I'm tired. Ryan and I were on the phone until about three in the morning. I can't imagine how tired he is with having to go to school today; at least I got to sleep in.

I drag my sorry ass into the shower. I have a meeting with some artist that wants to do a mini tour before the end of the year. Lovely. That means I'll be on the road for the holidays. Not something I really want to do, but Ian insists and Lord knows I can't afford to piss him off. He says I need to do something to make up for my "blunder". It's not like I went out on stage naked. I missed an interview. I can't imagine who Ian is bringing in to help my image.

But I have a feeling I'm not going to like it.

Walking into Ian's house is like second nature. I half expect to find *Anal Anna* lounging by the pool. I don't know why Ian has a house in Los Angeles, especially when I live in New York City and that's where we're from. Ian living here makes things extremely difficult. I don't want to be here. Being on the East Coast also puts me closer to Ryan and allows me to be in my own home instead of a hotel.

I know I'll find Ian in his office; I think he sleeps in there most nights. Voices carry down the hall. The closer I get, the more familiar the second voice is. My hand shakes as I twist the knob, pushing the door open slightly. The creak in the hinges gets their attention. They both turn and look at me. Ian's smiling and leaning back in his chair, his hands behind his head. I know he's done this on purpose. This is my punishment for wanting to be with Ryan and I have a feeling I won't be able to get out of this newly inked deal, whether I want to or not.

I want to turn and run out of the room, out of the house, when he stands. His movements are slow, calculated. He holds onto the arm of the chair like it's his lifeline. I'm trying to look away, but my eyes betray me. Coleman notices, his mouth turning up. I look away, closing my eyes. I can't look at him without reliving that night.

Meeting him at fifteen, we started dating a year later. It was intense and far too committed for being so young. Both of us were determined to be successful recording artists and let stardom go to our heads. Well at least he did. He couldn't or wouldn't say no to anyone, which was a slight problem for me, especially when I found another woman in our bed.

It only took one night for my life to turn upside down. We had been living together for about six months. I missed him and decided I needed to see him, regardless of being on tour. We had been on opposite sides of the country for far too long.

When I opened the door, it was like one of those Lifetime movies. Clothes spread out on the floor leading to my bedroom, champagne bottle tipped over and the moaning. I'll never forget that sound as long as I live.

I knew I shouldn't have opened the door, but I couldn't resist. My heart was already breaking. I just needed the visuals to split it in half.

They both looked at me, she smiled and he... he threw her off of him and came after me, apologizing as he chased me down the hall. I made it to the front door before he trapped me against it. He held me there, his naked body laced with her scent pushed against mine. He was crying, telling me how much he loved me and that she was a mistake. A stupid, stupid mistake.

I left that night without looking at him. I couldn't. The next day Ian had moving trucks at the apartment and I was front-page news. The break-up was messy and spread across the tabloids. Everything I did was scrutinized. Every date I went on we were hounded by the press. It was never-ending and the only way to make it stop was to stop dating.

"I didn't expect you to be on time."

I jerk up and stare at my uncle. I don't know why he has to be such an ass, but maybe he needs a reminder of who signs his paycheck. I stand in the doorway with no intention of moving.

"Are you going to join us?"

"No, I think I'll wait until your meeting is over before we start ours." I look down at my watch. "How much longer? I'm busy."

Ian lets his chair spring forward, his hands landing on his desk. He chuckles, shaking his head. "This is our meeting, Hadley. Why don't you come in and sit down."

I shake my head. "I'm fine right here. Quick escape for when I'm utterly disgusted with you. Don't worry though. The fill line is getting close. I'm sure it won't take much to set me off."

"So be it. As you can see, Cole is here and I'm sure you're smart enough to guess that you guys are going on tour. It's small, but nightly. There won't be any time for you to gallivant. There will be no meet and greets, either."

My fingers rub my temples. There are so many things wrong with this. Mainly that I'm going to miss Ryan's birthday and I can't have that.

"I'll need a day off in December."

"No."

"You're not my father, Ian. If I need a day off, I'm going to take it."

Ian stands, his hands pressing down on his desk. "You need this tour after your last little fiasco. You will not take a day off. You have a lot at stake here.

Don't encourage me to make a phone call. I have a list of people asking the same question over and over again. Would you like your friend to be front page news?"

"Watch me." I push off the wall and storm down the hall. I know I probably made a huge mistake, but I can't stand being in the same room with either of them. The footsteps behind me make me walk faster. His hand gets to the door before I have a chance to open it, blocking me. It's *that* night all over again.

"You're being unreasonable, Hadley."

I want to scream when he says my name. I haven't seen him since that night and now he's here making my life a living nightmare.

"Cole, move your hand so I can leave."

"We need to talk. I mean, we haven't seen each other in a long time and we should catch up. How about we go for some coffee?"

I shake my head, willing the impending headache to vacate its current residence inside my brain. My head feels as if it's going to explode, not to mention the tears that are threatening to leak down my face. I have nothing to say to Coleman Hollister.

"I don't want to talk to you."

His fingers move down the back of my arm. I jerk away, offended by him even thinking he can touch me.

"Don't," I say through clenched teeth. "You don't get to touch me, ever."

He leans forward, the scruff on his chin rubbing against my neck. "Ian told me about your newest infatuation."

"He told you?" I choke on my words.

"Of course he did. You know we're good for each other. We just got lost a little along the way. Don't think for a minute I'm going to let some little kid stand in my way."

He pushes off the door, leaving me standing here. Anger builds inside of me as I bang my head against the front door. I don't understand why things have to be like this. What does Ian think this he's going to accomplish? That I'm going to stop seeing Ryan?

Pulling open the door, I don't bother shutting it behind me. Childish, I know, but he can deal with the bugs. I realize quickly that I don't have a car. I have two options: sit on the steps and wait, or walk. I'll walk.

I look down at my feet and stare at my high heels. Why did I wear these today? Why did I even get dressed up to come to a meeting with Ian? I slip off my shoes and dangle them from my fingertips like some Hollywood starlet. At least the pavement is cool and not burning the pads of my feet. I could call a cab, but think I need this time to think things through. I know I need the good publicity that a tour can bring, especially with Coleman, but the last thing I want to do is spend any time with him. I know what happened with us was a long time ago, but I'm not over the hurt and it's taken me a long time to trust someone again.

I trust Ryan. Even after the homecoming fiasco, I trust him with my heart. I know that he didn't encourage Dylan in any way and was actually excited to see their homecoming pictures. I did feel a pang of jealousy when he showed them to me, but didn't want Ryan to know. He wanted to make this night special for Dylan, plus he didn't want his dad getting suspicious.

I come upon a park and take a detour. The cold grass feels refreshing on my feet. They ache from the rough concrete. I find a shady spot under a tree and sit down. The park is full of kids and either mothers or nannies. You can't really tell these days, especially here. The kids all look happy, running and screaming, while being chased around jungle gyms. They laugh when they're caught and squirm to be put down, only to start over. I can't help but wonder how these kids feel having their parents gone all the time. I don't know how I'd feel about leaving my child with a nanny all day.

My phone rings and I frantically dig in my purse. When I pull it out, Ryan's face is smiling back at me. This is a picture he took and sent to me before homecoming. He was all dressed up in a tuxedo again, but this time he captured the moment for me. The first time I saw him like this was at the charity ball and we both forgot to get a picture together.

"Hello?"

"Hey, how was your meeting?"

I close my eyes and wish I didn't have to tell him. But we promised each other no secrets, no matter how horrible mine might be.

"My meeting sucked, actually."

He laughs, which makes me feel a little better. He won't be laughing after I tell him why I don't want to tour with Coleman Hollister or that I could potentially miss his birthday. A day he and I have been waiting for, for what seems like an eternity now.

"Where are you?" he asks.

"Sitting in a park, watching all these little kids run around and have fun, remembering when I was little. My mom and I would leave right after school and walk to Central Park. I went to this private school in the city and we'd stop at either the pretzel stand or we'd get a bag of hot roasted nuts if it was cold out. I'd play while she graded papers for an hour before we went home to make dinner for my dad."

"That sounds like a good memory."

"It is. Just watching these kids makes me miss being a kid."

"Not me. I'm counting the days until I'm an adult." Ryan sighs. I know things at home are getting worse for him. His dad has taken away just about any freedom he had. Surprisingly his cell phone has remained a secret, for which I'm thankful. I'm not sure what I'd do if we weren't able to talk or text every day. I know I complain about not seeing him, but I'll take whatever I can get.

"Tell me about your meeting."

"It's boring," I whine.

"I don't care if you sat in a smelly old chair covered in cat fur and had to write your name a hundred times, I want to talk to you and something's on your mind. So I'm guessing it's about your meeting."

"When did my boyfriend become so smart?"

Ryan laughs. "It's because I have this amazing girlfriend."

I sigh and close my eyes and pray that what I'm about to tell Ryan won't change anything between us. One thing's for sure, I can't tell him why I'm doing this.

chapter
twenty-three

RYAN

We discussed emotions in health class today. Happy, sad, emptiness, longing, lust… they were all covered. Girls giggled, ooh'd and ahh'd and batted their eyelashes at some of the guys in the class. Most of the guys laughed when 'lust' was brought up, me included. These feelings I have for Hadley, now that I can start describing them, are increasing even though Dylan told me that they eventually go away and you just fall into a pattern of mundane reality, which apparently is where her parents are in their marriage.

I'm still fighting the urge to tell Dylan everything. After Homecoming our friendship seems stronger. As much as I wanted to back out and not take her, Hadley was adamant that I escort her for the night. She used words like *honor* and *keeping my word* as she yelled at me over the phone. This was just days after she yelled at me in the car. To say I was confused is an understatement.

I relented and took Dylan and we had a good time. I even danced a little, but only after Dylan threatened to expose my secret. I reminded her that no one would believe her and thought I had won the battle until she stated simply, "You'll be the laughing stock of the school." It only took me a moment to realize she was telling the truth and while her tactic may have seemed underhanded, when I told Hadley, she laughed.

When I started dating Hadley, I wanted her and Dylan to be friends. Now I'm not so sure. I can honestly say I'm not a fan of being ganged up on.

Dylan has changed back to the way she was before she found out about Hadley. I don't know if it was something Hadley said, but for whatever reason she's happy and wild again and I'll take that Dylan any day.

I never thought I'd be *that* guy. You know, the one who waits around for his cell phone to ring, constantly checking it just in case he didn't hear it. It's a girl thing. They are always looking and now so am I. I knew that dating Hadley would bring obstacles. I just didn't expect it to be like this. I thought that once her tour was done, she'd have more time, a bit more freedom, but that isn't the case. Her manager has kept her in Los Angeles and away from me for over a month. As pansy as it sounds to say it, I miss her.

I miss having her in my arms. I miss the smell of her hair. I miss the way she smiles when I kiss her or the way she plays with my hair when she's thinking. I fear that we're going to lose what we had now that we've been apart, or worse, she's going to meet someone else. Someone who can provide her with everything that she needs and wants and that she can be seen with in public. I know she wants that and I can't offer her jack shit.

The feeling of dread – an emotion we learned today – washes over me when she answers the phone. The cheery tone she usually has when she answers is missing. I try to mask my alarm; I don't want her to know I'm feeling this way because upsetting her is the last thing I want to do.

I want to know about her day. When I ask her, she plays it off as if it's no big deal, but it is to me. My life is mundane and repetitive, always sticking to the same schedule, even where she's concerned.

The silence is starting to scare me. Should I feel this way? Is she finally realizing the distance is more than she is willing to put up with? She doesn't have to. I'm the one who needs to hold on to what little bit of her I can get.

"Hadley?"

"Yeah, I'm here."

"Something wrong?"

She sighs and now I know. I take a deep breath and prepare myself for what she's going to tell me. It's not working. It's the distance. You're too young. Whatever the reasoning, I'll have to take it like a man.

"Ian's being unreasonable. He's sending me back out on a promotional tour."

"Okay." I'm not sure how to respond. This doesn't seem like such a bad thing. I know she's tired, but she's also a performer and this is her job. Believe me, I'd love to not work and get paid.

"You don't understand."

"What?" Vague Hadley is not my favorite.

"The tour is straight through until the end of the year."

Through the end of the year.

My birthday.

A day that she promised she would spend with me no matter what and now she'll be on tour.

"So no days off?"

"There's more."

I want to say *of course there is*, but I don't. I'm in no position to say anything.

Hadley sighs and starts talking. I listen closely, but really don't hear much after the words *ex-boyfriend, tour* and *together*. She's going on tour with her ex-boyfriend. One that I didn't know existed. Maybe she didn't think it was important to tell me about her ex, or maybe she thought he wasn't important to discuss. I feel he is.

"How serious were you with him?"

"We lived together. He was my first boyfriend. We were sort of thrown together because of our jobs, but…he cheated on me. I was on tour and really missed him so I came home and found him with someone else. I left and haven't seen him since. The break-up was all over the media and was messy. I just don't know why…"

She trails off, not finishing her sentence. I'm not sure what to think. I know that I don't have an opinion, but I'd like one. I don't know what I'd say though.

"This doesn't change anything, Ryan."

"Okay." That is a cop-out answer on my part, because in my mind everything has changed. She'll be spending all her time with this guy, one who knows her very well and I'll be here, waiting.

"Ryan?"

"What?"

"I know this sucks –"

"You're going out on tour with your ex-boyfriend and not just any ex, but one you've lived with and clearly had sex with and you're going to be spending every waking minute with him. I'm sorry if the visions going through my mind aren't what you think they should be."

"Ryan –"

"Is Alex going?"

"No." She says this so quietly I almost don't hear her. So no Alex to keep Hadley occupied or to intercede. Perfect.

I rub my hand over my face. I never knew what jealousy was until now. Everything in me is screaming that this is not good. Nothing good is going to come from this.

"Hadley, I know it's your job. I get it. I'm just… I don't know what I am." I lie. I'm jealous and hurt. Her manager did this. She was supposed to be off. We're supposed to be able to spend winter vacation together. I'll be eighteen. We had plans.

"I'll be there for your birthday."

"Yep. I gotta go. I have to work." I hang up. For the first time since we've started dating I've ended the conversation first and throw my phone onto the bed. It rings instantly, but I ignore her call. I don't have anything to say.

She calls back, I hit ignore and get ready for work. I can hear the phone vibrate against my bed, but I don't look. I can't. I don't want to look at her smiling face on my screen knowing that I'm losing her.

Did I really even have her?

Probably not.

She's Hadley Carter – mega superstar – and I'm Ryan Stone – nobody.

chapter
twenty-four

HADLEY

He hung up on me.

He isn't answering my calls. I never thought things would be like this and all because of Ian and his need for power. I need to tell him no. Tell him that this tour isn't going to be anything but a problem for me and that I won't do it. I don't need to. So what if some stupid article said I was in rehab. If my fans really want to believe that, then so be it. Ryan is more important to me.

I should've known Ian was up to something when he demanded that I stay in Los Angeles and not return to New York when Alex left. We're too close and he doesn't like that. He doesn't like that I listen to her and ask for her input on projects. I know he doesn't like it when Alex speaks her mind; she challenges him and to him that's disrespectful.

I try Ryan one more time, hoping that he'll answer. The phone rings and rings and by the fifth ring I know he's not going to pick up. Why should he? I just told him that I'll be spending the next six weeks with my ex-boyfriend. Ryan's smart enough to know that's night and day in this industry. There are daily rehearsals, interviews and travel. He's going to drive himself crazy with worry. I can't really blame him. I'd be worried too if he told me he was going on a trip with Dylan. I may have told him homecoming was a good idea, but I only did so he wouldn't lose his best friend. I'm a woman in love, I want him on my arm, *not my competition's* and whether Ryan sees that or not, she wants him and

I probably just delivered him to her on a silver platter.

I put away my phone. He has nothing to say. In all likelihood I'm going to miss his birthday and there isn't anything I can do about it. That was to be the night that I don't tell him no. The night when I give in to all my urges and finally be with him the way I've been dreaming about. I know Ryan wants to move things along and now he's worried about Cole. He didn't have to say the words, but his reference to sex was enough to convey that he thinks there could be something more. I can't blame him. I can't. He has every right to feel jilted.

I pull out my phone and try him again. Same result. I try Alex. She'll know what to do. I can't believe I didn't think about calling her right away. She would've been able to tell me how to handle Ryan.

"What's up, Buttercup?"

"I'm in trouble."

"Why, did you and Ryan tango and his parents find out?"

"No, worse." At least it is in my book.

"Worse? Details and hurry, because the suspense is already killing me."

"You're so dramatic. Anyway, Ian is sending me back on tour and Coleman is going with me."

Silence.

And more silence.

Alex clears her throat.

"Coleman as in Coleman Hollister, *the most eligible bachelor in the world according to People Magazine*, Coleman Hollister?"

"Uh huh."

"And you told lover-boy all about Coleman didn't you?"

"How'd you know?"

"Because I know you, Hadley. You were upset about Ian and the hottie jailbait called and you spilled your guts." I try not to smile when she calls Ryan jailbait. I should've called her first. She would've coached me on how to break the news to Ryan without having all this drama.

"Don't call him jailbait."

"Did you smile?"

"Yes, but still. Anyway, he's not talking to me. He's upset and I don't blame him, but there isn't anything I can do. Ian's still pissed from the last time I took off to see Ryan and said I need this for my image. He's threatening to tell everyone how old Ryan is."

"He wouldn't."

"I'd like to think he wouldn't, but I'm not so sure I can trust him to keep Ryan a secret. Besides, he's already told Cole so it's just a matter of time."

"He told Cole?"

"Yeah."

"Freaking shady."

"Tell me about it," I sigh heavily into the phone. I don't understand why things can't be simple.

"Here's the thing. Your image, it's fine. So what if one magazine thinks you went to rehab. You were gone for a weekend. It's not like you disappeared for a month and you were spotted in Jackson. It's not like there's a clinic there. There's only one image of you and Ryan and you can barely see Ryan. Someone would have to do a lot of digging to find dirt on you and him together. Ryan could totally play off the superstar crush that all the other guys out there have. I think Ian is up to something, Hadley. He's dirty and sneaky. And why bring Coleman in? Unless he's planning a bunch of staged publicity shoots and telling the media you guys are together, what's the point?"

I hadn't thought of it like that. I'd like to think my uncle wouldn't stoop so low, but maybe he would. Maybe there's more at stake than I realize. But Ryan's at stake for me. He knows this is my job and he accepts that, but I promised him time off and a special birthday and I'm not interested in breaking that promise to him.

"Do you really think Ian would do something like that?"

"In a heartbeat. Listen girl, something's fishy. I'm not there and all of a sudden you have this tour with Coleman. Remember when you guys broke up and Ian made sure you were moved out as soon as possible. There were pictures of Coleman coming home with flowers, only to find a moving truck there. Staged, totally."

"I don't know. Ian says there have been a lot of rumors about me that he makes sure never end up in the paper. He's making it sound like every time I take a misstep the media is making me out to be some type of drug user or something."

"That's such bullshit. You've never done anything stronger than aspirin."

"I know that and so do you, but what about everyone else? Is that what people think of me?"

"Let me ask you something. Why are you doing this tour? Is it for your image or to keep your secret about Ryan?"

I think about her question for a minute. "A little of both, I guess. I want his mom to like me and I felt like I was walking on eggshells when we met, but also for Ryan. He doesn't need people digging into his life."

"Have you told Ryan about what Ian said?"

"No."

"Why the hell not?"

"I'm afraid."

"Girl, I'm going to kick your ass. Tell him! He'll understand."

I sigh. "You're right. I'll tell him."

"Of course I'm right. Be honest with Ryan, he deserves it. He didn't grow up in this messed-up industry and if you have to, fly out to see him."

"I will."

"Okay, mama's yelling. I love you, Hadley, and so does Ryan. Let him prove it."

Alex and I hang up, leaving me with a lot to think about. I know Ian isn't perfect, but he's a good manager and I know the decisions he makes are for my benefit. My parents picked him because he has a good sense of business, dabbled in the music scene when he was younger and because he's family.

I look around and notice that the nannies are all gone and the sun is going down. I really need to call a cab. Walking back to Ian's is out of the question. Hell, at this point I just need someone to drop me off at the airport because I don't want to be here anymore. That would really send a message to Ian. His *checkbook* is missing again. The thought makes me laugh. I'd love to disappear and make him suffer for what he's doing to me. What is he thinking?

I stand and immediately wish I had done this more slowly. My feet are asleep. The annoying prickly feeling coursing through them makes me want to sit down right away. I don't. I take tiny steps around, not far enough away from the tree just in case I need the support. Each step is less painful, more annoying than anything.

I pick up my shoes. Still refusing to put them on, the cool grass sends a slight chill through me. I don't have an option but to walk through the grass without my shoes. I'd sink with each step I take in these stupid heels. I should stop wearing them. I'm sick of having to put on a show for everyone all the time. What about what I want? Comfort would be nice. I wouldn't mind not having to wear form-fitting clothes all the time. Maybe then I wouldn't be afraid to bend over or sit down.

As soon as I hit the pavement I immediately regret walking this way. Cole is leaning against his car, his arms across his chest and his legs crossed. He looks like he's posing for the cover of a car magazine. Thing is, if someone took a picture, he'd probably be asked the next day. He has that charisma about him. He can sell you on anything with just his looks. I should know. I paid dearly for it.

I pause when he steps forward. I'm not prepared to deal with him. The last thing I want is to talk to him, especially out in public. I look around for any photographers, wary of what Alex said to me. What if this is just all a set up by Ian, some ploy to get Ryan and me apart?

"Looks like you need a ride," he says with such sincerity that I almost believe he's an honest person. But then again, I could be over-analyzing everything when it comes to him.

"I'll walk." I set down my heels and step into them, surprised that my feet don't scream in pure agony. I make a mental note to start carrying around a bag. I'll make it couture or whatever, but something that I can keep some flip-flops in.

"You can't walk back to your hotel."

"Yes, I can." The first few steps are okay, but the hard concrete and each push of my foot into the toes of my shoes is an unwelcome feeling.

Cole grabs my arm, halting my steps. I pull away, turn and look at him. I hope I'm conveying the right amount of anger. He steps back and holds up his hands.

"I'm just trying to help."

"You've done enough."

"Babe, come on, we're going to be working together." He steps forward. "The long days and nights will be spent with each other. You know how things get on the road. You'll get lonely. I'll get lonely. I know how to make you sing."

I shake my head. I won't ever turn to him. I learned my lesson the first time. "Shut up, Cole," I say as I take a step closer. "I haven't forgotten what you did. What I said. How I felt. It's fresh every time I think about my boyfriend and being away from him. I wonder if he would do the same things that you did while I was away."

"You never let me explain."

I throw my hands up and scoff. "I'm not stupid. I know what sex looks like."

I turn and walk away from him. I was wrong. I can't work with him. I don't care if it's what's best for my career or not. I'll quit.

I make it three blocks before I have to pull off my heels. I'm doing more damage by walking in them. I'll just have to schedule a pedicure tomorrow. I ignore the honking of car horns, knowing better than to turn around. I pull my hair forward, shielding my face from onlookers. The last thing I need is for my picture in the tabloids with some flashy headline about me walking down Sunset with no shoes on.

Or maybe that is exactly what I need. The perfect headline that will send Ian into a tizzy and he'll have no other option but to give me what I need. Sounds dirty, but I'm willing to play if it means I can be with Ryan more.

I round the corner that will lead to my hotel. The home stretch, thank God. I have to stop when a car pulls into a parking garage. The window rolls down, the blue eyes I know so well staring at me before his face shows.

"Are you following me?"

He doesn't answer. He gets out of the car and comes toward me. I could yell and scream. Make a scene that brings out the police, but I'm not given any time. He scoops me up, cradling me like he did so many times when we were together. My arms go around him, hanging on for dear life as he swings us around.

The bright flash of light blinds me. The distinct sound of clicking fills my ears. I hide my face in his neck, realizing a second too late what I've done.

They're like vultures, getting closer, blocking Cole's attempt to get me into the car. He isn't saying anything, neither of us answering the same question being asked repeatedly. *"Are you back together?"*

I scream at the top of my lungs as soon as he shuts my door. I count the seconds until he's inside. Thirty seconds pass and then a minute. I turn and look. Is he talking to them? Are they blocking his way to the door?

He finally opens his door. The flashes start again. They are taking photos of me, shoeless and dirty with road grime. I know I said I didn't care, but that was before. Now I'm screwed.

"What the hell was that?"

He shakes his head as he starts his car. He's careful not to hit any of the paparazzi. If it were me, I'd run them over.

"That was me saving you. I just thought I had more time."

"What the hell are you talking about?"

"Ian called. Someone saw you walking down the street without your shoes. They told him you were going in and out of different bars and were staggering."

"Bull crap. No one knew I was out here but you. You set this up."

He pulls into my hotel and is out of the car before I can protest. My door opens and the valet helps me out. He takes one look at me and smirks. *Jerk.*

Cole follows me in, his hand on the small of my back. I want to push him off, but I owe him a thank you for saving me. He follows me into the elevator. I take one side, he on the other. I'm not sure why he's still here. He could've gotten off on the next floor, but he's still with me.

The car dings on my floor and he steps behind me. "What are you doing?" I ask without turning around. He pushes me forward when the door slides open, directing me down the hall.

My mouth drops when he opens my door. He smiles as he holds it open.

"Ian thinks you're about to head back east. I'm here to stop you."

chapter
twenty-five

RYAN

I'm avoiding the cafeteria today. It's not because of the meatloaf or lumpy white pile of gunk that they call potatoes, but because Dylan told me I need to lookup Hadley on the Internet. When I asked her why, she rested her hand on my arm and looked at me like I had just lost my dog.

I thought maybe the usual suspects would be talking about her in class. I tried to pick up on conversations, but no one was saying anything. I resolve that I need to go to the library and find out why Dylan would tell me to lookup Hadley.

I sign in at the desk, showing the librarian my student ID and wait for her to assign me a computer.

As I pull out the chair and sit down the machine stares at me, mocks me really, because I don't know what I'm doing. I haven't felt the need to search Hadley on the computer before, so why am I here now? I lean my head back and close my eyes. I picture her, in a dress and the cowboy boots she loves so much, leaning up against the oak tree outside of church. I'm standing there with her, my arm above her head. I like that I'm taller than her. I like that she has to look up at me.

We haven't spoken in twenty-four hours. I've ignored her because I'm angry and jealous. I knew this was going to happen. I knew that someone would come along and show her that I can't offer her anything. I'm a high school student going nowhere fast. Destined to be a shop foreman like the Stones before me, a family legacy that I have zero desire to be part of. What really sucks is that I'm powerless to stop either from happening.

My phone vibrates in my pocket. I know it's Hadley. She knows it's lunchtime. We talk at this time every day so why would today be any different? Because yesterday she told me she's going on tour with her ex-boyfriend and not just any ex, but one that she lived with. I know in my haste of being pissed off, I brought up sex. I can't help it. There are things that I want to try with her, but she doesn't let me. She stops me each time we're getting somewhere and I have all these…I don't know, urges, running through me and when I touch her, they increase and make me feel good. She makes me feel good. I just want to be with her.

I pull out my phone, her gorgeous face smiling at me. I ignore the call. One of these times I'm going to make a mistake by ignoring her. She'll just text me that we're done, that I'm childish and immature and not ready to handle an adult relationship. And she's right. I am.

My phone vibrates, this time with a text.

I love you, Ryan. I miss you. Please, we need to talk before it's too late.

Too late? What the hell does that mean? I hadn't realized we were on some type of time limit.

Too late for what?

I send the text back. Setting down my phone I shake the mouse to wake the computer. Pressing down on the mouse, the Internet window opens up. I type in my name and student ID so I can have access to the web. Everything I do on here will be tracked. I wonder what the principal will think when he sees that I'm searching Hadley Carter.

He won't think much because all the boys here talk about her, he'll probably think I'm normal except there isn't anything normal about me looking for her on the web. I feel like I'm crossing some imaginary line between us.

Her reply pops up. *Call me, please. I want to explain before you see the pictures.*

Pictures? Is this what Dylan was talking about? I look at my phone and the computer, my temperature rising. I've never been one to get too angry, but right now I'm on edge. What kind of pictures is Hadley talking about? And Dylan, what's she trying to tell me? I'm not sure how much more I can take. Yesterday it's the ex and today it's photos.

I type in her name and hit enter, closing my eyes before anything appears on the screen. I'm about to do something I'm going to regret, but I have to know. When I open my eyes, I wish I hadn't. I wish Dylan hadn't said anything and that yesterday never happened. I wish I could go back to the night of the concert and tell Dylan no because staring back at me is my girlfriend with her face buried in some guy's neck while he carries her. Best part, he's smiling, which tells me she's not hurt.

I reach for the mouse and click through the images. One labels the guy as

Coleman Hollister and says that he and Hadley are back together. *Back together.* So this is the ex-boyfriend. The one she loved before me, who knows her better than I do. The one I can't compete with. I bite my lip to stop myself from yelling. My fist slams down on the table, making the computer rattle.

I pick-up my phone, determined to throw it against the wall. Instead I open her message and reply.

TOO LATE!

I storm out of the library, the door slamming against the wall, almost hitting Dylan. I stop and look at her, she's rubbing her arm, but I don't care. I can't even comprehend what she's doing here. She knew what I'd find and encouraged me to look. Why would she do that? Does she hate Hadley that much or is she trying to hurt me?

She yells my name as I stalk down the hall. I don't know if she's following me. I lose myself in the swarm of kids coming out of the cafeteria. Their talking drowns out her voice. I don't want to talk to her right now, or even see her. I can't get over the fact that she knew.

My phone goes off again and this time I answer it hearing Hadley's cries. I want to scream and tell her to shut up because I don't want to hear it.

"Ryan, let me explain."

"What's there to explain?" I ask as I push open the front doors of the school. The fresh air feels good. I breathe in, hoping to calm down before I continue this conversation with her. My heart aches knowing this is the last time I'll talk to her, because even I know cheating isn't okay.

"Those photos… they aren't what they seem."

I laugh. "I may be naïve, Hadley, but I'm not that stupid."

"I never said you're stupid. I'm asking you to listen to me so I can explain what happened after you hung up on me yesterday."

"So this is my fault?" I cross the parking lot and wait for traffic to clear before walking across the street. I don't know where I'm going. I need to get away from this school and from Dylan and her stupid looks.

"I didn't do anything wrong!" She says this with such vigor it makes me stop.

"Why me, Hadley, huh?" I'm asking the question that has been plaguing my mind for months now. "Why did you pick me?"

"Why you? You know this, Ryan. When I first saw you, I felt something and that was without even knowing you. After we met, I knew you were the one for me. I'm in love with you. Why can't you see that?"

"Because I'm seeing you in the arms of your ex-boyfriend, the one I just found out about."

I take a shortcut through the park, keeping off the roads. The last thing I need is for my dad to drive by and see me walking down the street, talking on a cell phone that I technically don't own and I'm not allowed to have.

"I'm sorry about not telling you earlier about Cole; he's not a subject that I like talking about and definitely didn't want to bring him up. Had I known Ian was bringing him on this tour, I would've told you everything. I don't want to keep secrets from you."

"It's all excuses, Hadley."

"For what? I've done nothing wrong. Those pictures you saw, I have a feeling I was completely setup by Ian. I walked from his house back to my hotel and right before I got there, Cole showed up and told me that Ian was getting reports of me staggering in and out of bars. The next thing I know he's picking me up. The flashes started immediately and I hid my face out of reaction, not out of embarrassment. I wish I would've punched him or something, but I was too shocked and didn't realize what was going on until I was already in his car and the questions were being fired at me."

"And now you're going on a tour with him. Is this supposed to make me feel good?"

I sit down on the park bench. There are a few kids playing on the jungle gym. This is exactly what Hadley was looking at yesterday when she was stabbing me in the heart. How can something so innocent remind me of pain?

"What do you want me to do?"

"Not go on tour." The words are out of my mouth before I know I've even said them. I close my eyes and wish for the darkness to swallow me up.

"It's my job."

"I know it is. I'm angry and upset. I don't understand any of this. I miss you and the more I think about us and those pictures the more I get pissed off. Things seemed so much simpler when I didn't know you."

"Ryan?" her voice cracks. I know my words hurt her, but it's true. Before her I was just going through life as a blip. Then I met her and things changed. She made me feel alive and wanted. Now I just feel like shit.

"I'm sorry. I didn't mean it like that. I didn't have all these feelings before. This wouldn't be happening if you weren't famous and I don't know how to handle all of this. I want to be with you, Hadley, but I'm not sure if you want the same things."

"I do, so much."

"It doesn't feel like it. He had his hands on you and you allowed it. You let him hold you and touch you and I want to fucking scream. I don't want to share you."

"I know," she says softly.

"If you know then why did you let it happen?"

"By the time I realized what was happening, it was too late for me to stop it."

I lean forward, resting my elbows on my knees. My foot is shaking. If I don't get off the phone with her soon, I'm going to explode. Maybe I need to hit something to take out this anger. I could ask Dylan to print off one of the photos and tape it to the wall so I can beat the crap out of it.

"I don't know what you want me to say. I don't know how to handle all of this. I guess I should be thankful that no one knows about us because I'd be the laughing stock at school."

"Want me to tell everyone that I'm in love with you? Will that help make this easier for you?"

"Definitely not."

"Then what, Ryan? Tell me and I'll do it."

"I've told you, but it's your job so what I think doesn't matter. I gotta go."

"Why?"

"Because Dylan's here."

I hang-up before she has a chance to respond. I know it was a dirty thing to say, but I want her to feel the same pain that I'm feeling. Dylan sits down next to me and doesn't say anything. I lean back and realize she's a bit closer to me than usual. I don't move. I let her leg press up against mine. I encourage it, in fact.

chapter
twenty-six

HADLEY

His voice repeats in my head. You'd think I could remember something more pleasant, but I don't. I remember only '*Dylan*'. I want to believe that she found him because he's ditching school and she's there to be his friend, not the type to move in because she sees that he's having trouble with me.

Trouble we shouldn't be having.

I set down my phone and flip on the TV. Cole's voice sings through the speakers, I change the channel quickly. I don't want to be accused of enjoying his music while I'm being held captive, which reminds me, I need to call my parents and see what can be done about Ian. I'm not too keen on being kept in my hotel room by my ex; let alone keeping that information from my boyfriend. Somehow I think that had I let that little tidbit of information slip, I'd be single. I know I'd break-up with me if I were Ryan.

I stop on a movie that's playing. A woman is watching a guy and girl on a park bench. She's looking at them with tears in her eyes. I pick up my phone and pull up Ryan's name. His picture stares back at me, so handsome and sweet. I miss him and he needs to know that I do. Words are not enough under these circumstances. I look back at the room where Cole is and know what I have to do.

"Cole?" I yell in my whiny pay-attention-to-me voice. He used to come running when we first started dating, but that soon turned into an eye-roll even though he'd do what I asked of him.

He stands in the doorway, his arms raised over his head as he rests his hands on the door casing above him, causing his shirt to rise above his waistband. I look away. I don't need to remember what he looks like. I spent years erasing those memories from my mind.

"What do you need, Hadley Girl?" I hate pet names, especially from him. Maybe if Ryan gave me one I wouldn't care, but the bare whisper of one makes me cringe. I look back at the man that ruined most of me and stick my tongue out, a completely mature act for someone my age.

"I need some water and gum."

"Since when do you chew gum?"

"Since now and the store downstairs doesn't have the kind I want, so I'm letting you know that I'm going to the store." I get up and straighten my jeans. I step over to the mirror and fluff my hair and play with my lipstick, all things that he's used to seeing me do.

"You're not leaving."

I turn and glare at him. "You can't hold me here, that's called kidnapping. I'll call the cops if I have to."

Cole steps forward, shuffling his bare feet on the floor. "Ian will kill me if I let you out. You can wait. We leave tomorrow for the tour. One day won't kill you."

"Fine, I can wait for the gum, but not the water. I need water or I'll die."

"You're so dramatic, Hadley. There's water in the wet bar, drink that."

I walk over to the wet bar and look. Sure enough there's water, but not the kind I want. If he and Ian want to play games, they'll suffer. "This won't do. I don't like this kind."

"Of course you don't."

"What's that supposed to mean?" I ask, placing my hands on my hips for added attention.

"Nothing, I'll go get your freaking water. You know," he says as he slips on his shoes. "I never understood why you liked that generic water to begin with. You're a freaking pop star. Drink the good shit."

"I never asked for your opinion, Coleman."

His eyes narrow when I say his name. He never did like me using his first name because it reminded him of his mother. I cock my eyebrow at him. He shakes his head as he heads for the door.

"I'll be back in five minutes. Don't do anything stupid."

That's what you think.

The second the door shuts I lock it. I don't care if he's heard the lock engage or not. I need time to put a bag together and get out of here. Ian may be able to dictate where I perform, but he's not going to screw up my personal life.

With enough clothes for a few days and a couple of necessities, I sling my bag over my shoulder, pick up my phone and walk to the door. I hold my breath as I unlock it. I inch it open and cautiously look down the hall before opening it farther. I look in the other direction and only see one housekeeper. The path to the elevators is clear, but I'm not taking those. I jog down the hall to the stairwell and throw open the door.

I descend one flight of stairs before pulling out my phone and texting Alex, asking her to call the concierge desk and secure me a cab. I don't want to wait once I'm down there and run the risk of running into Cole, or even Ian, for that matter.

I rush down the rest of the stairs, breaking a sweat. I'm thankful for elevators because I can't imagine having to climb these, but the thrill of going down them so fast is exhilarating. When I get to the last step, only the door is standing between me and a bit of freedom. I push it open slightly and look for Cole and his harem of screaming fans that follow him around. That is one thing I could never get used to… his fans. He never cared if they followed us out on a date, or stopped us in the middle of dinner for an autograph. To him it was all business. To me it was an intrusive and unneeded deterrent in our relationship. It was like I was sharing him with the world and I hated it.

I walk down the long hall with my head down, sunglasses on. I wish I had put on a baseball cap or something to hide my hair, not from fans, but from Cole. I need this to work. I need to be with Ryan so he knows that he's the one and that being with Cole on tour won't change how I feel about him.

As soon as I'm out in the open, I spot the cab that is waiting for me. The driver is holding a sign with Alex's name on it. She's a freaking genius. I walk a bit faster until he makes eye contact, I wave and he opens the door.

"Airport," I tell him as soon as he's behind the wheel. "And please hurry," I say for added benefit. I look back at the hotel as we pull away and wonder if Cole has been back to the room yet and realize I don't really care. If Ian is doing this as some type of publicity stunt, he's in for a rude awakening because I won't be his guinea pig. I'd rather quit and never sing again than be thrown into his world of lies and deception.

Traffic is light and for that I'm thankful. The drive to the airport only takes twenty minutes and yes, the driver exceeded the speed limit. I hop out as soon as he stops, throwing money onto his passenger seat. He says something, but I don't acknowledge him. I look at the reader board to find the next available flight, one that will get me to Jackson or close enough that I can drive there.

My phone vibrates with a text from Alex. ***Your ticket is at the counter. Regular airline.***

I can't help but laugh at how vague she's being, talking in code. I run to our favorite airline and wait patiently, looking over my shoulder for Cole's blond hair. He has to know I'm gone by now and where I'm headed, unless of course he met a girl on his way to the store and became sidetracked. It wouldn't be the first time he's forgotten about me.

With my ticket in hand and through security I finally feel as if I'm breathing. Although there are still issues weighing heavily on my chest, seeing Ryan will help. Even if we only have a few hours, it'll be enough for me to tell him exactly how I feel and how much he means to me.

When I step onto the jet bridge I look behind me one more time. Satisfied that I'm not being followed, I descend down the walkway and onto the plane. I didn't look at my ticket until now and realize I'm not flying first class. I want to scream at Alex, but figure she did this to keep Ian off my tail. I'll have to buy her a nice present.

I'm anxious as the plane touches down. My leg has been bouncing for the last hour of the flight. I know I'm probably annoying the lady next to me, but I can't help it. I turn on my phone and wait, counting the seconds before my inbox floods with text messages. There are only two people I want to hear from: Ryan and Alex. The rest of them can leave me alone for the next couple of days while I fix my life.

I'm becoming more and more agitated as I wait for people to deplane. This process is so slow and I don't know how more people aren't scrambling to fly first class. When I'm finally on the jet bridge, I run to the rental counter. I'm banking on Alex having already set this up for me. It dawns on me that Ian would know which rental company I like so I look around and try to think like Alex. I spot the company that she is always making fun of and head there. I give the lady behind the counter my name and she smiles. I'm hoping it's because she has a reservation for me, not because she's a fan and is planning on asking for my autograph. Of course, if I would've developed a fake name like Alex has suggested so many times, I could avoid a potential situation like this.

The clerk hands me my paperwork and keys. I fill out the necessary information and head for the parking garage where my car is waiting. Just over an hour until I can hold and kiss him.

That is, if he'll come to me.

One hour and thirty minutes later, I reach the Brookfield town line and I realize I don't remember his address. I had it once, when I invited him to the charity ball, but never added it to my phone. I think about driving around, but wouldn't know where to go. I know he said the town is divided and remember him saying he wouldn't want me at his house.

I find the church easily enough and park, shutting off the car. I never took into consideration what time I'd arrive. I just needed to get here before it was too late. For all I know it already is. He hasn't texted me, only Ian, Cole and Alex have.

I pull out my phone and type *I'm at your church* and hit send before my heart tells me to chicken out and go back home. Maybe I'm not good for Ryan, maybe Dylan is the type of girl he needs, the kind that understands where he's from.

All I know is that Ryan is *who* I need. He's the air that I breathe in order to live. He's different and makes me different, too. The love that I feel for him is nothing like what I felt for Cole. I ache when I'm not with Ryan. I've been a fool to think that being apart would be okay.

I look at my phone, willing it to ring, giving me any sign that he's on his way. For all I know, I'm too late. He could be tired of me already and I wouldn't blame him if he were. I'm not sure I'd be able to let him go though. I'm in too deep.

I decide to wait on the bench by the tree... our tree. That seems silly, saying it's our tree, but it's where our first ever paparazzi picture was taken. Probably not something most people want to keep, but it meant something to me. I want Ryan in my life and he'll need to get used to those fleabags hanging around.

"You shouldn't sit out in the dark by yourself." I turn and find Ryan leaning up against the tree, his hands stuffed into his pockets. He's wearing a hoodie, his beautiful brunette hair hidden underneath the hood. I want to run and jump into his arms, but he doesn't look like he wants that and it breaks my heart.

"I wasn't out here long."

Ryan adjusts, leaning his back against the tree. It looks like we're keeping our space.

"Why me, Hadley?"

chapter
twenty-seven

RYAN

I almost didn't leave the house to meet her, but now that I'm standing here, looking at her, this is where I need to be. I'm not sure how this moment will end, either I'm walking away because I can't take the way I feel about her being on tour with her ex, or she'll show me that all my worries are for nothing. She could leave me. It's an option that I refuse to consider. She could be tired of my immature crap and be here to tell me that she's done. But why would she fly all this way when she could just text me. Keep it simple, with no emotions.

I ask her the same question I asked before. This time I'll be able to see her beautiful face when she tells me why she chose me. The logic behind us doesn't make sense. I come from nothing. Destined to be nothing and yet she pursues me and tells me I can be anything I want. She forgets that my chances of getting out of Brookfield are limited and that she's had opportunities people like me only dream about. Her parents have supported her from day one. Mine just expect me to brown-bag it to the mill once graduation comes. High hopes, my parents have.

I'm fighting the urge to sit next to her. I know that once I do, I'm done for. She can say anything and I'll believe her. Call it desperation or being whipped, I don't care. I'm in love with her and being away from her physically hurts.

I straighten when she stands. I've never seen her out of a dress. She's always been made up and flawless, until now. She's in yoga pants, tennis shoes and a zip up. Her hair is pulled back and she looks tired. I realize that I don't care that she's not in a dress. She's perfect just the way she is. Seeing her like this, it makes me think she's giving a part of herself to me that's usually reserved for behind closed doors. Even when we spent the one night together in her hotel room, she was the Hadley Carter everyone knows and loves.

But standing in front of me now is my Hadley.

She doesn't step any closer, keeping the gaping distance between us. Three large steps and I can have her in my arms. I move my hands from my pockets and place them between my back and the tree. I need to keep a level head and touching her will just cloud my mind.

I can see now why guys don't like to date. It's complicated and messy, but it has to be worth it in the end, at least that's what I'm hoping.

"You asked this yesterday and I told you, but maybe that wasn't enough, or maybe it's something I shouldn't say over the phone." She's closer now. I can see her tears trailing down her face and it makes me want to reach out and wipe them away. She looks up to the sky and smiles. She pulls the rubber band out of her hair and shakes her head. It's raining and she's basking in it.

"You'll catch a cold," I say as if I'm her parent.

"I don't care."

"You won't be able to sing."

"Good," she says as she looks at me.

I push my hood off as well, matching her. I step out from under the heavy cover of the tree and stand in front of her. Raindrops bounce off her eyelashes, making her look even more beautiful.

"I'm in love with you, Ryan. What I feel for you, it's different from anything I've ever felt before. From the moment I saw you, I knew I had to have you in my life. Whether we were just going to be friends or more, it didn't matter because not knowing you wasn't an option for me. That night after my show, you were sitting in the corner and all it took was one look and I felt this flood of heat and desire go through me, like I was on fire.

"You ask why you, but I'm saying why *not* you. You have the most beautiful blue eyes I've ever seen. I could spend hours looking at them. I love how your cheeks turn just the right shade of pink when I touch you. I love the way your hands make me feel, even when it's something as simple as holding my hand. I don't care that you live in a rundown house or don't drive a fancy car. None of that matters as long as I have you. You're the one I want to be with. I don't care about your clothes, your money, or some fancy house. I'd gladly give all that up just for you.

"This past week has been torture for me, not being able to talk to you and when we do talk things are strained. I found out a lot of things this week, things that apparently I did and didn't do. This is why Ian is being the way he is. I'm trying to figure things out, but I need for you to be patient and help me. I need to know that at the end of my shitty day, my boyfriend is on the other end of the phone listening to me vent and cry. I need you to love me for me and not who I am on the stage or in the papers. That person that you saw yesterday, that's not the *me* you know. This me, the one standing in front of you, she doesn't like Coleman Hollister and wouldn't be caught dead with him. This *me* is dying inside thinking that her boyfriend doesn't want her anymore. This *me* is so in love with Ryan Stone that nothing else matters.

"Now tell me, Ryan, why not you?"

I wasn't expecting an answer like that. I guess I didn't know what to expect. She looks at me, waiting for an answer. I shrug and step closer to her. "I'm plain and ordinary, Hadley. All I can offer you is me and I think that sometimes that's not enough, especially when I see you in the arms of that guy. You bring out these crazy emotions that I don't know anything about. I don't know how to control them or make them stop. I'm never going to be the type that can support someone like you. This place, it's not good enough for you and this is where I'm destined to be. My family expects me to wake up the day after graduation, put on some coveralls and go to the mill. You give me hope. You put these ideas into my head that I can get away from here and do something else, but what? I can't go to college and the only thing I can do is flip burgers. Are you going to bring me home to your parents and say, 'here's my boyfriend, the burger flipper'?"

"My parents won't care as long as you make me happy. They live in the same house I grew up in. It's a small three-bedroom home. My mom is a teacher and my dad is a banker, who takes the train to work, works long hours and falls asleep in his recliner at the end of the night. Anything you offer me is better than what I have now."

Hadley steps forward and into my arms. I hold her tight against my chest, burying my face into her neck. She's wet, cold and shivering, but I am too. We aren't too smart being out in the rain like this.

"I didn't like seeing those pictures," I mumble against her skin. "It made me feel… I don't know, like I needed to hit something and I've never felt like that before. I didn't like that."

Hadley pulls back. She reaches up and moves my hair out of my face. "I don't like him, not even in the slightest and I would never do anything to disrespect you."

"But you loved him at one time."

"I did, but he broke my heart in the worst way and I would never do that to someone I love."

I lean down and kiss her softly, which is too much for me to handle. I want so much from her, but not sure how to make that happen. I hate that I'm inexperienced and that everything I'm feeling is so foreign to me. I don't know if what I'm doing is right. It's times like this where I need my dad to be somewhat approachable. I know discussing girls with him is off-limits and he'd ban Dylan from coming over. I need someone to talk to, though. Maybe Dylan, she knows how I feel about Hadley and I know she's done things with guys before.

I kiss her again before pulling away. She looks like a beautiful drowned rat. Her hair is plastered to her face and her nose is red. I want to wrap her up in my blankets and keep her warm, but that's not an option. I pull her hand into mine and walk us to her car. I reach for the driver-side door, but she side steps and opens the back door and crawls in. I don't hesitate and follow her, shutting the door behind me.

She climbs forward and turns on the car, blasting the heat. I can't believe she left her keys in the ignition.

"That's not safe, you know."

"I wasn't thinking," she replies as she sits back. She's pulled her bag from the front seat and unzips it, pulling out some dry clothes. "Can you turn around?"

"No," I say. I adjust so I can watch her. She looks at me through squinted eyes. I should feel like a shit for denying her, but I want to see her. I can't help it. She looks down at the shirt in her hand and back at me.

"You should take off your sweatshirt before you catch a cold."

I nod and pull my wet sweatshirt over my head. I push my hair out of my face and stare at her. Her mouth drops open. I chuckle. She probably didn't think I'd be shirtless, but she texted me when I was in bed and I came right here to see her.

Hadley clears her throat and looks at her shirt before setting it down and peeling off her sweatshirt. The t-shirt she's wearing underneath is white and very see-through at the moment. She crosses her arms. Her fingers grasp the ends of her shirt and lift it up and over her head.

"Don't," I say as I set my hand on hers before she can put her dry shirt on. I want to see her, hold her, like this. There can't be that many consequences. I'm almost eighteen, she can't go to jail for something I'm asking for.

"I shouldn't be like this."

"No one is going to know, Hadley. It's not like I'm going to tell anyone. I love you and you love me. How can this be wrong?"

I pull the shirt gently from her hands and set it on the console. My arm reaches around her waist and I pull her toward me, her back resting against my chest. I've been waiting to have this feeling, being skin to skin with her. I let my fingers glide along her arms, feeling as her skin pebbles. She links her hands over the top of mine and brings them over her, showing me where touch her. I can't help but groan when she pushes down on me. Wearing sweatpants was the best decision I could've made.

I bite down lightly on her neck as she moves against me. My eyes close as she moves my hands to her breast. She holds us there, adding pressure to my hands. I inch my hand into her bra and feel her for the first time. I can't... I don't... the feeling is too much. The fire in my stomach, I feel like I need to let go, but not here. Not like this. I need to stop this even though I want her, even though I've been begging her to let us be like this.

"Hadley..." She turns, cutting me off with her mouth. The kiss is deep, urgent. I can feel her need in the way she's moving. She maneuvers around, straddling me. Her hands move along my chest to the waistband on my sweats. This is it. She's not going to stop and I'm powerless to stop her.

chapter
twenty-eight

HADLEY

The feel of Ryan's skin against mine set everything in motion. I've wanted him since the night of my show. It was the mere mention of him being in high school that stopped me from pursuing more from him and now here I am, in love and in desperate need to feel him against me in any way I can.

I have a burning desire when I'm in his proximity. I can't deny my attraction. It doesn't matter if he's standing across the room; he spurs enough emotion in me to make me lose my mind. I can't make proper decisions when he's around. When he pulls me against him, when he touches me so lightly that I have to have his hands on me, I know I'm in too deep to stop.

The way his hands feel against my skin, they're perfect. Showing him the way to touch me is one of the most intimate things I've ever done. I didn't mean to push against him. The thin fabric of his sweatpants urged me. He groaned. He freaking groaned and all I can think is that we are in the backseat of my rental car. Why did I get into the backseat? I did this. I put us in this situation.

The way my name sounds as it rolls off his lips spurs me into a decision I know this is wrong. I seek out his mouth, letting him know that I'm in this. I'm not saying no this time. I turn and straddle him, he feels good and I know he wants me. I know he wants this for us. I know it shouldn't happen, not like this. Not here and not after I flew here to see if he still wanted me.

I can't help it. I need to touch him. I explore his chest. My lips follow the path my hands make on his skin. He pulls away from me when my hand touches his waistband. I sit back and look at him. His eyes are hooded.

He wants this and so do I.

"Let's go to my house," he says so quietly, it's as if he's trying to keep his words a secret. I know it pains him to say those words. Bringing me home has never been an option and it's something I've accepted. I know he's embarrassed by his home. I get that. For him to suggest we go to his house shows me how much he loves me, how much he's willing to put his feelings aside so that we aren't having sex in the back of my car, in the church parking lot.

Ryan pushes my hair off my shoulder. He's so tentative, going with what feels natural when it comes to us. "I want to have sex with you, but not here... like this. I can't offer you much, but I can at least offer you a bed."

"We could get caught." I know we'll get caught. Parents have a sixth sense when their child is having sex in the house, although it could be the squeak coming from the bedroom that is the dead giveaway.

Ryan shrugs. "I've heard the guys talking in the locker room and they're always talking about having sex in their cars and trucks, at least that is what they are telling each other and it's not like I don't want to do it, I do. I just don't want you to feel cheap or like I don't care."

Blue lights flash through the fogged up windows, followed quickly by a flashlight. "Shit. Shit. Shit. Shit," I say as I scramble off Ryan's lap. I look for my shirt, sliding it over my head just as the officer taps on the window.

I look at Ryan, who's whiter than a ghost, staring at me. I throw his sweatshirt at him, but he doesn't flinch, even when it hits him in the face.

He shines the flashlight in the window, tapping again. I have to lean over Ryan to push the window release down. I don't let the whole window down, just enough that the officer can see inside.

"Good evening, officer," I say, hoping to kill him with kindness.

He looks at his watch and back into the car, shining his light all around. "I think we're way past evening, wouldn't you say, Ryan?" He points his flashlight directly into Ryan's eyes. His arm comes up to act like a shield. It doesn't escape me that the police officer knows his name.

"Yes, sir."

"I suppose you have a good explanation as to why you're out at this hour, in a running car, sitting in the church parking lot?"

"Just talking," I answer immediately. I rub my hands up and down my legs, trying to calm my nerves. The officer looks at us like we are a bunch of lying teenagers. He's right. He should look at us this way. He steps away from the car and does something with the radio on his shoulder. I can't tell what he's doing, but I need to use this distraction to get Ryan to snap out of it.

"Ryan?" I pull his face toward mine, forcing him to look at me. "We weren't doing anything wrong so we need to answer his questions so he'll leave, okay?"

He nods and puts on his sweatshirt that isn't even dry yet. I lean forward and shut off the car. I forgot it was running and is probably out of gas. I don't dare step out of the car, although I want to move up front and get the hell out of here. I can't believe I let things get this far. I should know better.

The officer steps up to the car. I smile, hoping to convey some sort of "I'm sorry and it will never happen again" image. He's unreadable, his lips in a straight line. I think if he was to smile, his face would crack and break like old plaster.

"Hadley Carter?" I swallow hard when he says my name. I look down. I can't look at him as I nod in assent. "I need you to step out of the car."

Ryan finally acknowledges what's going on. He grabs my hand as he opens his door. I follow him out. He shuts the door behind and pulls me to him. I get this chivalry act, but it's not going to help.

"What brings you to Brookfield, Miss Carter?"

"Um –"

"She came to see me." Ryan speaks with confidence. The officer looks at him doubtfully and that pisses me off. He shakes his head while he writes something down.

"It's true. I flew in and texted him when I got here." Ryan pulls me closer, wrapping his arm around me.

The officer nods as he continues to write in his notebook. He walks around the car, flashing this light in the windows.

"What's in the bag?"

"Clothes, I flew into Jackson and drove straight here. I didn't have time to check into a hotel yet."

"Where are you guys off to?"

"Excuse me?" Ryan speaks up. I'm thankful he's not just standing here. I know he must be scared, but really, what does he have to lose. I look like a freaking child predator here.

"Your dad reported you missing about two hours ago and I find you in this car with Miss Carter and her luggage."

"It's a backpack, hardly what you'd consider luggage."

The officer steps in front of us and turns off his light. "That's not how I see it. What I see here is an impressionable young man from a good family getting mixed up with big-city money like you. What I see is an older woman taking advantage of a young boy. A boy that may not have everything he needs out of life and you come in here with your money and flash it around. What I see is a woman about to kidnap this boy to cause him harm."

My mouth drops open at his accusations. I hate that he's close to accurate. I did come in here and show Ryan that I can offer him something different, but I only did it because I love him and want to be with him. I never suggested we run away together. His birthday is close. If we've waited this long, we can wait until he's eighteen.

Besides, he needs to finish school and get his diploma and then we can be together whenever we want. He can travel with me and work on my tour if he wanted. Although we've never discussed that, I'd want him with me. But never would I force myself on him.

Ryan steps forward, dropping his arm until our hands link together. "Whoa, Officer Daniels, you don't know anything about me and Hadley. I'm here because I want to be and she's nothing like that. She didn't do anything or force me to do something that I didn't want to do. We've been together for a while now. She's my girlfriend."

"Is that what she tells you?"

"It's what I know. We're in love, that's why she's here. She came to visit."

"Son, people visit at homes, not in parking lots. Haven't you been listening to Reverend Monroe's sermons?"

"Yes – and if you were listening too, you'd know Hadley's been at church with me and my mom, so my dad is mistaken. So what if I'm not in my bed. I haven't left Brookfield."

"Save your story for your dad." The officer steps forward and grabs my arm.

"Don't touch her." Ryan pushes his arm off me and moves me behind him. He stands in front of me, guarding me. His shoulders are shaking. I reach out and rest my hand on his back, hoping to calm him down, but things just turned from bad to worse.

Officer Daniels stares down Ryan, his face taking on a menacing look. I cower even though Ryan is shielding me. Officer Daniels takes a step forward, his hand on his gun. Ryan stands his ground, not moving. I don't know how he's so calm. The only thing I know is that we are in some serious trouble.

"I'm going to forget you touched me because of your relationship with the Rosses, but you need to move out of the way so I can arrest Miss Carter."

"Arrest her for what?" Ryan scoffs.

"Harboring a runaway."

"I didn't run away! I'm here because I want to be here."

"That's for a judge to decide, now step away."

"No!"

Officer Daniels draws his gun and points it at Ryan. I clench his sweatshirt in my fists, tightly. My knees are about to give out. This can't be happening. This is a dream. I'm going to wake up any moment now and be back in my hotel where Cole is watching over me, babysitting me, because I can't take care of myself. Ian is right. I'm trouble.

"Ryan, I'll go with him."

"You didn't do anything wrong," he says, turning around to face me. I know it's never good to turn your back on a gun or an officer trying to arrest somebody, but he did. He cups my cheeks and presses his lips to mine.

Another car pulls into the parking lot, the blue lights flashing, alerting the homes around the area that something is going on. When the other officer steps out, the first thing I notice is the handcuffs dangling from his fingers. I close my eyes and lean my head against Ryan's chest. Everything I thought could go wrong with us is nothing compared to what's about to happen.

"I love you," he whispers against my forehead. I fist his sweatshirt, hanging on to him. They descend on us at the same time, a calculated move that I'm sure they practice repeatedly. Officer Daniels grabs Ryan and pulls him away from me. I scream for Ryan as the other officer steps behind me, wrenching my arms back. He's holding my arms tight, squeezing them until I lose feeling in my fingertips. He pushes me to the trunk of my car and slams my head down on the hood, kicking my feet out wide. Through my tears I see Ryan in a similar pose, both of us being handcuffed.

When the officer pulls me up, I see blood coming from Ryan's mouth. He looks at me, I mouth 'I love you' before I'm pushed into the backseat. The door slams and radio is blaring with police code that I don't understand. The cops meet and compare notes; the one who arrested me is looking back at his car and laughing. He pulls out his phone and types something before putting it back in his pocket. My luck, he just tweeted that he's arrested me. This is not how our time together is supposed to be.

The officer gets in and puts his car into gear. He's talking but I'm not answering. I know enough now to know that I need to keep my mouth shut. I'm in enough trouble. I don't need my mouth getting me into anymore.

I close my eyes and lean my head back and allow the tears to escape. There's no stopping them once they start. I cry for the day I met Ryan and changed his life, because obviously I've done nothing but damage him. I cry for what's going to happen to him and how he's going to feel when I break his heart. I have to do what's right for him, even though it's going to kill me. I can't offer him anything but drama. If it's not pictures, it will be an interview question taken out of context. It will be a promotional event where a reporter reads more into a hug. Nothing I say can prepare him for my life. It was stupid of me to think we could be a normal couple, that I could be a normal person. I'm nothing but a cancer to him and I need to leave him alone before I damage him for good.

Ian was right…

chapter
twenty-nine

RYAN

What just happened?

I don't even know. One minute we're talking about going to my house and now I'm in the back of a police car, in handcuffs, with a busted lip. I don't understand how everything turned sour so fast. We weren't doing anything but talking.

My dad... since when does he check in on me? I could stay up all night and watch the door and he'd never come in, so why now? My mom wouldn't tell him I've been sneaking out. At least I don't think she would.

I can't believe Officer Daniels touched Hadley like that. When he did, it was like all the anger I've been feeling about those pictures came to surface. I wanted to pound his face in, but something told me to hold back. This rage... this anger... it's nothing I've ever felt before, and I hate it.

My dad is standing outside the police station when we pull up. I'm sure he didn't expect this, but I don't care right now. I want him to leave me alone. I wish I had the balls to tell him that I hate my life here and that I want out. That I don't like the way he treats my mother. I don't want to work in the mill. That I wish he were more of a dad, the kind that took time to teach me how to throw a baseball or toss a football. That he encouraged me to be more than he was.

Another officer opens the backdoor and pulls me out by my arm. My dad steps forward and touches my lip. I jerk my head away. Not only do I not want him touching me, but my lip hurts.

"You're lucky he found you first, because if I did, you'd have more than a busted lip."

I look at the officer holding onto my arm and ask, "Did you hear him?"

"I didn't hear a thing," Officer Daniels replies in his hillbilly voice. Of course he didn't. "Where is Mr. Ross?" I ask, but am met with silence.

I'm pushed into the station, taken to a room and thrown into the chair. I almost tip over, causing the officer and my dad to laugh. I don't get it. I didn't do anything wrong.

"Mr. Ross," I yell, but the door is slammed before my voice can carry out of the room. He's always been friendly and nice to me, but now, here I am being treated like some common criminal. I need Mr. Ross. I need his help.

The officer leaves, leaving my dad in the room and no way to defend myself. Great, just what I need. My dad pulls out the chair across from me and sits down. He folds his hands, pressing his index fingers to his mouth. If he thinks I'm going to talk to him, he's crazy.

"Where were you going?"

I look down at the table and count the specs of red mixed in and wonder if that's blood. I should've asked Dylan a long time ago if her dad was a violent man.

"Who's the girl?"

No answer.

He leans forward, pulling my chin up so that I'm looking him in the eye. I try to move away, but he's pinching me, holding me in place.

"I suggest you answer, boy, because in case you've forgotten, you live under my roof."

"I haven't forgotten," I mumble. He releases my chin. I try to rub it on my shoulder to relieve the pressure, but it doesn't do enough to ease the ache. I'm sure I'll have a bruise there now, too. I wonder what my mom will say when she sees me. Probably nothing, I'm sure. She'll sit on the floor and pray, asking God to forgive her son and all his sins. She'll shut down, stare out the window and act like I don't exist.

"Where were you going?"

"Nowhere."

He slams his hand down on the table. I hope he broke it.

"Answer me."

"I did."

He rubs his face and sighs, though he hasn't ever cared before. He makes things this complicated, it's not like he's ever sat down and asked me how I'm doing or paid a bit of attention to me. I've just been another mouth to feed and someone he's had to put second-hand clothes on.

"I'll ask you again. Who's the girl?"

I shake my head. That's one question I'm not willing to answer. If he wants to beat me, so be it, but he's not getting any information about Hadley.

"You're not going to tell me? You don't think I already know about you and her. You don't think I know that you've been sneaking out of your room at night since September, that you've spent the night with that whore?"

I look up when he calls her a whore; she's anything but. "Go to hell. You don't know shit about our relationship," I say through gritted teeth.

He stands, his chair colliding with the wall. He leans over the table, his hands flat, arms spread out wide. He's intending to scare me and I'm sure he would be if I weren't so pissed off.

"You're seventeen years old. She's an adult. She's a pedophile. She's the type your mother and I have been protecting you from. Any adult who takes advantage of a young, innocent boy deserves to rot in the fires of hell."

I bite my lip to keep from screaming out, but I can't hold back. "You're wrong. You're so wrong. You don't know shit about her I. She didn't take advantage of me. She fought me every time I tried something with her. I want to be with her and she wants to be with me and there's nothing you can do about it. You're so screwed up in your own world that you have no idea what life is like for me. I hate you. I hate that I'm seventeen years old and the first girl to show me any attention, the first one to see ME, you try to do all you can to ruin it."

The door opens and in walks a lady dressed in a suit, carrying a briefcase. My dad eyes her up and down and shakes his head. He's such a chauvinistic pig. I wonder how I didn't turn out like him. Moreover, I wonder how my mother can stay married to someone like him.

"I didn't hire a lawyer," my dad spews.

"No one said you did, Mr. Stone. I'm here on behalf of Miss Carter. She's retained me to represent Ryan."

"No, your services aren't needed. You can leave."

"Very well." Only she doesn't leave. She sets down her briefcase on the table and looks at me. "Ryan, I need you to tell me to go. You're old enough to consent to have a lawyer present and Miss Carter has asked that I assist you in any way needed. The choice is yours."

I look from her to my dad. His face is red. His hands are clenched at his sides. I know that if I ask this lady to stay, things at home aren't going to be good. I should probably start fearing for my life once I walk out of these doors, but I also know Officer Daniels can press charges against me and I'll need help with that.

Either way, I'm screwed. One thing I do know is that I want out of these handcuffs and I think this lady is my ticket.

"Ryan, don't you dare." My dad knows what I'm about to do and for the life of me I can't understand why he doesn't want me to have help. Does he plan for me to sit in jail or do an excessive amount of community service? Why wouldn't he want me to have a lawyer to help me out of this mess that I'm in? That's what dads should want for their kids.

I look at the lawyer, who is ignoring my dad. I like her already. "You can stay." She nods and pulls out the chair next to me, sitting down. She opens her briefcase and pulls out some papers, slamming it shut. I jump, my nerves getting the best of me.

"My son is a minor. You need to leave."

"Your son is of sound mind and at the age of consent. He doesn't need your permission."

"Consent for what? He's not an adult."

"Mr. Stone, I'm going to ask you to leave if you can't be quiet."

"Again, lady, he's not an adult. He doesn't know what's good for him."

"Mr. Stone, I assure you that what you have planned with the police department here will not work. I've seen the report you filed and I intend have it withdrawn."

"You can't." My dad leans over the table and points his finger at her. "That whore raped my son and she'll pay."

"WHAT?!" I yell. "She did no such thing. Are you crazy?" I try to stand, but having my hands in cuffs proves this to be a difficult task.

The lawyer puts her hand on my shoulder and waves her other hand in the air. The door opens as if she was a magician and another officer comes in. "Please escort Mr. Stone out so I can speak with my client."

"Let's go, Joe."

"This is bullshit. That's my son."

"I know, but the law's the law." The officer, who I've never seen before, follows my dad out of the room. His voice grows louder and louder as he shouts throughout the station.

"I'm Jessica Danville. As I said earlier, Miss Carter has retained me. Now, while I don't know her personally, my firm, which has offices all over the world, has represented her for years. I'm here to help, Ryan. Your father has made some very serious accusations against our client and we'd like to get this cleaned up."

I take in what she's saying, repeating the words over in my head. She's not here to help me, but to make sure everything is okay with Hadley. I'm not sure how to process that.

"Can someone take off these handcuffs?"

"Sure." She gets up, goes to the door and opens it. The officer that took my father out comes in and takes off the handcuffs. My arms ache from being in the same position and my wrists are red, the skin rubbed raw from the metal. I lean forward and rest my head down on my arms, willing the pain to go away. I'm not angry anymore, just emotionally drained. I feel like I could cry for hours if I let myself, but I won't. I can't.

When she sits back down, she rubs my back. I really don't want her touching me, but right now she's the only friend I have in here.

"Am I going to jail?" I ask. My voice echoes against the table because I'm too ashamed to look her in the eye and ask that question.

"No, Ryan, no one is going to jail. Chief Ross has spoken to Officer Daniels and he is willing to forego pressing charges against you. You have a good ally in Chief Ross."

I pick my head up, resting my chin on my arm. "Well, that's good. What my dad said about Hadley, that's not true. She didn't do anything like that to me."

"Tell me about your relationship."

I sit up and look at the mirror. I wonder if Hadley is on the other side or if it's my father telling anyone who will listen to him that I can't speak for myself.

"Everything you say in here is private. They can't use it against you."

I nod. "We met at her show and she invited my friend, Dylan and I, to her hotel room for an after-party. We've been seeing each other ever since."

"Sounds like a whirlwind romance."

I shrug. I don't know what it sounds like, except it was destined to fail from the start.

"When can I see Hadley?" I need to see her, to know that she's okay.

Jessica opens her briefcase and pulls out a sheet of paper, laying it in front of me and hands me a pen.

"What's this?" I ask.

"Just a document I need you to sign. It states that anything that has happened between you and Miss Carter will be kept confidential. Once you leave here, you're not to speak to or seek out any contact with her until you become of legal age."

I push the paper away and shake my head. "No! There's no way Hadley is okay with me signing this."

"She is and she asked us to draw it up. It's for the best. She wants you to sign it, Ryan. She needs to put what happened tonight behind her and focus on her upcoming tour."

I can't stop shaking my head. Tears come and I don't fight them. "She doesn't love me?"

"That's not why I'm here. You sign this and you're free to go. No charges will be filed for assaulting an officer and everything goes back to the way it was before you crossed paths with Miss Carter."

Everything goes back to the way it was.

Everything.

No more Hadley. No more wondering if she's with someone else. No more beating myself up over why she's with me. I continue being the nobody that I've always been and she continues being everyone's sweetheart. She continues to live her life while I suffer the heartache of letting myself love her when I knew it was a mistake.

"This is what Hadley wants," Jessica says as she pushes the paper forward.

I reluctantly scribble my name and set the pen down and count. Ten seconds and the piece of paper is in her briefcase, the pen in her hand and she's up and out the door without even looking at me.

I get up and follow her out. "Wait," I yell, but she doesn't turn around. I see Hadley, she's there signing something at the counter. "Hadley?"

She turns and looks at me, before turning back and taking keys from the desk clerk. She doesn't look at me again as she walks toward the door of the police station flanked by Jessica and a man I don't know. She turns briefly before exiting, but gives me no sign that everything will be okay.

The door slams, sealing her off from me.

chapter
thirty

HADLEY

Hearing Ryan call my name was almost enough for me to nix this whole deal, but when I looked at him, battered and bruised because of me, I knew I had made the right decision. My heart, though, definitely isn't agreeing with my head. I can't close my eyes because when I do, all I see is him. His face, sad and tear-stained is staring back at me asking me why, begging me for an answer. I want to ask the lawyer who's driving to turn around so I can go back to him and tell him that I'm sorry, that I didn't mean it, but I can't. I'm nothing but poison to him. I should've known better from the start. Clearly my relationship with Coleman is the prime example of how screwed up everything is when I'm around. He's nothing, but I couldn't even keep him happy.

I hand my keys to the lawyer. I'm so bad I don't even remember his name. I know he told me when he slammed his briefcase down on the table and started ranting about how he's up at the ass crack of dawn to come save some spoiled brat. I didn't argue because it's true. I had no choice but to call Ian. My parents couldn't get me out of this jam; only he could. When I told him what was going on all he said is that he'd take care of it. I expected him to yell and say 'I told you so', but he didn't. I don't think he even sighed or said my name. Moments later this guy walks in and my life changes.

He gets out and retrieves my bag from the rental. I refuse to drive the car back to the airport. I'll pay the fine. I don't care. I can't get into that car. Not after everything that happened, and everything that didn't. He stopped us, not me. I was ready and didn't care. I wanted him. I needed him. I still do, but I can't have him. Not now, not ever.

I can't look at the church either, too many memories. That's what I see. The two of us standing under the tree with him leaning into me. Holding me as if I'm the most precious thing he's ever seen. I am to him, at least. To me, I'm nothing but trash. I don't deserve the decency I'm being afforded right now. These highly paid suits coming in to make everything go away because of who I am. That's not right. Breaking his heart shouldn't have been just a simple piece of paper. I should've had the guts to walk up to him and tell him I'm leaving. Give him an explanation about why we aren't going to work and how the age thing is just too much. But I'm a coward. I know he'd say that his birthday is soon and we can hold out. He's right, I should be able to, but I can't.

We stop at an area rest stop so I can freshen up. I have no doubt my arrest has hit the social media sites. I guess Ian is at least prepared for it. I found it ironic that the officer who interviewed me is Dylan's dad. Of course, I only found out after he told me in the interview room how upset I made his daughter when I started dating Ryan. I knew she liked him, but there's a difference between her and I – Ryan loves me and I love him – I just can't show it right now.

I'm changed and somewhat cleaned up and back in the car. I'm being dropped at the airport where I'm to catch a flight to New York to see my parents. We're having a family meeting without Ian. He'll fly in tomorrow sometime with Cole so we can start this tour. I can't imagine what Ian has told my parents. I don't really care, because honestly, I think they're going to be disappointed with me regardless. It won't be so much about Ryan, but about the way I handled myself. I know better and should've acted with more maturity and not let my hormones dictate what I did. I could've easily waited until he turned eighteen and just come back, but no, I had to have him, keep him like he was some type of souvenir.

After stopping at my apartment to shower and change, I pull into my childhood home. I was hoping Alex would be here, but she's with her mom. I know if I called and told her what I had done, she'd be waiting, but I can't do that to her right now. Her mom needs her. The drive to my parent's house happens in a blur. I can't stop crying. I want to crawl up into a ball and bury myself under the blanket of misery that I've created.

I walk into the house, expecting it to be empty. My dad, dressed in jeans and a t-shirt, is sitting on the couch. He's waiting for me. His hands are folded and resting in his lap and he's looking out of the window. It's the way he used to sit each time I'd leave for a date or for a show, always worried.

I set down my keys on the small table just inside the front door. "Is Mom home?" I ask, breaking the silence.

"No, sweetie, it's just us." His eyes are kind when he looks at me. He stands, opening his arms. I can't move fast enough. I collapse into his arms as he holds me tight in his embrace. I don't care how bad I've screwed up; a girl always needs her daddy and I'm so thankful for mine.

He rubs my back, shushing my sobs. "It's going to be okay."

I shake my head. "No, it's not. I messed up so bad, Daddy."

"Everything will be fine. Come on. I'll make you some lunch and we'll talk." He wraps his arm around my shoulder, guiding us into the kitchen. He pulls out the stool for me, just like he does for my mom, and waits until I'm seated before walking around to the other side. I watch as he looks through the cupboards and refrigerator searching for something to make. I can't help but smile when he pulls out the makings for tomato soup and grilled cheese sandwiches.

I like watching my dad cook. While I was growing up, he would cook once a week. Mom and I would get pampered and served dinner. He'd set the table with candles and flowers and it didn't matter what he served, Mom always said it was the best meal she'd ever had. That's what I see when I look at Ryan – a lifetime of memories waiting to be discovered.

When I close my eyes and think about him, I see him walking around our kitchen, the morning sun shining through the window. He's in boxers and a white undershirt standing at the stove, cooking. If I let my imagination wander, I see a little girl running and attaching herself to his leg. I stand off to the side and watch. That vision will never happen, especially after what I've just done. He'll never forgive me. I won't ever forgive myself.

Dad sets a bowl of soup in front of me and a plate of quarter-cut sandwiches in between us. He hasn't cut my sandwiches since I was ten years old, a time when everything in life was so simple and my one dream was to become a singer. Now my dreams are a pile of nothing because the one person I thought I could share them with, isn't here and it's my fault. Even if I apologized I don't expect him to forgive me. I did the one thing I asked him not to do: I broke his heart. I could see it on his face when he called out my name. It pained me to not smile at him, to hold back from running into his arms.

"Ian called," he says this in a tone that would suggest Ian calling is an everyday occurrence and it may have been at one time, back when he was trying to sell my brand, but I can't imagine he keeps my parents up to date on me. That's my job and recently I've been failing.

"I figured." I take a deep sigh, turn and look at my dad. "I fell in love and made some terribly wrong decisions."

"You've been in love before."

I shake my head. "Not like this. With Cole, I think I loved him because he was there and we had spent so much time together. Our love grew that way, but with Ryan..." I pause and smile at that sound of his name coming off my lips. "With Ryan, it was instant, like a bolt of lightning passed from him to me."

"So what's the problem?"

I look at my dad in questioningly, furrowing my brow. "Ian didn't tell you?"

Dad sets his spoon down, picking up his napkin and wiping his mouth. "He said that you've gotten yourself into a bit of trouble with a guy and that you were coming home and that he'd be here tomorrow. Being in love isn't trouble if you ask me."

"I am in love, but it's wrong."

"Love is never wrong, Hadley." He says this with such confidence I almost believe him.

He picks up his spoon just as I blurt out: "It is when he's only seventeen."

He looks at me and tomato soup drips down his chin. I grab my napkin and wipe it away. He sets his spoon down again and turns. "Seventeen?"

I nod.

"Why?"

Shrugging like a child would be the easiest answer to give, but I'm not going to discount what I feel for Ryan. That wouldn't be fair to him. "I know it deep in my heart that he's the one for me, regardless of his age. When I first saw him, Dad, I knew. It was later that night that I found out his age and by then I was so lost in him that I couldn't see straight."

"Hadley –"

"No, let me finish. I want to get this all out there so you know why I'm here and why Ian is coming. We met at a show. His friend won a contest and she brought him. I had Alex talk to him and then I had an after-party so I could spend time with him. We spent all night talking and I fell asleep in his arms. When the sun woke us up, he kissed me. It was his first kiss and for me, it felt like I had never been kissed before. I asked him to the charity ball and he came. I went to church with him, I met his mom and everything felt so good."

"I hate asking this because I know you're an adult, but did you have sex with him?"

"No, I wouldn't, but when Ian invited Cole on this tour, things changed for us. Ryan became jealous, not that I could blame him, and we were fighting, so I went to see him, to tell him how I feel. I wanted to be with him so bad. We were in my rental and I was pushing for it, but he stopped me. We were about to go to his house when the cops showed up.

"His dad had reported him as a runaway and I was arrested for harboring him. We weren't running anywhere, but the officer didn't believe us and now… I did the worst thing I could've ever done to protect him from my crazy world."

"What's that?"

"I made him sign a no-contact order until he turns eighteen, which is just a few weeks away, but the worst part is I shut off his phone. I was paying for his cell phone because his parents won't allow him to have one and I *needed* to talk to him." I cover my face and break down. When I say it out loud it makes me realize I chased this boy. I gave him no option but to fall for me. "I'm so stupid."

Dad wraps his arms around me. "Come sit down, let's talk." I follow him back to the living room and sit next to him on the couch. I pull my leg underneath me and he mimics my position. It's funny, my dad with his salt and pepper hair sitting just like me. "Sounds like love got the best of you and that's okay. Sometimes you feel so much that common sense goes out the window. The important thing moving forward is that you're making the best decisions. Everyone has an error in judgment every now and again. You just happen to live in the limelight so when you, or someone like you, does it, the consequences are greater."

"What do you mean?"

"Not that I'm condoning what you did, but I think in a normal setting dating someone a bit younger isn't frowned upon. It may not be ideal, but definitely not a bad thing. Love doesn't know age."

"I'm not good for him," I say, choking on my words. I wipe away my tears and cover my face.

"I find that hard to believe. I know you better than anyone, except maybe your mom and Alex, and I know you're a good person." My dad pulls my hand into his. "Tell me about the no-contact order."

I shake my head, biting my lip. "They were going to charge him with assaulting an officer and the lawyer Ian sent suggested it. I didn't want to, but after thinking about it and realizing that Ryan's changed who he is to be with me... It wasn't right. I wasn't right for him. The changes he was making weren't for the better and I didn't want to see him become someone he hates because of me. But I love him so much and it hurts."

Dad pulls me into his arms. "You know your mom always says if you love something, set it free. If he comes back, he's yours."

"And if he doesn't, he never was."

"I'm sure he'll forgive you."

"No, he won't. I broke his heart."

I rest my head on my dad's chest and let him comfort me. If Ian thought that my dad was going to yell and scream at me, he's sadly mistaken. Ian doesn't have to worry because I'm doing that enough for myself. My last vision of Ryan is enough punishment to last me a lifetime and that's what I'll have, because there's no way Ryan and I will ever cross paths again.

I made sure of that.

chapter
thirty-one

RYAN

I can't believe she walked away from me. I need an explanation. What did I do? I look around. Everyone in the police station is staring. Are they feeling pity? Are they thankful that Hadley Carter is gone and out of their sleepy town?

I could make a run for it, make it back to her car before she does and demand that she take me with her. Beg her to rip up that stupid piece of paper and tell those lawyers to get the hell away from us. We can run, leave Brookfield and never come back. I'm only a few weeks from turning eighteen; surely no one will care. Everything that has happened between us has been because we're in love, nothing less. She didn't force herself on me. I welcomed her.

His strong and domineering voice shakes me from my reverie. I turn and look, wishing I hadn't. His face tells me everything that I need to know. He's going to make me wish I were spending the night in jail. My dad pushes me toward the door. I try to resist. I try to keep my feet grounded but it's no use. I look at the desk clerk and wonder if she knows what's going to happen when I walk out this door. Do they know what kind of man my father is? Right now, even I don't know, but after seeing him in that room, I have an unhealthy fear of him.

He's too calm as we drive home. He's even singing to himself. I can't hear what he's singing about, but it seems to keep him happy. I'm tempted to reach over and turn on the radio in his truck, wondering if it even works. I know that turning it on would piss him off. Maybe I should rock the boat while I'm already in for it when I get home. I want to hear music, is that so wrong? I want to hear her voice. I want to be a normal teenager.

My mom is standing in the window when we pull up. She disappears quickly, not opening the door or waiting for us. The enigma that is my parents is really starting to freak me out. I don't know if it was Hadley who opened my eyes or what, but the way my mom acts is weird and my dad... I never want to be like him.

I try to beat my dad into the house. I want to make it to my room where I feel the safest. He grabs me by the back of the sweatshirt and heaves me across the living room and onto the couch. I hear a pan drop in the kitchen and wonder if she's watching or whether she's nervous. Does she know what he's capable of?

I try to move, but he's on me before I'm able to defend myself. He presses his knee into my stomach, his other hand clamping down on my throat. I've never seen this side of him. The look in eyes is menacing. Deadly.

I try to remove his hand off my throat, but he tightens his grip. I push his face, extending my arm as far as I can. I stretch enough to get him off of me and allow my leg to move and help alleviate some of the pressure on my stomach. His hand slips from my neck, causing him to collapse on top of me. We both grunt from the pressure.

I take a deep breath and choke. The burning in my lungs is making breathing difficult. If I don't move, he's going to kill me. I kick and scramble as he tries to pin down my arms. I never knew how strong he was until now. He pushes down on my face, cutting off my air. I gasp and slap at his face, my legs working to get him off of me. Where the hell is my mother?

"If you ever disgrace my name again, I'll end you." I know he's telling the truth. The tone of his voice is enough to drive the point home. His knee grinds into my stomach with such force I feel like I'm going to throw up. It's now or never. I can't stay like this or he will kill me.

I raise my knee hard, not once, but twice. He jerks forward, losing his hold on my throat. I cough hard and move away quickly. I look at him, withering on the floor. He's bent in half, holding himself.

"Ryan?"

I look sharply at my mom. She's standing there, with a dishrag dangling from her hands, tears streaming down her face. She's shaking her head, her lower lip trembling. "Dylan's outside. You should go," her voice cracks.

"Mom?"

"Go, Ryan. Please go before he hurts you even more."

I try to speak, but nothing comes out. I nod and run down the hall to my room. My door is already open, my room torn apart. I grab a few pieces of clothing, my phone, money and backpack. I don't know if I'm coming back here, but I'm hoping to never see his face again. I don't stop to look at the scene in the living room or even say goodbye to my mother. She allowed this to happen. She allowed him to put his hands on me.

Dylan is a statue in her car. The usually peppiness is missing. I open the door, she looks at me and we both gasp. Her face is tear-streaked black from her make-up. I can't imagine what I look like. I get in and barely have the door shut before she's speeding down the road. We don't talk. The radio doesn't play. The tension between us is thick. I can feel it radiating off her. She's been so vocal about Hadley hurting me that she knew this day was going to come. I just didn't listen. And I'm not ready to accept that we're done. I know Hadley did what she had to, to get us out of trouble. I only wish she asked me first.

I pull out my iPhone and text Hadley, watching the screen while I wait for the message to say it has been delivered or read. But it doesn't change. I try again and again. The same result each time. I hate doing this in front of Dylan, but I have no choice. I press Hadley's name. I need to talk to her. I don't care what that ridiculous piece of paper said. I'd gladly spend the night in jail if it gives me the answers that I need.

Nothing happens with the call. I try again, nothing. I tap the phone to my head, thinking. Why isn't my phone working? I shake it and try calling her, nothing. I hit it against my hand, nothing.

Dylan pulls over, but doesn't shut off the engine. She stares out the window at the open space. Wheat fields are all you can see. If you look long enough, stare hard enough, the sky touches the never-ending fields. It's a cool illusion when you're a kid and you're out here looking. But looking at it now makes me want to run until I can reach the edge where the two connect and hope there's something better for me out there.

"My dad knows his officer hit you. So does my mom. He's pissed. You know he doesn't condone violence at the station. She's upset, angry. They fought and when your mom called she threw the phone at my dad. I don't know anything else except that Hadley's gone."

"Yeah," I say, for lack of anything better to add. I'm not sure how to respond or if there's even a right thing to say.

"You're coming back to my house. My dad will apologize and take care of things at the station. I know you made the first move or whatever, but that doesn't give Daniels the right to hurt you like that. He knows better and for him to hit you..." she trails off, wiping more tears from her cheeks. "Anyway, Mom says you're staying with us."

Dylan puts her car in drive and turns back onto the road, heading toward her house. I never expected I'd be staying with her, or that her mom would react the way she did, but to say I'm thankful would be an understatement. Maybe I can leave when I'm eighteen as planned. Take what money I have saved and buy a bus ticket out of here. That was my plan until I met Hadley and now everything has changed.

Mrs. Ross is standing at the door when we walk in. She takes me in her arms, enveloping me the way a mom should. Dylan joins us and they cry. I don't understand why they're both crying. I'm not, but I should be. Maybe this hasn't sunk in yet, or I need to be away from people. I can feel the ache in my heart getting stronger and know it's just a matter of time before everything explodes. When she releases us, she pats down my hair, avoiding eye contact. I know she's staring at my lip. She looks up and smiles as she cups my cheeks.

"Come you two, I made brownies."

Dylan pushes my shoulder to get my feet moving. The smell of freshly baked brownies makes my stomach growl. I realize I haven't eaten since the night before, not that I know what time it is now, but I'm starving. We sit across from each other, each with our own plate and a glass of milk. I devour mine, while she picks at hers. I snatch one off her plate before she can slap my hand and stuff it in my mouth. This is the only time I get sweets like this; my mom would never dream of baking anything.

Mr. Ross comes in and sits down across from me. Dylan rolls her eyes at him. She gets up and moves to the sink, taking her coveted brownies with her. Mrs. Ross joins us, choosing to sit down next to me. Mr. Ross clears his throat and lays his hands on the table.

"Officer Daniels was a bit out of line when he punched you. I've always treated you as if you were my own and I expect my department to do the same. Today they treated you like every other teenager we deal with when it probably wasn't necessary. We should've re-evaluated and listened to what you were telling us. I'm sorry, Ryan."

"Okay." I say, not sure how to respond. I've never had an adult apologize to me before, but I've also never had an adult hit me either. Today was a whole slew of firsts for me. "Thank you," I add for good measure.

"What happened to your neck?" he asks. My hand instantly goes to my neck and rubs it. My skin is raw and hurts to touch. I pull my hand away and shake my head. "What about your chin?" I look down at my empty brownie plate to avoid answering.

His chair scrapes the floor and before I know it, he's on the side of me. He bends and kisses Mrs. Ross on the cheek and sets his hand on my shoulder. "You don't have to tell me, I can figure it out by the look on your face. You'll stay in the guest bedroom until you're ready to go home." He pats my shoulder one more time before walking away. I jump slightly when the front door slams shut.

"You know where everything is," Mrs. Ross says as she gets up, but not before placing a kiss on my cheek. The way she treats me makes me realize how inept my mother is with her feelings, but then again, she did call Dylan and ask her to come pick me up, so maybe there is some hope.

The bed is a welcome comfort, much softer than the one I have at home. I helped paint this room last summer. Dylan calls it bleached green; her mom calls it sage.

I lean back, rolling over on my side to look out the window. The dark sky is settling in even though it's not yet dinnertime. It's only going to continue to get dark this early. I hate winter. The cold, dark nights leave so much to be desired. Thoughts of the last few days replay in my mind as I focus on the swaying tree outside the window. The pictures of Hadley, the way she told me she loved me, the car. It all seems like a blur, like a dream really. I close my eyes and wish that when I open them I'd be holding her, her skin pressed against me, my lips finding hers in the dark. I want to be back in the car, holding her and not saying no, not holding back from what we both wanted so desperately.

I pull out my phone and try Hadley again. My text sits there, not delivering, staring back at me. Her picture mocks me; she's smiling, but I'm not. I don't want to believe that I can't reach her, that we can't at least text. I don't want to believe that she's made it impossible for us to talk. Why would she do that? I close my eyes and fight the tears. I will not cry. I won't. I'm not an emotional person and I'm definitely not starting now. I guess that's a trait I've learned from my parents. No emotion so people don't think any less of you.

I roll over and scream into the pillow, my fist pounding into the bed. I'm trying to be quiet, but know they can hear me. Why did she leave me? Tears stream down my face. I wipe them away angrily, unable to stop their flow. I'm not supposed to cry. Guys don't cry. Yet here I am, crying like a damn baby because my girlfriend just dumped me.

She dumped me.

I say the words over and over in my head and don't want to believe them. My body hurts. My hand rests on my chest, my fingers tugging at my shirt trying to ease the pain. She's gone and there's no saving our relationship. She left me. She left me behind after promising me so much.

I shouldn't stay here. I should go as planned. Leave when I turn eighteen. I have enough saved for a bus ticket. Yeah, that's what I'll do. I'll go to New York and look for her. Age won't matter then. We can be together.

The bedroom door squeaks open. I don't have to turn around to know that it's Dylan. She sets something on the table beside my bed and sits down. She's so tiny the bed doesn't even dip.

I startle when she reaches out and touches me. Her arm wraps around my waist and she rests her body along mine. She gets as close as humanly possible. We've never been like this and I'm not sure how I feel about it.

"Ryan," she whispers my name so softly it reminds me of Hadley saying my name earlier. I try to block that imagine out of my mind, but I can't. From the sound of her name to her leaving me at the police station, I can't shake it.

"I know you're hurting. I know it's not the same, but I've been there. I've been in love and it hurts like hell when you're not ready to quit and someone else is. Things get better, I promise you. And I also promise you that whatever happened this weekend and what's going on now, no one will ever know about it from me. I'll keep your secrets, Ryan."

I roll over and pull Dylan's hand into mine, not afraid to let her see how much I'm hurting.

"You'll be okay," she whispers. She rests her head on my chest and holds me while my heart shatters into a million pieces.

chapter
thirty-two

HADLEY

Waking up in my childhood bedroom isn't anything like what you see on television. My room isn't bubblegum pink with posters of boy bands adorning the walls. My prom queen tiara isn't hanging from my vanity with my singing trophies. Nothing like that exists in this room. Now, this is where guests sleep. They crawl into a queen-sized bed with decorative pillows. They can watch TV on the flat screen mounted to the wall. They never know that this used to be a girl's room.

The walls are yellow, it's calming and inviting according to my mom. I have no problem sleeping here. In fact, I like it. It brings back memories. Sometimes I miss the safety of my parents' house. I bury myself deeper into the pillows. I don't want to start the day. I don't want to think about yesterday and what it means. I don't want to constantly check my phone hoping he'll call, knowing that he can't. Maybe I shouldn't have turned off his phone, but I had to. I'd be too tempted to contact him. The desire to hear his voice is already pounding in my head.

My parents took today off work to help me deal with Ian. I told them it wasn't necessary, but they insisted. My dad said I'm still his baby girl and if he wants a day off to watch over me, no one is going to stop him. I didn't want to show him how much his words had affected me, so I curled up on the couch and rested my head on his leg. My mom sat at the other end holding my legs, much like they do when I'm sick.

I finally drag myself out of bed and into the kitchen. Dad's cooking and Mom's sitting at the bar sipping her requisite cup of coffee and reading the paper. I sit on the stool next to her and steal a piece of her toast.

"What do you want for breakfast?" Dad smiles at me as I sit down.

I shrug. "Whatever you're making is fine."

He winks before turning back to the stove. Mom pushes the rest of her toast over to me as she closes the newspaper. "How'd you sleep?"

"Fine, actually. But anything is better than a hotel bed."

"I don't know why you insist on staying in a hotel when you're in L.A. Why not just buy a place?"

"Because I don't want to live there, Mom," I say as I pick at the toast. My dad sets down a plate with eggs over easy, bacon and hash browns.

"What time will Ian be here?" she asks. I look at the clock and sigh. He and Cole took the red-eye, which arrives in New York at six and that means any minute.

"They're probably on their way now unless they checked into the hotel first."

"Well, it will be good to see Cole."

I give my mom the stink eye. I know she loves him, but come on. She puts her hand on my wrist and gives it a squeeze.

"I'm just saying it will be nice, not that I want you guys back together."

"Uh huh."

I give her a kiss on her cheek and head back to my room. I dig through my old dresser for some sweats and a t-shirt. I wasn't planning on staying the night, but as soon as Mom came home last night I realized that I needed my parents.

I quickly hop in the shower. I know Ian will be here soon. He never misses an opportunity to rub it into my parents that he controls my everyday life. But after getting me out of that mess in Brookfield, I owe him. I have no idea how he plans to collect, but I'll be ready. I have to be the good little girl from here on out. No more messing up.

No more falling in love.

Ian and Cole are here when I'm finally presentable. Well, as presentable as I'm going to get while lounging at my parents'. My hair is up in a messy bun, no make-up on and I'm wearing a tank top and sweatpants with flip-flops. Everyone stops talking when I walk into the kitchen. Ian looks at me and says nothing and shakes his head, but it's Cole and the way that he looks at me that makes me smile despite how I feel about him. He's frozen mid-bite, his mouth hanging open and spoon dripping milk back into his bowl of cereal.

Some things never change.

"Close your mouth, dear; no one likes to see what you're eating," Mom says to Cole, making me laugh. He closes his mouth and clears his throat. I sit down next to him, his eyes watching my every move. Creeper. Ian is across from me, a pile of papers in front of him. He picks them up, shuffling them around. Dad pulls out a chair and takes a seat, my mom following suit. I guess this is it. Time to detail how messed up I am and what I have to do to fix it.

"Last week we had a discussion about your behavior. I admit I employed some shady ploys to keep you in your hotel, but when I tell you that I did those things to keep you safe, I mean it."

"I know," I say, catching Ian off guard. He looks up quickly, his bangs falling in his face. That's the one thing about Ian that I've always liked: he doesn't look like a manager. He's not walking around in a suit and tie, carrying a briefcase. He's dressed for the music scene.

"You know?"

"Yes. I can see that now."

"It took you getting arrested to see that I'm only trying to help?"

I put my face in my hands and sigh. I feel Cole's hand resting on my leg, his way of showing comfort. I wipe away an errant tear and look at Ian. "That was a wake-up call. I'm not going to apologize for Ryan. I'm in love with him, but I'm not healthy for him."

"He's a distraction." I don't agree or disagree with Ian. He's right. At least that's what I'm going to tell myself. It's not going to matter how bad it hurts or how much my heart is breaking. Ian's right. "Can you promise me he won't be a distraction during the tour?"

As much as I hate it, I nod. "I promise."

"Last night a reporter called and is giving me until the end of today to give him something juicy on you. Your rental car was reported in the parking lot. He heard it on his scanner and he started digging. He knows you were arrested, but doesn't know why. I can make this go away or we can let him run with the article, your choice."

I lean back, preparing myself for the inevitable. "What do I have to do to make it go away?"

"You're going to go public with Cole. This reporter will get an exclusive and he'll be happy." Cole's hand tenses on my leg. He didn't know about this. Something like this will surely ruin his bachelor status. He'll have to play nice as well. He can't afford another cheating scandal.

"Cole and I aren't together."

"You'll act it each time you leave the tour bus or hotel. I'm not saying you need to kiss him in public, but you'll hold hands, feed each other ice cream – hell, you'll even allow him to put sunscreen on your back. I don't care what it is, you're together."

"How does that help Hadley's image?" I'm so thankful my dad speaks up, because I don't know if I can get the words out.

Ian leans back in the chair, looking at my dad. "She needs someone the media likes and that's Cole. They've been together before and with them being on tour, it's expected. The tour is short, so they only have to act for a while."

"I don't like it," Mom adds. "I don't see how it helps."

"See, Liberty, that is why this is my job. This reporter is going to write an article about your daughter being arrested. Along with that article, he'll dig and find out why. Would you rather her pretend to be with Cole, a man she knows, or would you rather her be disgraced for screwing around with a seventeen year old? Because if it's the latter, I can guarantee you this will be her last tour for a long time. No one will want her around."

My mom gets up from the table and walks into the kitchen and starts slamming cupboards. I can't imagine what it was like to grow up with Ian as your brother. He's entirely too bossy for my liking.

"What about you, Austin? Are you willing to go along with this sham so I can get your daughter on the straight and narrow?"

"I'm with Libby, but I also don't want Hadley's name dragged through the mud. I'll support whatever Hadley decides to do."

Cole leans into me, his scruff tickling my cheek. "I'll do whatever you want," he whispers in my ear. I nod and move away slightly. I can't have him this close.

"Fine," I say, looking away from Ian.

"You know things could be worse, Hadley."

"I know." I can't take any more of this intervention. I get up, grab my hoodie and head outside. I need fresh air. I sit in the rocking chair on the back deck and watch a bird look for food. Doesn't he know he should be south by now? The door opens and closes. I can tell by the overwhelming scent of his cologne that it's Cole. He sits down and starts swinging us back and forth. I hate that he can do that and I can't. It sucks being short.

"You screwed up, Hadley Girl."

"Shut up, Coleman, I don't need to hear it from you, too."

"What's this guy got?"

I look away so he doesn't see my tears. I'm not sure I can explain it to Cole without hurting his feelings. Cole and I were in love once and I thought that was enough, but with Ryan, it's so different, I can't explain it.

"You can tell me, ya know."

I shake my head. "I can't."

"Do you love him?"

I nod.

"More than you loved me?"

"That's not fair."

He reaches over and pulls my chin toward him. He wipes my tears away. "Hadley, it's okay to love someone else. What we had was great and I screwed that up. I was young and stupid, but if I could change it, I would. I never wanted to hurt you. If you're in love with this guy, then he's the luckiest guy I know." His voice is so quiet and soft. I know why I loved him so much. He pulls me into his arms and holds me. The sad thing is, this isn't acting. He's being genuine.

"I can't be with him. I'm not good for him and it was stupid for me to even think I could have something with someone who isn't part of my crazy life."

"You're life isn't crazy; it's normal."

"It's anything but normal, Cole."

Cole leans away so he can see my face. "Don't worry, I'll make everything better."

Yeah, that's what I'm afraid of. If Ryan was an error in judgment, Cole is a colossal mistake.

chapter
thirty-three

RYAN

I missed a week of school thanks to Dylan. It was at her insistence that I not go to school until the bruising around my neck was less visible. I told her it wouldn't work, but she forged a note from my mom saying I was ill. Mr. and Mrs. Ross didn't like that, so things changed quickly. I don't know what happened the night Mr. Ross left me sitting at the table and I didn't ask. My parents haven't called and asked me to come home though and I'm not sure how I should feel about that. I hope that my mom can at least call and check on me. I'll have to visit her at work if that doesn't happen soon.

Returning to school is not high on my priority list, but I can't say that it is for any teenager. I'm trying not to count the days since I last spoke to Hadley. I'm trying not to remember what we were about to do before everything changed. If I had kept my mouth shut, maybe things would be different now. I carry around my phone – the phone she bought for me – hoping that it will spring to life at any moment. It's the only piece of her that I have and I can't let go. Each time I think about her, the anger starts. At night, when I'm alone, I lie in bed and cry, waiting for that stupid phone to ring, or vibrate, or beep or something that signifies my connection to her is not a figment of my imagination. Maybe this is why my parents sheltered me so much, so I wouldn't feel the pain of heartache.

I can only hide a few of the bruises and they aren't as dark, but I'm keeping my head down, tucking myself into the new hoodie that Mrs. Ross bought for me, one of my new pieces of clothing. Dylan told a few kids that I was thinking about taking up wrestling and the marks were from working out. That earned me a few pats on the back and a requested meeting with the wrestling coach. The nice thing is I'm not being stared at. No one knows about what happened and they definitely don't know about my dad. I want to keep it that way.

The only problem living with Dylan is that I have no freedom. Everywhere I turn she's there making sure I'm okay. But being at Dylan's gives me things I've never had before like a radio, TV and computer. I'm allowed to watch TV, even though I haven't a clue as to what we watch at night, but I do know it's all done as a family and I like that. And I have laughter. They're always laughing. I wish I could join in, but I can't. Each time they laugh, I think of Hadley and wonder if she'd think the same thing was funny. When that happens, I excuse myself and retreat to the guest bedroom.

I know I can stay here as long as I want. It's nice to be wanted by someone, even if it's not Hadley or my parents.

I left this morning before Dylan woke up. I needed to walk in the crisp air and work out some aggression. I've thought about asking the wrestling coach if I could use the punching bag in the weight room. I figured if I can picture Hadley's face, the way she looked leaving the police station; I could take my anger out on the bag. I also wanted to come in and use the computer in the library where Dylan isn't looming in the hallway or looking over my shoulder. If I had told her this, she'd make sure it didn't happen. Dylan is doing everything she can to help me forget these past few months, even if I don't want to forget them. Now I sit in front of the library computer, which is the same computer that showed me pictures of her and her ex, which resulted in her showing up here, and us being arrested. I type in her name and pause, my finger hovering over the enter key. There's a side of me that wants to know what she's been doing these past few days, but I'm also afraid.

I keep asking myself "what if I meant nothing to her? What if I was just something to pass her time?" I want to say that I know the answers, but if someone asked me today, I wouldn't know what to say because nothing seems real. How do you just disappear from someone's life like that? How do you almost give yourself to them one minute and in the next want nothing to do with them?

I need to stop thinking about her, but I can't help it. Everywhere I turn, she's there. I want to believe that when I turn eighteen, she'll be standing outside waiting for me. We'll run off together and this will all be a stupid nightmare.

I hit the enter key and shut my eyes, waiting for the images to load. I've learned from Dylan that the newest items always show first. I'm going to believe that she's coming back to me. When I open my eyes, I bite my lip to keep from screaming out, but it's not enough to contain the rage building inside of me.

A week ago she was my girlfriend. A week ago she was kissing me, touching me. Now, merely seven days later, she's kissing him, and it's right there for everyone to see. She holds him like she held me. He's touching her, touching her like I've done… like he's done so many times. It's clear, right? This is what they call the writing on the wall. She doesn't want me, never did. I was just her charity case.

I shove my chair back, hard. My hands push against the table for leverage. The computer wobbles, but Dylan appears beside me, steadying it with her hands. She straightens the computer, not making eye contact with me. She must think I'm some pathetic loser. That's what I think of me. I can't believe I've been so naïve this whole time. I turn away, afraid to look at Dylan or even have her look at me. I want to scream out and throw the computer across the room. How can she do this to me? Did I mean anything to her?

I stand up, kicking the chair. It does nothing to quell the anger inside of me. I pick up the next chair and throw it across the room. I don't know if it hits anything. I don't care. I hate feeling like this. I look for something else to throw, eying the computers sitting on the table. If I damage them, maybe they'll throw me out of school and then I can be the pathetic loser that everyone thinks I am.

Dylan steps in front of me. I look down at her. Her face is calm, reserved. She stands in front of me with her hands down at her sides.

"It's going to be okay, Ryan."

I shake my head. She steps closer, pulling my hands into hers. Her chest presses against mine. I shouldn't be standing like this with her, it's not right. I'm with Had… no, I'm not. I'm not with anyone anymore, so who cares how I'm standing. I shouldn't care.

I look down at Dylan. Her gray eyes stare back at me. They don't hold pity, just kindness. "I need—"

"Time," she says, interrupting me. She's right. She's been right this entire time; I just didn't want to listen. "Come on, we need to get to class."

She leads me out of the library, bypassing the chairs that haphazardly lie on the floor. I have no doubt I'll be called down to the office today and punished, but that's fine. Right now, I'll take whatever someone wants to give me.

Dylan doesn't let go of my hand as we walk the halls. The attention feels nice. I won't lie. Girls are smiling at her and guys are once again patting me on the back. It feels like I'd done something remarkable like save a life and suddenly everyone knows who I am. I'm not sure if I should feel good about this or not.

We stop at our lockers. When she lets go of my hand I feel a loss, but not like when I was with Hadley, just… different.

I feel like I'm in the twilight zone. Guys that I've never spoken to are fist bumping, saying hi and nodding in my direction. When I sit down for lunch, three classmates sit down, too. I look around for Dylan, who is watching me. A smile breaks out on her face as she walks to the table.

"What did you tell these guys?" I whisper to her as she sits down. She shrugs and starts unpacking her lunch. I poke her in the side, but all she does is smile.

I'm included in conversations like we've always been friends. I don't think I've ever listened to what these guys talk about. The guys invite me to a party this weekend and Dylan tells them that we'll be there. I'm not so sure how I feel about that. I don't know what the shift is. I haven't changed. But maybe I should enjoy it and think about staying in school for the rest of the year.

I walk into my mom's office. Her eyes light up as she rushes around her desk to give me a hug. Her arms wrap tightly around my neck and she holds me, much like she did when I was a baby.

"I'm so happy to see you. I miss you." She steps back, leaving her hands on my shoulders and looks at me. I know she sees my new clothes and if she's upset, she doesn't show it. She looks behind her, probably checking to see if her boss is coming before leading me over to her desk. I know her boss is strict, but I have a feeling this is the only place I can see her without seeing my dad.

"I miss you, too. Is everything okay at home?"

"Things are fine, Ryan. You don't need to worry about me."

"But I do."

She rests her hand on my cheek and smiles. "You're such a good boy, you didn't deserve what happened." I have no reply for her because I don't think anyone deserves to have that happen. It's one thing to lose your girlfriend; it's entirely another to have your dad turn violent on you.

"I'm scared for you," I say. Her lips tighten into a faint smile.

"Listen to me. I can take care of myself. You don't have to worry about your dad. The Rosses, they have my permission to let you stay at their house. You'll be eighteen soon and can do anything you want."

"What about you?"

She shakes her head. "He doesn't touch me, I can promise you that."

"If he does, will you leave?"

"Yes, Mr. Ross and I discussed that this week. You're very lucky to have them. They love you, but not as much as me. I'm so sorry, Ryan. I should've been a better mother."

I'm not sure if I should believe her or not, but I do. I tried to be mad at her for the way she acted, but Mrs. Ross explained how when someone emotionally abuses you they take away all your self-esteem and that it took a lot for my mom to call Dylan that day.

Her eyes glisten and I smile at her, hoping to keep her tears at bay. This is the most talkative I've ever seen my mom and I like it.

"I'll come by next week," I say as I stand and give her a kiss. "I love you, Mom."

"Love you, too."

I wave as I walk out the door and head for home. Home... such a strange word for me now. When I pass the newsstand, the familiar blond hair mocks me. I know I shouldn't stop, but I have no control over my feet. She's there on the cover with him. The headline blurs. All I see is her on her tiptoes, kissing him.

chapter
thirty-four

S tanding off to the side of the stage, I watch as Cole interacts with his fans. The female contingent is in full force for this show and he loves every moment. For the most part the tour is going really well. Each show is sold out and we've added more dates. I think Ian was shocked when I didn't refuse the additions. Truth is, I love being on tour. Being on stage gives me such exhilaration. I need it to feel satisfied. It keeps my mind off things.

I didn't want to come back here, to Jackson, but Ian insisted. I balked at doing this show, begging Ian to cancel, but when the show sold out within minutes, Ian wouldn't budge. Alex is supposed to be here already and I'm starting to get nervous. Her plane landed over two hours ago and it doesn't take that long to get from the airport to the venue. I didn't have to ask her, she just knew I'd need her, especially since the day is *tomorrow*. I've tried not to think about how things ended with Ryan. In fact, I try not to think about him period. Out of sight, out of mind, right? It's easier this way, better really.

Ian surprises me when he drapes his arm across my shoulder. He's been happier, too, since the tour started and I'm sure it's because my *issue* no longer exists. I also think he's over the moon about the display Cole and I have been putting on. Well, more of a display for me, not so much for Cole. Late night conversations with Cole lead me to believe he wants more. I wish I could say that I'm immune to Cole, but the truth is, I'm not. I never have been and it's always been a fight. But I'm not in love with him. Not the way he wants me to be. I care for him and he'll always be a part of my life, but that's all I can be for him.

Ian whistles – you know, that annoying loud thing people can do when they put their fingers in their mouth – right in my ear. I elbow him and he just smiles. This is the nice side of Ian. I know he wishes he could be like this more, but I stress him out. I cause him more work because of my inability to think straight. I made a vow when the tour started that I'd work hard and be America's sweetheart.

I've been waiting for that reporter to renege on his deal with Ian. Each day I scour the Internet looking for anything related to my time in Brookfield, even though I don't want to remember the result.

"You ready?"

I nod. I'm always ready when I'm about to perform. Cole and I recorded some duets when we were dating, but never released them until now. That was part of the agreement. I would sing with Cole and Ian would make sure we had everything we needed on this tour. One thing I asked for was no *Anal Anna* and Ian agreed. It just means he lost interest and I'm okay with that.

The fans chant my name. I close my eyes and savor the sweet sound of their voices. It's moments like this where I can forget everything. Word spread fast that Cole and I are performing together, giving me this surreal feeling. It's not that I don't like performing with Cole; it's just that the song means something different now. The fans though, they think we're together and believe we're singing to each other. Ian pushes me lightly, getting me moving. He's had to do this a few times. When I open my eyes, Cole is beckoning me out on stage with a wicked smile on his face. The crowd erupts. I look and see both of us on the jumbo screen. He looks like he's in love and for a brief second I wish I could return the sentiment.

When I reach him, he places his hand on my hip, pulling me closer. His lips graze my cheek, causing the crowd to go wild, only they don't know that he's whispering in my ear that he's tired and really wants to go take a nap. I try not to laugh and the smile that spreads across my face entices the fans.

I'm handed a microphone and our stagehands bring out two stools. Cole helps me onto one stool before sitting on his own. The band starts and we wait for our cue. Cole starts, his words, once having meaning, are now just words he sings to make the girls go crazy. They love him and they should. I haven't looked at the crowd. I'm afraid. Not that I expect him to be here, but my heart is hoping he's standing right up front, maybe holding a sign telling me how much he loves me and that tomorrow everything can be different, that he has forgiven me for being such a bitch.

Only when I open my eyes, he's not there. In fact, from the looks of it there aren't that many guys in the first few rows. There isn't a sign. There isn't anyone trying to get my attention. I don't know what I was expecting, but it isn't this. My heart starts to ache with thoughts of him. I close my eyes again and breathe in deeply before belting out my lyrics. I think of Ryan and how much I miss him as I sing.

The song finishes. When I open my eyes and look at Cole, he knows what I just did. I can see the hurt on his face, even though he's trying to mask it. He looks back at the crowd and waits for the next song to start. I clear my head. I have to be fair to him. We're supposed to be play-acting for the public. I can't do anything stupid.

After three more songs, Cole and I leave the stage. We're going to have a half-hour intermission before I go on. I follow him as he stalks off. I can tell he's talking to himself by the way his hands are flying around. He throws his microphone at one of the techs. I shrug and apologize when I hand him mine. Cole throws open my dressing room door and stands in the middle of the room. I shut the door behind me, hoping that Ian will give us just a few minutes so I can explain, even though I have no idea what I'm going to say to him.

He turns. His face is red and full of anger. I get that he's upset, but we aren't a couple and I'm allowed to miss the one I love.

"What the hell was that, Hadley?"

"What?" I ask, throwing my hands up in the air.

"Seriously, you don't know?"

"Obviously not," I say as I move by him. I sit down at my vanity, resting my head in my hands. I can't stand vague. When he acts like this it really pisses me off.

"You missed your cue. Twice."

"What?" I look up at him and he's staring at me. The expression on his face tells me he's serious. "I did not. I know when to come in, Cole, I wrote the damn song. Remember?"

"Yeah, I remember, but I just sat through it and so did the fans. You missed it and that's not like you. You're supposed to be acting like my girlfriend and there you are thinking about some piss-ant teenager, making me look like a fool."

"You don't know what you're talking about." I get up and move over to my rack of clothes. I pull out a couple dresses and throw them onto the couch. Throwing my clothes feels good so I keep doing it until the rack is empty. I pick up my shoes and start throwing them across the room. When they're out of reach, I reach for the vase of roses and throw it against the wall. The glass shatters sending shards all over the place.

Cole grabs me from behind, locking my arms down with his. I fall to the ground. He goes with me, holding me in his lap. I cry hard for the loss of the boy that I love and can't have and for the man I just humiliated on the stage. I've destroyed Ryan, just like Cole destroyed me and there isn't anything I can do to fix it.

Cole lets me cry. He doesn't tell me everything will be okay or that he'll fix it. He can't. He's not going to sugarcoat anything for me. He's realistic and right now I hate him for it. I need him to tell me that he'll track down Ryan and bring him to me, that he'll make sure Ryan forgives me for being a self-centered bitch, but he doesn't. He holds me, keeping my arms locked so I don't do any more damage.

I try to calm down, matching my breathing with his. It's not as easy as it sounds, but thinking about his chest moving up and down against my back brings things into perspective.

"You have to go on in a few minutes, Hadley."

I shake my head. He's wrong. "We just came off stage, Cole. I have thirty minutes."

He rests his head against my back. I feel his lips press against my skin. "I love you, Hadley, probably more than I should, but you've got to get over this. I know you love him, but sometimes you have to put those feelings on hold and live your life. This is not the right time for either of you and you have to accept that."

"We should never have come here."

"I know. I don't know what Ian was thinking, but it's not good and right now your fans think there's something wrong with you, so you need to go out there and show them that you're the Hadley Carter they paid to see, not the one they just witnessed singing to her boyfriend."

"Fake boyfriend," I whisper.

"Yeah, fake boyfriend," he sighs. "It doesn't matter what I am, we have a deal and you need to keep your end."

"I know."

Apparently that satisfies him because he lets me go. I slide the rest of the way to the ground and pull my knees to my chest. I wish I could cancel the rest of the show, fake the flu or something, but I can't.

The door opens, I don't turn around because I know who it is and as excited as I am that she's here, I don't want her to see me like this.

"It's okay, Coleman, I'll take care of everything." I feel him shift behind me and hear the door close. Alex runs her fingers through my hair. She knows how to make me feel better.

"I want to go see him. Tomorrow he'll be eighteen and everything will be fine. We'll go in the morning and be back before the bus leaves."

Alex moves and sits in front of me. She looks tired. I reach out and trace my finger under the bags. I hate seeing her like this. She shakes her head, pulling my hand into hers.

"I went to Brookfield, that's why I'm late. I thought if I could bring Ryan to you, things would be better – not that things are good – but you know what I mean."

"He didn't want to come?" My voice shakes when I ask.

Alex shakes her head. "He doesn't live at home anymore, sweetie. He ran away the morning after you left him."

"No," I whisper before breaking down in her arms. I've just lost the one I love more than anything and don't know how to find him.

chapter
thirty-five

RYAN

I'm eighteen today.

This is supposed to be the turning point in my life.

Today everything was meant to change.

Only I'm alone, staring at the white ceiling.

I reach under my mattress and pull out Hadley's phone. It's been hiding. I couldn't stomach looking at it day after day so I hid it. I didn't need the painful reminder of what it meant at one time not so long ago.

Freedom.

Love.

A life away from Brookfield.

Now it holds lies.

Deception.

Pain.

I turn it on and wait for the apple symbol to disappear. I hold it in my hands waiting for that distinct chime to alert me that I have a message. The chime – her ringtone – her song – doesn't sound.

I pull up her name, the only contact I ever put in here. The only person I ever wanted to talk to with this phone. Her porcelain face stares back at me. Before today I thought she was the most beautiful thing I'd ever seen, but now I see flaws. I see someone who used me to make herself feel better. I see someone who took advantage of me because I didn't know any better, but not anymore.

Dylan has taught me in this past month what it's like to care for someone simply because you can. Her father taught me to speak my mind and not be afraid to answer when asked a question.

I want to tell Hadley that I'll never forgive her for what she's done, but I'll never see her so why do I need to say that to her? Fact is, she's not even watching. I'm not stupid, at least not anymore. I know she shut off my phone. As easy as it was for her to give it to me, it was just as easy for her to take it away. She's treated me like a petulant child and not the lover she said I was.

I get out of bed and move quietly down the hall, careful not to wake anyone. The stairs to the basement creak with my weight. They're old and in need of repair. Mr. Ross and I plan to do this over winter vacation. It's the least I can do to return their hospitality and love.

I turn on the overhead light. It sways back and forth casting shadows along the walls. Chills wash over me. I get the feeling that someone is watching me, lurking in the corner waiting to pounce. I take a deep breath, calming my nerves. There isn't anyone down here, just an old basement. I'm an adult now. I shouldn't be scared of the boogeyman. I walk carefully into Mr. Ross's workshop and pull the cord to turn on the light. This time I hold the bulb from moving back and forth so I can focus on what I need. The black handle is easy to spot. I pull out the hammer, turning it from side to side, inspecting the large metal object before laying it on the table.

My phone feels heavy in my pocket, but after I'm done it won't. I won't have to see it anymore. I drop it onto the table and bring it to life. Her smiling face mocks me, reminding me what her lips felt like against mine. I pick up the hammer and bring it down once, hard. The crack is satisfying, but it's not enough. I can still see her. Her brown eyes sparkle as if she's telling me a story. Her kissable lips make her face light up with her bright smile.

I fell hard for her and she let me, encouraged me, but no more. I bring down the hammer hard, hitting the picture dead on. The glass spider webs making her invisible, but I can still see her, feel her on my skin. Again and again I pound my phone until nothing is left. It's in pieces. My life is in pieces because of her.

A soft hand rubs up and down on my arm, a head resting on my shoulder. She whispers in my ear that everything will be okay. How does she know? I lift my head slightly to look at her. Her dark hair is pulled back in a loose ponytail. She doesn't wear make-up or worry about what she looks like when she wakes up in the morning. For the first time I'm really looking at her and she's pretty, beautiful.

Her thumb dances along my cheekbones and I sigh into her, telling myself she'll never have to see my so broken again. From here on out, I'll be strong. She grins when my hand reaches out and touches her hip. I didn't plan for that to happen; it was natural, as if I needed to touch her.

"Happy Birthday, Ryan," she whispers.

My lips crash onto hers. She gasps before she kisses me back. Her mouth opens slightly, but enough to let me taste her. I pick her up and set her down on the worktable. Now she's my height and I like that. My hands cup her face as she moves her hands over my arms, igniting my flesh. This is different from the way I've felt before. Dylan locks her legs around my waist, pulling me closer. My hands move on their own volition, from her face to her shoulders, down her arms, resting on her hips and finally I cave, allowing myself to touch her under her nightshirt.

Her mouth leaves mine. She marks my skin as hers, leaving a path of energy coursing through my body. Her hands tug at my shirt, lifting it. I step back and raise my arms and let her take it off of me. Her fingers glide over my skin, her lips follow leaving a trail of goose bumps.

My fingers run through her hair. I don't want her to stop. She's making me feel good, making me forget.

"You're so beautiful, Ryan," she says against my skin.

A loud bang above us breaks our reverie. We jump and she pulls away before I can touch her or return the sentiment. Someone's awake and in the kitchen. We're busted, both of us downstairs, Dylan half-dressed.

Dylan unlocks her legs so I can pick up my shirt. I slide it over my head without breaking eye contact with her. She looks away, her face falls. I'm not sure what I just did, but I do know that I don't like seeing her look sad. I pull her chin toward me and kiss her deeply.

We hold hands walking down the hall. I made the contact first. I wanted to feel what I felt this morning with her in the basement. Maybe she gives me a newfound confidence that I never had with Hadley, or maybe it's just that she's different and understands me better than anyone.

A few of her girlfriends wink at us as we walk to our lockers and each time Dylan pulls me close and kisses me on the cheek. I walk her to class – also a first for me – and let my lips linger on hers longer than allowed in school.

"See you at lunch." I take a step back, then another as she watches me. I'm bumped into, sorry's are muttered, but I never take my eyes off of her as she stands there watching me. Her smile is infectious. For the first time I look at her, *really* look at who Dylan Ross is, and I'm very thankful that she's in my life.

I sit down at my desk and pull out my book. When I open it, there's a sticky note stuck to my assignment. *Happy Birthday* is all it says and I know it's from Dylan. I take out my wallet and place it in there carefully. That's something I'll save forever.

"'Sup, Ryan."

I look over at Jake Miller, who just sat down. We've never spoken before, at least not in casual conversation. "Not much," I answer as I put away my wallet.

"So, party at Dylan's tonight?"

Mr. and Mrs. Ross are out of town this weekend for a police convention, but I didn't think Dylan would invite people over.

"It's your birthday, right?"

"Yeah."

"Yeah all right, party. Happy Birthday, man." He pats me on the back and prepares for class.

All throughout my day that's how things go. Kids I've never talked to come up and wish me a happy birthday and tell me they'll see me later. A few ask me what I want for a gift and I just shake my head. Only Dylan has been buying me gifts the past few years so I only expect one from her.

When I see her at lunch, I grab her hand and pull her out into the hallway, walking down the deserted corridor and pushing her up against the lockers. I place my arms on either side of her and look down. She's devious. She knows why we're out here. She reaches up on her tiptoes and kisses me lightly.

"You'll have fun, I promise."

"You promise me a lot of things, but fun isn't one of them."

"People are excited. This will be good. They want to know you."

I can't deny that it wouldn't be nice to have some more friends, especially guy friends. It's always been Dylan and I'm not complaining, but sometimes I think it would be nice to have a buddy. I remember what Mr. Ross told me about my feelings. Feelings have words and words need to be expressed and no one can get into trouble for expressing themselves.

"I need to see my mom after school and then I have to work."

"Only until nine, right?"

She knows my schedule and I like that she does. I nod.

"That gives me enough time to decorate and wrap your gift."

"You didn't have to get me anything."

"I know, you say that every year." She's right, I do. When it's her birthday, I buy her a book or journal, never knowing what to get her. Her gifts are always wonderful because she puts thought into it, which is what I'm learning to do.

"Can I kiss you?" I ask her. She nods as my lips meet hers. Her fingers thread through my hair, making me hungry for her. I hang onto the top of the lockers afraid to let go for fear she'd disappear. She's bringing all my emotions to the surface with the way she touches me and the new me really, really likes that.

chapter
thirty-six

I barely make it off stage before Ian is dragging me down the hallway to my dressing room. He throws open the door and pushes me in. I stagger before catching myself. Alex and Cole are right behind us. Cole shuts the door and locks it.

"What the fuck was that?" Ian spits out.

I turn away and try to collect my thoughts. I pick up a rubber band off my vanity and pull my hair back. Ian spins me around to face him. "We had a deal, Hadley."

"One bad show isn't breaking any deals, Ian. I'm allowed to have a bad show."

"No, you're not," he roars. "Those people don't wait in line in the freezing cold and spend their hard-earned money so you can have a bad show. They expect nothing but the best when you step out there. We've talked about your image, Hadley, and this little stunt will cost you dearly. It won't matter if you and Cole announce your engagement, the media is going to have a field day once all the blog posts go up."

Ian grabs his head as he screams out in frustration. "I don't get you. I really don't understand how you can perform night after night and get up on stage now and forget your words. These are songs you know in your sleep. You don't forget them. When you're up on that stage, nothing else matters, but you…"

He stalks over to me, his finger pointing at my face. His teeth are clenched and his normally coifed hair is standing on end. "You just keep screwing up and expecting me to fix it and I'm sick of it."

"Ian, that's enough." I expect to hear Alex's voice, but it's Cole. He pushes Ian's finger away from my face and stands in front of me. "She had a bad night; if anyone knew what was going on, they'd forgive her. We should never have come here."

Ian rips his hand out of Cole's and starts pacing. I'm just one giant screw-up after another. It doesn't matter what I do. Everything ends up in shambles. I lean my forehead on Cole's back and wrap my arms around his waist. Right now he's my safety net.

"You have to make this show up to them."

"Why?" Cole asks. "This is her second show here in months. Somehow I'm thinking you planned this because everything has been going so well you needed as excuse to railroad her again. You hate that we aren't front-page news anymore now that everyone thinks we're back together, so you're creating some drama. Jesus, Ian, let her be human for one moment. She made a mistake, let it go. It was a bad night, it's over, time to move on."

"Cole's right," Alex adds. "I can't help but think you set her up for failure with this show. You know what happened here last time."

"What do you know, you're just a clinger."

"Excuse me," I say, coming around Cole. He sets his hand down in front of me, halting my movements. "You can't talk to Alex like that, she's my best friend. Aside from Cole, she's the only one who knows how I'm feeling."

"Unbelievable," he mutters as he storms out of the room. We're all quiet, waiting for him to start yelling at the road crew or some indication that he's still lingering, but we hear nothing. Cole pulls me into his arms as I break down. He scoops me up and carries me over to the couch, setting me down gently.

"I'm going to go so she can change," he says to Alex. She quickly wraps her arms around me, much like earlier tonight, as I sob. I'm such an idiot for thinking I'm strong enough to handle being away from Ryan. I should've listened to my heart and not my head, because clearly my head is so far in the clouds that nothing makes sense.

Alex helps me change into my sweats before the crew comes in to pack up my things. We are due in another city tomorrow and have a long night ahead of us. Alex packs my essentials for me while I gather my purse. We walk arm in arm out of the dressing room and down the long hall to the bus. When we pass Cole's dressing room, it's empty. He's likely already asleep on the bus. Lucky him.

We step outside and the flashbulbs are instant. People yell my name and grab at my clothes, startling me. The media isn't supposed to be back here and I can't help but think Ian set this up because of what Cole said to him.

Questions are flying at me right and left about Cole, which I've learned to ignore, but when one says Ryan's name, I freeze. Cameras go off, the constant clicking sound of the shutter irritating me.

"Who's Ryan Stone?" a reporter asks. I'm dumbfounded, unable to move. I feel Alex pushing me, her other arm blocking my line of sight, but I don't move. He told them. Ian told the reporters his name. Something he promised he'd never do. Ryan's name is repeated over and over again as if my silence is answering all their questions. It won't matter what I say from here on out, they will hunt him down like vultures until they find out who he is.

I'm lifted off the ground and carried onto the bus. I bury my face into Cole's neck as he mutters death threats and Ian's name. He carries me to our room, the room we've been sharing on the bus under the pretense that we're a couple because Ian says you can never trust your own crew. He lays me down and slides in behind me.

Alex walks in and hands him something. "Here, get her to take this; it will help her sleep and maybe forget."

"Somehow I doubt that," he says.

The door clicks quietly. I sigh and wonder where the tears are. How come I'm not crying?

"Can you sit up?" he asks as he adjusts behind me.

"I'll be okay."

"I have no doubt, but you need some sleep and your mind will race all night and I need sleep, too, so your tossing and turning will just piss me off."

"You're so kind," I say as I sit up and take the pill and glass of water from him. He smiles as he downs the rest of my water. Jerk. He leans over and kisses me on the forehead. He lingers there for a moment before pulling away. I know he wants more, but I can't. Not with him.

He turns his head slightly and looks at me. "I'm sorry I fucked us up." With that he gets up and leaves me alone in the room. I hear the bus start up and wonder if Cole has decided to drive it himself, leaving Ian behind. Wouldn't that be such a nice surprise?

I lie back down and close my eyes. I hope that I don't dream, because if I do it will be nothing but a nightmare until I wake up.

When the sun blasts through the window I think Cole forgot to shut the curtains. I roll over, only to find he isn't in bed and hasn't been according to the untouched sheets on his side. I look around and realize we aren't on the bus anymore, but in a hotel room. I get out of bed and hit the bathroom, brushing my hair and teeth and washing my face. My eyes are red and puffy from too much crying and not enough water before going to bed. I'm going to end up paying for it tonight.

I open my door quietly and step out of the room. The suite is smaller than what we usually stay in. Alex is up and reading in the chair by the window. She smiles at me before continuing to read.

"Where's Cole?"

"His room is across the hall."

"How'd we get here?" I ask as I pour myself a glass of orange juice.

"The bus broke down last night. You were passed out cold. Cole carried you up here."

"Where's Ian?"

"He's meeting us at the venue later. He decided to fly."

I nod. "Must be nice of me to pay that bill for him."

I sit down on the non-descript brown couch that is uncomfortable against my bare legs. I pull out my phone and look at my calendar alert, *Ryan's Birthday*. I should've deleted it when I removed him from my life, but I couldn't bring myself to do it.

"I'm going to go take a shower," I announce. I don't wait for Alex to acknowledge me before I'm up and moving back to my room. I shut the door and lock it. Pulling out my phone I look up the contact information for my cell account. I turn on some music so no one can hear me talking. When customer service comes on I ask them to activate Ryan's number and as easy as that is, I feel apprehensive about what I'm doing.

I jump in the shower quickly so I don't cause suspicion. I change into shorts and a t-shirt and let my hair air-dry. I have no idea where we are or how much longer we'll be here, but I don't care. The press saw me at my worst last night; I'm done caring. When I come out of my room, Cole is standing at the bar, making his breakfast. It doesn't escape my notice that he's shirtless, his sweatpants hanging way too low to be legal.

Alex is napping in the chair with her book resting on her chest. I can't imagine she got much sleep last night. I'm such a great friend, not. I take this opportunity to pull up Ryan's name and hit send. It rings and rings, but no voicemail. Maybe he never set it up or more likely I never showed him how to so why would he bother with such a thing? I text *Happy Birthday, Ryan*. I want to add more, but I don't think we can adjust back into any type of relationship. I watch as my text says delivered and know he'll get it when he has a chance to look at his phone. I hope that wherever he ran away to, he brought his charger. He had to know once this day came, I'd reach out to him, even if I didn't know it myself.

"Who are you are calling?"

I look up at Cole and send my phone into sleep mode. "No one. I was just texting my mom."

He looks at my questioningly, but doesn't say anything as he walks to the table to sit down. I walk over to the balcony and look out the window and watch cars pass. We must be near the highway.

"Why are you eating in here?"

"Your room is bigger and has what they consider *room service*."

"Where are we?"

"About two-hours from Jackson."

"Lovely."

I bring my phone to life and look at my text. He still hasn't read it, but I can be patient. It was stupid of me to call anyway, maybe he's found a job in his new town and he's working. Of course that's why he didn't answer, because he wants to hear from me, especially today, even though I broke his heart and left without telling him why.

Yeah, keep telling yourself that, Hadley. Of course he's waiting for you to call and ruin his life some more.

chapter
thirty-seven

RYAN

When I open the door to my mom's office she stands and shouts, "happy birthday!" I've never seen her like this and for a moment I wonder if she's been drinking. I can't hide the grin on my face as she rushes over and envelopes me in a hug. I hold her tight, not wanting to let her go and trying to savor this moment and embed it where I'll remember it most.

She steps back. There are tears in her eyes. Something changed for her and I don't know what it is. "I can't believe this day is finally here." She pulls my hand into hers and takes me into the conference room. When I walk in, her co-workers yell out "Surprise!" scaring the crap out of me.

"Wow," I say as I look around the room. There are streamers hanging from the ceiling and everyone is wearing party hats. There's a cake on the table, too. Everyone starts singing. I feel my cheeks heat up. I must be as red as a tomato right now. My mom puts her arm around me, leads me to the chair and motions for me to sit down. She lights the eighteen candles and I blow each one out, making a wish like Dylan used to when we were little. I can't remember the last time I did this. I look up at her and silently thank her for making my day special.

Mom cuts and serves cake to everyone, giving me an extra-large piece. I anxiously dig my fork in and take a big bite causing her to laugh. It's the second most beautiful thing I've ever heard. I close my eyes and clear my head. I won't think about *her* anymore, not like that. I don't need her to survive. Besides, I like how things are with Dylan and that's definitely something I want to explore.

"This is great, Mom, thank you."

She pulls out the chair next to me and sits down. Most of her co-workers have gone back to their offices. I'm curious what she had to do to get them in here. I suppose the offer of free cake was enough.

"I'm sorry I couldn't get you anything."

I set my hand down on hers. "This is perfect," I say, because it is. I never expected this – especially from her – and I'm going to enjoy every moment that I can with my mom.

I stay and chat until I'm dangerously close to being late for work. She sends the rest of the cake with me, making it incredibly hard to run down the street, but I'll manage. I want to share this cake with Dylan tonight so I need to make sure I'm not wearing it all over the front of my shirt.

Work goes slowly. For a Friday night, we're dead. I keep hoping my boss will let me cutout early, but since I'm the one who always asks to stay late, he never gives me a second thought. He does offer me a ride home, so that's nice. It's about an hour walk from the restaurant to Dylan's house.

Walking up the driveway I can feel the house vibrating. The music is so loud. I'm surprised the neighbors haven't called the police. Although I suppose when it's a police officer's house, the town turns a blind eye. I open the door and find people dancing. Some are holding red cups while others hold bottles. I knew Dylan liked to drink, but never really took her for someone who would bring it into her parents' home.

I make my way through the crowd and into the kitchen. Only a few people linger in here, around the food table of course. I don't know very many of these people and a lot of them I've never seen before. I put the rest of my birthday cake into the refrigerator. I don't know if it should go in there or not, but I don't want anyone eating it and I'm certainly not going to stand guard over it all night.

As I come around the corner, Dylan jumps into my arms. I stagger back as I catch her. We hit the wall behind us and she instantly starts laughing. I wonder if she's been drinking. My curiosity is cleared the moment her mouth touches mine. She tastes sweet. Her tongue is cold, but welcome as it moves against mine.

She pulls away and smiles. "How was your mom?"

I beam at her. I love that she's asking about my mom and encouraging me to maintain a relationship with her. I could so easily avoid her and forget about everything, but Dylan tells me I'll regret it in the future if I act like that now. She's right, of course.

"We had a party," I say. "There was cake and her co-workers sang to me."

I put her down, not because I'm tired of holding her, but it seems awkward holding her like that with people staring. "I brought the rest of the cake home. Maybe we can have some later."

"I'd like that," she says as she straightens out my shirt, slipping her hand underneath. I lean down and kiss her on her forehead; I don't know why, but it feels like the most natural thing in the world for me to do. Before, I felt like I was always blundering when I was with Hadley. How can things be so different? How can everything feel so natural with Dylan, who I've known for most of my life, than with Hadley, who I have no doubt that I was…still am in love with? I'm comfortable with Dylan. I don't have to try and be someone I'm not when I'm with her. With Hadley, I felt like I was always on edge, like I needed to be this down-and-out kid she was trying to save. Maybe what I had with Hadley was simply lust. First-time attraction and raging hormones and she was my outlet.

I know I want things with Dylan to be different. They have to be. I can't compare her to Hadley. There's no comparison. She's been my best friend for years and maybe we were meant to happen. It should've been sooner, in my opinion. I wish I had never met Hadley Carter. The pain I've endured because of her is enough to last me a lifetime and it's something I could've done without.

Dylan hands me a cup and promises me that I'll like it. Thing is, I'm not really interested in getting drunk. I'd rather keep my senses and spend the rest of my birthday with her in my arms. She takes me around and introduces me to people I don't know. There are kids here from other schools as well. I've heard about parties getting out of hand, but for the most part this one seems mellow.

We dance. I get to hold her in my arms and feel her up against my body. She's not shy and I'm not sure if I like that or not. She has one hand underneath my shirt, her fingers dance along my waistband giving me just enough satisfaction. She pulls me down closer to her so she can press her lips against my neck. Each movement she choreographs as if she's the conductor and our bodies are the orchestra.

As the night goes on, people come and go. Only once do I hear glass break, which leaves me standing in the middle of the room while Dylan rushes off to make sure nothing valuable has been ruined. My arms felt empty and cold without her in them. When she returns she looks frantic, crazy almost.

"What's going on?"

"Nothing, I just think it's time for people to start leaving, if you're okay with that."

"Of course I'm okay with that. I would have been happy to celebrate just with you."

"Okay, good," she says before rushing off.

I start to pick up the garbage that people leave in their wake. She shuttles people out, most of them don't even say goodbye. I find that a bit rude since she graciously opened her house to them.

Once everyone is out, we finish cleaning up the mess. I carry black bags of bottles out to the garage. We'll have to take them to the store tomorrow before her parents get home. The last thing I want is for her to get into trouble or for them to think I did this and ask me to leave. Although if that happened, I'd just take a bus to New York and start living my life – there's no way I'd go back to my parents. When everything is cleaned, furniture replaced and the house smelling nice, Dylan excuses herself to go take a shower.

I sit on my bed, listening to her sing in the shower. She's loud. Her voice carries through the walls. It's funny, all the time I spent with Hadley, she never once sang out loud. Maybe it was because that's what she did for a living, but listening to Dylan makes me realize how real she is when she's around me. When the shower shuts off, I jump. I don't know why I'm so nervous. It's not like I'm expecting anything to happen.

I step into my doorway just as Dylan comes out of the bathroom. Her hair is wet, leaving drops of water all over her shoulders. The hot pink towel she's using to cover herself leaves very little to the imagination. She walks over to me, my mind forgetting that I'm standing in just my boxers, as her finger trails down my chest, resting when it reaches the top of them. I swallow hard, afraid to make any sudden movements or errant outbursts.

"I…" I clear my throat and try again. "Shower," I spit out, earning a wicked grin from her. My hand runs through my hair, pulling at the ends. I don't know what I'm doing here, no freaking clue how to proceed, but I think I want to… No, I know I want to.

Dylan kisses my chest, lingering there for a moment before walking down the hall to her room. I lean out of the doorway and watch as her hips sway back and forth. Taking a deep breath I hightail it to the shower and rush through getting clean.

I take a chance and go to her room when I've finished. I didn't put on a t-shirt when I got out, hoping she'd want to kiss me again. I stand in her doorway. She's lying on her stomach, her legs bent at the knees and crossed at her ankles. They move up and down as her head bops like she's listening to music. Her hand moves back and forth, turning pages of a magazine or book.

I've been in her room before, but never like this. Never with the intent to touch her, kiss her. I've never had impure thoughts about her either, and now they're running rampant through my mind. I walk into her room, my steps quieted by the plush carpet. My heart beats faster the closer I get to her bed. If she knows I'm here, she's not calling me out. My knees brush the side of her bed, but she doesn't stop moving her legs up and down. I want to reach out and make them stop, but I can't.

I reach out and run my fingers down her back. Her legs still and she pushes aside her magazine. I don't know what I'm doing, but this feels right. When I get to the hem of her shirt, I pull it up, showing more of her back. Her dark-as-night blue panties grab my attention. She scoots over on the bed, giving me space to sit next to her. Taking her cue, I kneel down and move her shirt up more. She moves away, sitting up on her knees. Her arms cross, her hands picking up her shirt and pulling it over her head.

Her breasts are bare. I don't know where to look. My eyes travel from her eyes to her breasts and back. I want to touch her and think she wants me to as well, but what if she doesn't? I had to lead up to this before and now everything is happening so fast and in the back of my mind I remind myself that I don't know what the hell I'm doing. I want to touch her. Her eyes close when my fingers graze her nipple. It hardens against my fingertips. I touch the other one. She leans back, breaking our connection. I crawl over the top of her, touching her again. She opens her eyes when I settle in between her legs. Her smile is breathtaking, she wants this... me. Her fingertips travel up and down my back, pulling me closer. Our mouths are inches apart. Our foreheads rest against each other, lips touching lightly. She pushes on my ass, creating friction. I can't hold back. I kiss her hard, not waiting for her to meet me halfway. My arm shakes from holding myself up. I'm afraid I weigh too much. My fingers roll over her nipple as she pushes me into her again. Her back arches as I kiss down her neck. I've been so afraid I wouldn't know what to do, but my body knows. It knows how to make her feel good.

Taking her nipple in my mouth, I bite down lightly. Her hand flies to my hair and pulls, which feels good. I add more pressure and move my hips more, alleviating the pressure that's building. She moans and I like it. I like knowing that I'm causing these reactions. She rolls us over, shocking me. I didn't realize she was this strong. She straddles me, her mouth moving over my chest. She bites down on my nipple and now I know what it felt like and why she liked it so much. She moves down, kissing her way toward my hard-on. I reach out and grab her arm. I don't think I'd be comfortable with her doing *that*. She sits up and grinds, adding pressure to my groin. I sit up, hell-bent on moving her, but she pushes harder and rocks, creating much needed friction.

"I want to do this with you," she whispers against my lips as she moves a bit faster. The soft sounds coming from her make me believe she's getting pleasure, too.

I can't speak, only nod. I want this. I want to experience this with her. She jumps off of me and walks over to her dresser. She comes back with a condom in her hand. I swallow hard over what I'm about to do. She hands it to me and slides off her panties. I try not to look, but I can't help it. I follow her lead and push off my boxers, my erection springing free. I try to push it down, but to no avail. If she thinks it's funny, she doesn't laugh. She climbs back on top of me, kissing me all over as she works her body over mine. Her hand slides into mine, taking the condom from me.

She's done this before, but I'm trying not to think about that as she opens the package and slides the latex rubber on me. The sensation alone is going to make me cum and I know that would be embarrassing. My body tenses when she centers herself over me. I don't think it's supposed to be like this. She's supposed to be underneath me.

"Relax, let me show you." She picks up each of my hands and places them on her hips. I push her down lightly, feeling myself enter her. Her eyes close, but I watch. The sensation of being in her rocks my core. I feel the need to scream or something. I don't know. My hands grip her hips and move her up and down. I can't believe I'm doing this. I can't.

Dylan moans and moves up and down faster, causing an intense buildup in my stomach. I grunt hard as my body releases. She falls forward, kissing my chest and rocking against me slowly.

"Happy Birthday, Ryan," she says against my skin.

I wrap my arms around her and worry that I didn't satisfy her and I don't like that fear. "Can we do that again? I think I'm supposed to last longer and maybe touch you."

"Says who?" she asks, laughing.

I shrug. "I read it in a magazine."

"Yeah, we can do it again." She looks at me when she says this, the glint in her eyes says so much more than words. I have a feeling I'm about to learn a lot from her.

chapter
thirty-eight

HADLEY

I think I have a problem.

Sure, I paint a happy smile on my face each time I step out of my hotel room and loop my arm into Cole's. I pose whenever there is a camera around. I feed him ice cream when fans are lurking. I do everything I'm asked.

But it's getting to be too much and Cole agrees.

After the *incident* – that's what we're calling it – we're certain that Ian set me up. The problem is we can't prove it. We've tried. Alex has a lot of contacts and she even tried to find out who tipped off the photographers about Ryan, but none of them are budging. I can't believe they like Ian that much to sell me out.

I told my parents. At first they didn't believe me, but when my mom bought the magazine and read the article she finally relented that maybe her brother is a bit off his rocker. She suggested Cole and I quit the tour, but she doesn't understand what that would do to both of us. Neither of us is willing to forgo the tour and upset the fans just to stick it to Ian. My dad on the other hand, is looking for a new manager and was quite shocked to find out that Cole didn't have one.

Getting rid of Ian will be hard, but will be better for me… I think. I know he does his job, but it's the way he manipulates me to get what he wants. First with the staff he hires and now with the media. He's supposed to protect me, not feed me as live bait to the sharks.

The tour is almost over. This makes me happy and sad. Each night, I'm looking. Looking for any sign that Ryan is in the audience or out front trying to buy tickets. I don a disguise and walk around the concourse pretending I'm a concertgoer so I can mingle with the crowd in the hope that he's out there. Each night I come up empty. I stay awake long after everyone has gone to bed and text him, but I never receive a response. His phone rings and rings, never being answered by the one voice I so desperately want to hear. I know I screwed up, but I thought he knew I'd call him on his birthday.

No, he didn't know. I gave him no indication that I would. I shut off our lifeline like a selfish bitch in order to protect myself and started a very public relationship with my ex. He'd know about that, I'm sure. Dylan would show him. She would make sure of it. She didn't like me with Ryan because she wanted him for herself and I handed him to her on a silver platter. I have no doubt he knows about Cole and me and there isn't anything I can do about it because he doesn't answer his phone or return my texts. If he'd just return one, I'd go to where he was and get him and bring him here with me. We can live in my apartment and not have to worry about what people say.

I'm going to look for him when the tour is over. I'll go back to Brookfield and start there, maybe hire a private investigator. I can't believe he ran away. I know he talked about leaving, but I thought he'd wait until he graduates. A diploma can mean so much more when looking for a job.

The sun is up when I finally retire. He's not going to answer or return my text. I crawl into bed and close my eyes. Life should be so much easier, but it's not. My door opens slightly. I turn and find Cole standing in my doorway. He walks in and sits on my bed.

"What's wrong?"

"Can't sleep," he says as he slides down the bed, resting his head on the extra pillow. I roll onto my side and face him.

I'm tired of pretending and he must be, too. He's been so good, though. He's the devoted boyfriend, always holding my hand, tucking my hair behind my ear at the right moment. He never complains that behind closed doors our relationship is platonic. He's been without a partner for months now, just to help me. He's really the best, most perfect fake boyfriend any girl could ask for.

I don't know why I can't love him again. He's proven that he's changed. That he's trustworthy and patient. He's a catch and any girl would be so lucky to have his blue eyes look at her the way he looks at me. His blond hair is always kept short and away from his eyes, unlike Ryan's. Both men are so different and yet could own me completely. I know Cole would welcome the opportunity, but I just can't get Ryan out of my head.

"You should write a song with all that thinking you're doing." Cole's voice is rough.

"I haven't written songs since you and I did. I don't have a passion for it."

"You should try, it might help."

I shake my head. "What are you doing in here?"

He shrugs. "I was thinking about you and us and this whole pretend thing. I'm not sure how much longer I can go on. My feelings have never gone away and the lines are so muddy right now."

"I'm sorry," my voice breaks as his hand cups my cheek.

"You don't have to be sorry. I just want some of you back. I miss the happy and carefree girl that I love so much."

A warm tear hits my pillow. Cole moves closer. He rests his forehead against mine while his hand still cups my cheek.

"What's up, Hadley Girl? You seem so distant since that night and I don't know how to fix things for you."

I run my fingers through his hair. His eyes close and he hums softly. He's always liked this and I used to do it when he was sick. "You can't fix this, Coleman. I just need to get over him."

"I know what would help."

I push his shoulder lightly. "I don't think sex is the answer." I roll over, giving him the proverbial cold shoulder.

He pulls me close, wrapping me in his arms. We are spooning and in this position I can feel everything. "Cole?" I question as he adjusts himself.

"Can't help it."

"Yes, you can."

"No, I can't. You're hot and you turn me on. All day long we pretend to be a couple and sometimes we sleep in the same bed. It's starting to get to me."

"Sex isn't the answer."

Cole moves so that he's on top of me. Everything is familiar, second nature. "You're right, it's not, but it's a solution."

I have a problem, a big one. It's the indecisiveness I create for myself on a daily basis. Sleeping with Cole last night was a mistake. He held me while I cried, which made me feel even worse. It's not that the sex was bad, it wasn't, never has been. It's my erratic brain telling me I've done something wrong. Cole assures me that everything we did was right and perfect.

Maybe he's right.

Maybe I should just give in and listen to my brain. I know that would make Cole happy and I'd be comfortable. I mean, that's what people go for these days, right, comfort? I know him and he knows me. What more does a girl need?

I need love and trust. Not everyone needs those feelings, but I do. I don't know how to move past Cole cheating. If I did, we probably would've gotten back together. There is nothing stopping him from doing it again.

I slide out of bed and walk into the bathroom. I have no doubt he's awake and staring at my naked backside, but I don't care. I lock the door for good measure. I don't want him sneaking in thinking we are going to repeat what we did hours before. That was so stupid.

The hot water drips down my back. As much as I want to stay under this drizzle I can't stand being in here. I get out and wrap myself in a towel. When I open the door, he's sitting on the edge of the bed. His face looks pensive. This is exactly why we're a mistake.

He reaches out, pulling my hand into his. He turns my hand over and kisses my palm.

"Cole—"

He stands, cupping my face and kisses me softly. "I know." I want to reach out and pull him to me. Why can't I love him? He kisses my forehead and leaves me standing in our room with more pain in my heart than I know what to do with. "I'll meet you on the bus, Hadley Girl."

Alex is dancing. This wouldn't be a shock to me except we are cruising down the highway and she's standing in the middle of the tour bus living room, dancing. I sit down and watch her, enjoying her carefree moment. She's my best friend. I love her and I don't know what I'd do without her.

The song finishes. She takes the seat next to me. She throws her head back in exasperation and starts laughing.

"What's so funny?"

"I'm just thinking that I'm about to go crazy if we're on this bus any longer."

"We need a spa day when we get back to New York."

"Definitely."

"I slept with Cole," I blurt out. Alex doesn't look shocked at all. Am I that easy to read?

"I figured it was just a matter of time."

"What's that mean?" I ask. I bring my knee up under my leg and face her. She mimics my position.

"Cole's good-looking, you're beautiful and you've had to pretend you're in love. It was bound to happen. I guess it would be different if you fought all the time, but you don't. He protects you. I think he's still in love with you."

"But I love Ryan."

Alex shakes her head. "Do you? Or are you in love with the idea of someone like Ryan? Someone who isn't part of your world?"

I sit back and ponder what she's saying. She knows me better than anyone else, so why can't she see that I'm in love with Ryan.

"I thought you liked Ryan?"

Alex smiles, but shakes her head. "I do, but if you were in love with him, you would've fought for him. There wouldn't be a no-contact order and you wouldn't try to call and text him when you think we're all asleep. You need to let him go."

I look up at her sharply. She shrugs.

"You're not as sneaky as you think you are, Miss Carter."

"Whatever," I mutter. I lean over and rest my head in her lap. "I'm so messed up, Alex. I think I need some professional help."

Alex runs her fingers through my hair. It's calming and helps me relax. I do need help, but at what cost? Alex is right. I need to let Ryan go and move on. I just don't know how. I promised myself after Cole that my heart would always be guarded. That I'd never let anyone in again and then I met Ryan and things changed.

Things could've been perfect.

chapter
thirty-nine

RYAN

"Shit, shit, shit," I say under my breath as I jump into my pants. Dylan is scrambling to put on her shorts and a t-shirt all while trying to fix her hair. I high tail it out of her room and down the hall to mine, shutting the door quietly. My heart is pounding. I can feel my pulse trying to break out of my skin. My hands are shaking from nerves. I can't believe her parents are home. They were supposed to be having dinner and catching a movie. That should've given us at least three hours. They weren't even gone for one.

This is not good.

I sit on the bed and wait. Mr. and Mrs. Ross are walking down the hall. I jump when they slam their door. I'm afraid to move. My nerves are shot. I know Mr. Ross is going to burst in here any moment now and kick my ass out for having sex with his daughter… under his roof. I don't even know why I ran to my room. I could've sat down at Dylan's desk and pretended to study. I guess it's better than thinking I had to jump out of the window. Instead I'm sitting here, in my jeans with no boxers on because they are on Dylan's bedroom floor where she flung them. To make matters worse, I'm still wearing a used condom.

How did she even know they were home? She all but threw me off of her and whisper yelled at me to get dressed. I definitely wasn't listening to anything but her. I was trying to satisfy her and do what she liked. I'm going to have to ask her because if she's not into it, I… I don't know what. I do know I need to get to the bathroom and take care of things. I'm getting a bit uncomfortable sitting here in my jeans.

"Ugh!" I rub my hand over my face. I can't stand it anymore. I get up and throw open my bedroom door and startle Mrs. Ross. She jumps, bumping her head on the wall. "Crap," I say as I reach for her. "Are you okay?"

"Yes, you just scared me. I figured you were sleeping like Dylan."

She's sleeping? How can she pretend to be sleeping when her parents almost caught us? "I was just gonna take a shower." Yeah, that's what I'm going to do.

Mrs. Ross's smile drops when she looks at my bare chest. I should've probably grabbed a t-shirt. I try to cover myself when her eyes look at me sharply.

"Since when do you have a girlfriend?"

"Um…"

"Are you being safe?"

I look at her questioningly.

"I know a hickey when I see one, Ryan. I know you're trying to hide it, but you're eighteen and I know you're going to… you know, but please be safe. Do you need me to buy you some condoms?" Her face is red, probably matching the same color as mine.

Awkward.

"I think I'm okay, Mrs. Ross." She pats me on the shoulder and continues down the hall. I take this opportunity to escape into the bathroom before Mr. Ross comes out of the room. I'm still curious as to why they're home so early, but think I might hang out in my room for the rest of the night. I definitely don't want any more uncomfortable conversations, especially with my sub-parents.

I thought last night was awkward but that is nothing compared to how things are today. Dylan isn't talking to me. She's not holding my hand and she didn't wait for me to walk her to class. I don't know what I did, or what changed.

Now I'm walking down the hall by myself and I don't like it. Even before we started dating we were together, except those few months where I was so wrapped up in myself that she couldn't stand to be near me. I feel a small pang in my heart. I don't know what's going on, but losing Dylan is not an option.

I race down the hall, her head barely visible through the sea of students. I reach her just before she turns into the classroom. I pull her hand into mine and weave us through the other students, away from both our classes. She doesn't say anything when we end up at her car; maybe she knows. Of course the only problem with this plan is that her keys are in her locker and we're now standing outside. Thank God it's spring.

"We're going to miss class."

I shrug, not really caring. "What's wrong?"

"Nothing," she looks away. She can't even look at me when she lies. I hate that. I pull her chin forward and slouch down so that we're eye to eye.

"Don't lie to me. Something is wrong. I can feel it. Are you pregnant?"

Her mouth drops open, her eyes go wide and she pushes me hard. "Why would you ask me something like that?"

"I don't know, Dylan." My arms go out wide in frustration. "Yesterday..." I shake my head. "I know we almost got caught. Honestly, I'm surprised we haven't been caught yet – we've been having sex under their noses for four months. We're just biding our time here."

She doesn't say anything. I've learned this is typical chick behavior, especially when they want to be dramatic.

"Your mom thinks I have a girlfriend."

"You do."

I shake my head. "She doesn't think you and I are together. She saw the marks you left on my chest and called them hickeys."

"That sounds gross."

I nod, and shove my hands into my pockets.

"Can I ask you a question?"

I walk closer to her and lean up against her car. "Yeah."

She fiddles with her hands and sighs. This can go on for another half-hour if I don't tread lightly. Before I crossed the line and kissed her, there were things I didn't know about her. Now I can read her like an open book. She can't hide anything from me, which is why we're standing out here now skipping class.

"Do you ever worry we aren't going to make it?"

"What?" I scoff.

She turns and leans against her car. "Close your eyes."

Doing as she asks, I close my eyes.

"Imagine five years from now. You're dancing and when you open your eyes, do you see me?"

Five years? I don't know where I'll be in five years, but I imagine myself dancing, holding her close to me. I even add some music to keep up the pretense.

"Now look down at who you're dancing with and tell me who you see."

My throat swells a little when the imaginary me opens my eyes. It's not Dylan that I'm dancing with. My eyes flash open and she knows that I didn't see her. I reach for her, pulling her into my arms.

"It doesn't mean anything."

"Yes it does," she mumbles against my shirt. I feel her body shake and know tears are coming. "I don't see you either, Ry."

She looks up at me. I wipe her tears and kiss her, holding her to me. Deep down I know this is going to be the last time I get to.

"So what do we do?" Sometimes I wish she wasn't so matter-of-fact about everything. Why do we have to do anything? Can't we just stay together and take it one day at a time? I shake my head. I'm not ready to let her go. "Do you love me?"

"What kind of question is that? Of course I do."

Dylan shakes her head. "You love me because we're best friends and we've been dating, but do you love me like you love Hadley?"

I roll my eyes. "I don't love Hadley."

"You do and I'm okay with it. I know you don't love me the same and I don't really love you like that. Last night, I wasn't afraid that my parents would find us having sex, but that they wouldn't approve because they treat you like a son and I didn't like having those thoughts."

I step back, putting some space between us. When she says things like that it makes me think. I shudder at the thought. I know exactly what she's talking about and agree, except for the Hadley part. I couldn't care less if I never see her again. As far as I'm concerned, she never existed.

The rest of my day is a haze. I still walk her to class, but the routine quickly changes. I'm not kissing her goodbye or holding her hand. I'm not really sure how I feel about that, but looking at her as my sister makes it much easier to keep those feelings away.

It doesn't take long for word to spread that we broke up. By the end of the day, she has a date to prom and I, once again, am alone. We drive home in silence, mostly because I don't have anything to say. This morning when I woke up, I had a girlfriend. Now, I have nothing. I'm back to where I was in December.

When we walk in, Mrs. Ross is baking cookies and she's singing. This means she has good news. Dylan and I sit down at the table and pull out our homework. Mrs. Ross sets a plate of cookies in between us and stands there with her hands folded in front of her.

Dylan and I both look at her. Our heads move in slow motion. Mrs. Ross looks funny, like she has a plastic smile. She looks at Dylan, then to me.

"Ryan, would you like to invite your girlfriend over tonight for dinner?"

Dylan chokes on her cookie, which makes Mrs. Ross pat her back. Nothing like being put on the spot.

"No thank you, Mrs. Ross, she's not really my girlfriend." Dylan kicks me lightly under the table. I look at her, raising my eyebrows. What was I supposed to say?

"Okay. Dylan, would you like to tell me why you applied to NYU?"

Now I'm the one looking at Dylan, my eyes wide. She's never mentioned going to New York for college. In fact, she's never mentioned college at all.

"I... um... I sent in an application with the essay that won first place last year. I didn't think I'd have a chance."

"Well, it seems not only did you get in, but they gave you a full scholarship." Mrs. Ross pulls an envelope out of her pocket and sets it down in front of

Dylan. She looks from the envelope to me and to her mom before jumping into her mom's arms.

I'm happy for her. I am, but wish it were me.

When they're done celebrating, I give her a hug.

"Will you go with me?" she asks when I release her.

"Seriously?"

"Yeah, I can't go to New York without you."

I close my eyes and nod. I pick her up and spin her around. She laughs, holding my neck tightly. When I set her down, Mrs. Ross hugs the both of us.

"I'm okay with Dylan going as long as you're there with her, Ryan."

"Yeah, I'll go," I shout loudly.

chapter
forty

I throw down my headphones and push the microphone out of my way. My producer stands, his hands pressing down on the table that holds his mixing board. He's leaning over it, staring at me through the glass. If the look on his face is supposed to be menacing, he's missing it by a mile. I can't do this anymore. These songs, the ones I thought I wanted to sing for my new album, aren't cutting it. I wrote them shortly after I left Ryan. Putting my feelings down on paper helped a little, but I never thought I'd be standing here in a studio recording them.

I'm not sure I can do it. There is so much anger. Pain and sadness fills my lyrics, but when I say the words, I hate them. I hate myself for letting Ryan go. In my mind, he was going to wait. He was going to be ready to take me back, forgive me for my stupidity and everything would be perfect.

He was the smart one. He moved on. I can't blame him, even though I want to. How come he didn't know I'd be back? Because I didn't know I'd be back, that's why.

I can't do this, not today. I pick up my bag and sling it over my shoulder. I open the door only to find Ian standing there with his arms against the doorframe, blocking me from leaving. He's shaking his head and his lips are curled into a sneer.

"Get back in there and get this done."

"I'm not feeling it today. I need to leave."

Ian straightens. This is his 'I'm the boss' stance. It works with the media and others who cower to him, but not me, not anymore. Not after everything that has gone down in the past few months. He's supposed to be my friend, my confidant. I should be able to trust him, but he showed his true colors, repeatedly.

"I don't think you understand."

"No, Ian, I don't think *you* understand. Your contract with me is up in a couple of months. If I was you, I'd start kissing my ass in the hope that I'm willing to re-sign with you."

"Excuse me?" He steps back, which I don't expect. I figured he'd push me into the room and shut the door so he can read me the riot act.

I step forward, finding a bit of confidence within. "You heard me. Don't act so shocked. Yes, I know your contract is due for renewal and you bet your ass that I'm shopping around. You work for me, not the other way around."

"You wouldn't fire me. We're family."

I scoff. "You can't throw the word 'family' around when it's convenient for you," I say as I point my finger at him. "If you know what's best for you, you'll move out of my way."

"You're a spoiled little bitch, you know that?"

I shrug. "Whatever, Ian, I don't care what you think. Not anymore."

I walk past him, purposely bumping my shoulder into his. I slam the door behind me, hopefully conveying my anger. I doubt it did though. I opt for the stairs. I don't want to see anyone out front. I don't want to be stopped by the nosey receptionist who is supposed to order my lunch this afternoon. I just want out.

As soon as I'm out on the street, I'm heading to the local coffee shop. Today is not the day to be accosted by fans, but I see it coming. I can't even stand in line without someone pointing and whispering. Yes, people, believe it or not, Hadley Carter buys her own coffee. Better call the paparazzi and let them know that I do mundane things. The cashier asks for my autograph and I stare at her. Really? Isn't there some unknown code where people waiting on you know better than to ask for an autograph?

I slap down my money and tell her she can keep the change. I don't even know how much that is, but I'm hoping it's nothing more than a few pennies. I take my coffee and smile. I hear the word *bitch* as I turn my back.

Whatever.

I'm done.

I pull out my phone and call Alex. "I quit," I say as she answers.

"Okay."

"Is that all you have to say?"

"No, but I do think you need a break. You've been through a lot and you didn't take any time after you and Ryan. And then there's Cole and the media all over you because he's dating someone new and they're desperate for a story that isn't there. So, I don't blame you."

I stand at the corner and wait for the traffic to clear or for the signal to change. As beautiful as it is today, the streets aren't that crowded. I walk into Central Park and find a bench to sit on. There are a few street performers, but none who catch my attention. What I'd really like to do is sit here with my guitar and just play for people; people who don't care who I am or what I do for a living.

"You need to talk to someone."

"I'm talking to you."

Alex laughs. I know what she's talking about. We discussed me going to see a therapist when I was on tour, but of course when the tour was over, I went right into the studio. Can't let my fans down. Maybe Alex is right. Maybe I do need to talk to someone to help me deal with what's going on in my head, because we all know the song writing isn't cutting it. Usually that's my therapy, my release, but not this time.

"What do you think?"

"I think people will think I'm nuts if they find out."

"No one will find out, Hadley, but I think you need this. You never saw one after the first time with Cole and then there was Ryan and now this very public relationship with Cole again. Talking to someone will help you deal with it all."

"Okay." I don't want Alex to list all my problems. I know them. I've always thrown myself into my work and never dealt with what Cole did to me or what I did to Ryan.

"Okay?" she asks.

"Yeah, call someone for me." I don't say goodbye. I need to get off the phone before I change my mind. Within minutes Alex texts me with a name, location and a time, a time that is an hour from now. I have a sneaking suspicion she had this set up for a while now.

"So," she says, she being Dr. Patrick with her jet-black hair wrapped tightly in a bun perched high on top of her head. She greeted me the moment I walked in, like she had a nanny cam in the hallway; either that or she has no other head cases lining up to see her. She likes black. Her black pencil skirt goes with her black stilettos and black jacket only accented by a red cami to match her red lips, all while I'm sitting on a black couch. Maybe she needs someone to talk to.

"So," I reply back. I keep my hands folded and rested on my knees. I really don't know what I'm doing here. Am I supposed to give her my life story or wait for her to ask me what's wrong?

"Sometimes people come in here and just sit and others spill. I'm not saying you have to do either, just remember that no one judges what you say here. This is an open forum. I only take notes when there's something I want to ask you again or remember for our next session. You don't have to worry about the press or your manager finding out about what you talk about. Your assistant, Alex, was very clear about what you expect."

Her voice is smooth and the words tumble out in a gentle cadence; it's amazing how she eased so many worries just like that. I sit back, a little bit more comfortable. She doesn't smile or even change her position. She's good at her job and she knows it.

"You like black?" I didn't mean this as a question, more of a statement, but didn't know how to end my thought.

"Believe it or not, it's calming. If everything was white, you'd think clinical and hospital and you wouldn't want to talk. Red brings out anger and yellow makes it seem like I'm forcing you to be happy. Black allows you to be relaxed."

"Some would say black is death."

"Some would, but it gets people talking."

She's right, I want to talk and I do. I start with Coleman and tell her everything. How we met, fell in love and I thought I had found the one for me until I caught him with someone else.

"But when I met Ryan... my soul knew he was the one I was destined to be with, but everything was against us."

"Like what?" she writes down something, asking her question without looking at me.

"Completely different lifestyles and not just because of my job, but we were even raised differently. My parents doted on me where his didn't acknowledge he was around. It was hard for me to see him not have basic necessities, like new clothes. I wanted to take care of him, but knew he'd never accept my help."

"It's not uncommon for people to come from different social economical classes and have one want to take care of the other."

I shrug. I think Ryan would've been okay if I bought him more, but he would've gotten into trouble.

"It's not just social status. There's an age difference."

"What is it?"

"Five years."

Dr. Patrick adjusts in her seat, uncrossing and re-crossing her legs. "Five years isn't that big of a gap, Hadley. Many people have an age difference larger and make it work."

"He was seventeen when we dated." I drop my eyes before I can see the look on her face. I don't need to know that she doesn't approve even though she doesn't know us. I can hear her pen moving across the page, that's how quiet it is in here. There isn't the sound of a clock with its tick tock, tick tock to break the silence. Not even a bird outside chirping. Just the sound of writing as she puts down all the questions she's going to ask.

"How did his parents feel?"

I rub my hands down my pants. They're sweating and I know she's going to judge me. I should feel ashamed, but I don't. I love him. I'll wait a lifetime to see him again if I have to. "Only his mom knew, but she didn't approve. No one approved except my friend, Alex, and she still had her reservations. Like I said, we were doomed from the moment we met."

"When was the last time you spoke with him?"

"That's just it," I say, shaking my head. "We got arrested when I went to visit him and my manager made a deal with the police, or whoever, that they wouldn't charge Ryan with assaulting an officer. In exchange, Ryan signed a no-contact order stating he couldn't contact me until he turned eighteen."

"When is that?"

"Six months ago."

Dr. Patrick sets down her notepad and leans forward slightly. "So what's keeping you from reaching out to him?"

I readjust and sit more comfortably on her leather couch. I know why doctors use couches: it's so you can lie down and tell them your woes and feel better about yourself while you're encased in fine Italian leather.

"I had bought him a phone and turned it off so I wouldn't be tempted. On his birthday, I'd had enough and needed to hear his voice, but he never answered. He never replied or read my text messages. The message is clear, I just can't let go."

"What about going to visit him?"

"He ran away the day after all this happened." I shake my head, fighting the tears to no avail. I wipe at my cheeks, roughly, needing the pain to feel human. "I don't know where he is. I lost him because of the people in my life. My manager made him sign that stupid form and I lost him."

She stands and hands me a tissue. I'm surprised I'm able to smile and thank her.

"Tell me about your manager."

"He's my uncle and he's an idiot. His contract is up soon and I'm really thinking it's time we part ways. He's good at his job, but he's like a spoiled child and does the most unbelievable things when he doesn't get his way."

"And Coleman?"

I clear my throat. "I love him, but not the way I love Ryan. When I look at Cole, I see a friend who has been a part of my life, but not my future. I wish I did because being with Cole could be so easy. I know everything about him and can easily fall into a routine with him, not to mention we are in the same field. But he's not what I want."

"Here's what I want you to do. Write down what it is you want and when we meet next week, we'll talk about the healthiest way to achieve that goal, okay?"

I nod and dab at my eyes.

I breathe in deeply when I'm outside, taking in the sounds of the city and wonder where Ryan is and if he's happy. I hope that he is. I hope he's getting everything out of his life that he wanted and making a name for himself.

chapter
forty-one

Graduation.

I can't believe this day is here. My mom will be there today, in the auditorium, watching me walk across the stage to receive my diploma. I still haven't spoken to my dad. Mom never brings it up and he doesn't try. Apparently I meant nothing to him. I think my feelings would be hurt if it weren't for Mr. Ross.

After Dylan and I broke up, he saw that I was down and started taking me to the gym. Working out has been my salvation. It gives me something to do. I also got my driver's license. Once I turned eighteen, I didn't have to take driver's education and Mr. Ross insisted I learn to drive. I don't have a car, but Mrs. Ross lets me drive hers when I need to.

I stare at the ceiling, biding my time before I have to get ready for graduation and reflect back on the last ten months. So much has changed since I started my senior year that it's hard to believe I'm the same person I was at the end of August. No one but Dylan knows about Hadley. We don't talk about her or what happened or how I made the biggest mistake of the year by even thinking I had a chance with her. I do think that if I hadn't met Hadley, Dylan and I would've never taken our relationship to the next level. A relationship that we haven't exactly stopped, we just aren't dating. 'Friends with benefits' is what she calls it. She's had one boyfriend since me, but that didn't last very long.

I ended up taking Dylan to prom and we had a blast. Our prom was held at a hotel in Jackson. At first Mr. Ross was adamant that we not go, or go and come home. He even offered to pay for a driver, but Mrs. Ross said it was just one night and we were about to move to New York, so what was the big deal. The night of prom, Mr. Ross reminded me that he had a gun and I wasn't to touch his daughter. If he only knew, I may be dead now.

I would've never thought my year would end the way it has, especially considering the way it started, and I have Dylan to thank for that.

"Umf," I grunt when Dylan jumps onto my bed, landing on top of me. I wrap my arm around her shoulder as she rests her head on my chest. Our relationship is pretty solid and probably a deterrent for anyone who wants to date her. I feel bad about that, but I'm not sure how to change it.

"You're getting too buff."

I look at her out of the corner of my eye. "I thought chicks dig muscles."

"They do, but when we get to New York all the chicks are going to be chasing you down the block and I'm going to be right behind them with my broom."

"I need a girlfriend, don't you think? Unless we're getting married and having lots of babies."

Dylan slaps my stomach. Earlier in the year that would've hurt, but now I barely flinch. I like who I've become in the past few months. I walk with confidence now. I still don't have many guy friends, but I'm willing to make those changes when we move next week. I'm going to be a new person and leave behind this underdog.

"Knock, knock." Mrs. Ross is standing in my doorway, not even caring that Dylan is lying on my bed. I think she knows, but as long as we aren't getting into trouble, she doesn't say anything. We're allowed in each other's rooms as long as they're home and the doors stay open. For the most part we follow the rules.

Dylan and I sit up. Mrs. Ross comes in and sits on the edge of my bed. I can tell she's been crying. I know she's not excited about Dylan moving, but I told her I'd make sure she's taken care of. We rented a two-bedroom apartment. Her parents will pay for our rent since they're saving on dorm costs and I'll find a job to cover the rest of our expenses, like food.

"What's up, Mom?" Dylan asks as her mom shakes her head. They embrace and I hear crying, my cue to escape. I'll let mom and daughter have their crying fest.

I find Mr. Ross in the garage working on Dylan's car. We are taking it to New York, so he's been putting a lot of money into it.

"What's going on?"

"They're crying."

He rolls his eyes and hands me a wrench. "Let me teach you how to change the oil."

We spend the next hour under her car learning how to change the oil and where to watch for trouble. He teaches me things that every dad should be teaching his son.

"I want to thank you for everything you've done for me this year. If it wasn't _"

He sets his hand down on my arm, silencing me. "I did it because you deserved to have someone care about you. I sat back far too long and that incident woke me up. You needed someone to help you grow into a man and I needed someone to show me that I could make a change. You've turned into a standup young man and for that I'm proud. You could've taken what happened and turned down a path of self-destruction, but you didn't." He sets his hand on my shoulder, but I go in for a hug.

"Thank you."

"I should be thanking you. You've changed things around here; it's definitely for the best." He pats me on the back and moves back to the car. He's a decorated police officer. I can't imagine sharing his feelings is easy for him to do.

The garage door opens to gasps. I turn to find Mrs. Ross standing there with her hand over her mouth. I look at her questioningly. Mr. Ross ignores her.

"Get inside and cleanup. We need to leave in half an hour and your hands, both of you," she points at Mr. Ross, "are filthy." She slams the door with emphasis, getting her point across.

Mr. Ross slaps me on the back. "Just think, Dylan is just like her." He chuckles as he walks back into the house. I follow behind and see him grab Mrs. Ross and plant kisses on her while she fights to get away. Someday I'll have a love like that.

"Dylan Jane Ross."

I standup, whistling loudly when her name is called. Her parents stand too. Students were told to stay seated, but I can't help it. I'm proud of her and excited to start a new journey with her. I continue to clap until she's seated. She turns and looks at me, giving me the death glare. I shrug and take my seat, waiting for my turn. As other names are called, I grow anxious. I know my grades are good, that's not the problem. The issue is, what if I can't make it out in the real world, away from people like the Rosses who have provided me with the means to grow up properly. What if I fail?

"Ryan Michael Stone."

I stand and walk down the steps to loud cheers. Dylan does the same as I did for her, as do her parents. But then I see my mom standing in the crowd. She's jumping up and down and waving. I hate that I don't live with her, but it's been the best thing for me. I think our relationship is stronger for it, I just sometimes wish my dad wasn't the way he is. There are things I missed that other kids have done, like fishing and Boy Scouts. Why couldn't *my* dad be like those dads and want to do those things with me?

As I'm handed my diploma, the principal shakes my hand and we turn and have our picture taken. I'm sure this man doesn't even know my name. He's never had to call me to his office, he's never given me an award and I've never done anything to be on his radar, good or bad. I'm not leaving a legacy behind. I didn't letter in varsity sports, or have my name in the paper for doing something extraordinary like my classmates. I wasn't a criminal. I didn't paint the side of the school building for entertainment. I came to school daily. I went to each of my classes and turned in my homework on time. I studied and did well. Well enough that I could probably go to college, but can't afford to send myself. I started high school as a nobody and am leaving just the same.

When I move to New York, I'm going to a community college. Mrs. Ross helped me fill out the necessary loan applications. I'll have to pay the money back, but at least I'll have an education. It may not be the big fancy school that Dylan is going to, but it's something and it's for me.

Most importantly, it gets me away from the mill and Brookfield. I'll be doing something different. I won't follow in my father's footsteps. I'll be better. I don't know what I want to do, but a counselor will help me figure that out. Dylan suggested being a banker because I'm good at math, but all I can think about is climbing the stairs to the roof of our new apartment and lying out under the stars. I can't wait to hear the horns honking and the sirens blaring.

I'm about to live a dream. One that I knew I wanted, but made possible by two people who took the time to care and help me achieve this goal. Sure, I could've moved there a long time ago. I've saved enough for a bus ride, but would've been living on the street, begging for a job and a place to sleep. I have a head start now.

As I walk back to my seat, Dylan winks at me. I sit down and flip open the top and see my name scrolled across parchment paper. It tells me that I've achieved the standards set forth by the state and that I'm a graduate.

If you asked me in September if I was going to graduate, the answer would've been no. I had every intention of following Hadley around. I don't know if she would've asked me to or not, but I had hoped. And if she hadn't, there was a bus ticket with my name on it, destination unknown, just as long as it was away from here.

Dylan asked me last night if I'm going to see my dad before we leave. I told her, honestly, that I didn't know. He's made no effort to try and be a dad and she reminded me that I haven't tried to be a son. She's right, of course.

When I look out to the crowd and see the other parents standing for their children, the parents videotaping and the ones holding bouquets of flowers, I can't help but wonder why mine are the way they are. Why would parents have children if they don't want to dote on them and be proud of them?

We all stand as the principal announces us as the graduating class. As practiced, we pull off our caps and throw them in the air, each of us ducking as they come falling back to the ground with their pointy ends first.

Dylan waits for me as I descend the stairs. I grab her hand and pull her into the aisle, holding on to her tightly. We may not be together, but there isn't another person I'd want to start my next journey with.

chapter
forty-two

I love the winter. I think this is why I refuse to leave New York. There is nothing better than walking down the streets of Manhattan and seeing the storefronts decorated or the fresh smell of roasted peanuts and cashews on every corner. The sounds of children having fun at Rockefeller Center or the joyous screams when someone has just been proposed to coming from the ice rink are what make this place special.

My black leather boots pound the sidewalk. I'm late. This is nothing unusual and is likely expected, but I'm trying. Ever since I started with my therapist I've taken a more laid back approach to things. If I want to sing, I'll sing. If I want to write, I write. I work for me and no one else. That is probably the most important lesson Dr. Patrick has taught me – I'm important to *me*. I had forgotten that over the years. Everyone wanted something from me, except for my parents and Alex. Even Coleman wanted something. I was just too blind to see what it was.

I pull open the heavy wooden door to O'Malley's. I haven't been here in about a year, but this is where Coleman wants to celebrate his birthday. Alex and I live not too far from here, within walking distance, so this is our hangout. Family-owned and versed on keeping the privacy of their clients, it quickly became a place for me to relax.

Strong arms encase me before I even have a chance to take off my scarf.

The smell of Old Spice, barley and hops tell me it's Mr. O'Malley. He picks me up off the ground and spins me around. His laughter is contagious and soon I'm laughing with him and hugging him back. I've missed him. When he sets me down, he kisses me on each cheek. His face is lit up like a kid on Christmas morning.

"It's been far too long, Hadley." His words go right to my heart. He's right. I have no excuse for staying away except for work.

"I know and I'm sorry, but I promise you, I'll be around more often. How have you been?" I unbutton my coat and hang it up on the wooden pegs along the wall. I feel safe leaving my stuff there. Mr. O'Malley isn't going to let anyone walk off with someone's personal belongings. He's like a shark that way.

"I'm well and the missus is doing well now that the grandbabies are a wee bit bigger."

"That's good," I say as I rub my hands together to create some warmth. I don't realize how cold I am until he hands me a cup of coffee. I wrap my hands around the mug, basking in the warmth.

I look at the door as it opens and smile. Alex and Cole are here and she looks happy. It's been a long time since I've seen her happy. Mr. O'Malley walks over and gives her the same greeting. He pats Cole on the shoulder and nods. He's never forgiven Cole for cheating and I have to say, it's taken me years to do it, but I have.

With the cup of coffee clutched in my hand we walk to a back booth and sit down. In the last year they've expanded and added a pool table and dartboard. They've also added some flat-screen TVs, no doubt to watch sports.

We know the menu well and decide quickly what we're having for dinner. Each of us orders a pint, appetizers and our main course. This is Cole's birthday and this is how he wants to spend it. I was surprised when he asked if we could come here. I thought for sure it would be a night of club-hopping with gyrating music. I have to admit, this is nice and almost perfect.

Before long the bar becomes too busy. The door is constantly opening and closing and Mr. O'Malley is greeting each customer as if he's known them for years. That's the thing about this place, once you're in, you're in for life. I guess it's like the mafia, but not as violent.

Alex talks about going dancing later, earning eye rolls from Cole and me. We'll relent, we always do, but the thought of getting dressed up and going back out into the cold doesn't really sit well with me at the moment.

Mr. O'Malley brings out a traditional Irish cream cake and starts singing to Cole. He turns red and tries to hide his face, but Alex doesn't allow it. I pull out my phone and videotape his embarrassment, something I'll save for later when he's pissing me off. Secretly, we all know Cole loves the attention he's getting and when he blows out his candle he's smiling like he just won a Grammy.

With Cole's cake boxed up and Alex's pleads to go dancing, we reluctantly leave our table. I'm hoping to call it a night when we get back to our place. At least that is my goal. I'm just not in the dancing mood tonight. I follow behind

Alex, with Cole leading the way. Alex pulls up short, causing me to ram right into her, breaking open the box holding the rest of Cole's cake.

"What the hell, Alex?"

She turns and looks at me. She's whiter than I've ever seen her dark complexion get. If I didn't know better, I'd think she's playing a corpse in some horror thriller.

"What's wrong? Are you sick?"

She clenches my arms tightly and my mouth drops open in pain, but don't want to say anything to cause alarm. Whatever has her spooked is doing quite a number on her.

"We should walk out the back."

"Um, no," I say. "My coat is up front where I always put it. What's your problem?"

She looks over her shoulder, shaking her head before looking back at me. Her eyes are sad and for the life of me I can't understand why. She steps aside, taking the broken cake box from my hands. I look in the general direction and see nothing out of the ordinary.

Along the wall, the booths are patrons, which is normal for a Friday night. Others line the bar, a few of them yelling at the TV and some basketball game is on. With the clank of the pool table, I look over there for any clue as to what would make Alex freak out like this.

It doesn't take long, just the mere look in his eyes, to know why she stopped the way she did. He stands there in a dark t-shirt and jeans, looking far different from what I remember. His hair is shorter, but his arms... they're large and defined with muscles. His shirt is tight enough to show that he's definitely changed over the years.

I'm afraid to move or even blink. He stares right back as he holds the pool cue in his hand. My gaze is broken when she comes into the picture. She leans up on her tiptoes and whispers something in his ear that makes him smile. Who knew that witnessing such an act would make my heart ache so terribly? I bite my bottom lip hoping to keep my emotions in check. Her hand rests on his arm as she looks at me. She's telling me everything I need to know. They're together.

I can't look anymore and tear my eyes away. I don't know what I'm doing. One half wants to forget that I even saw him. The other half wants to walk over there and ask how he's doing and how long he's been in New York. Surely, if we were frequenting the same bar, we'd run into each other. But then I remember I didn't go out for a long time so I could get my life in order. I make the best decision for me and take a step toward him.

His eyes don't leave mine as he watches me take step after step to get to him, closer to him. His friends continue on with their game, ignoring what's going on in this imaginary bubble that I've created. I size him up the closer I get and can't believe how much he's grown and how much I miss the baby face that he had. He's all man now, an adult and it shows.

He hasn't moved and doesn't motion for us to sit down or anything. Maybe this is a mistake and he's going to dismiss me like I did him. As much as it would hurt, I deserve it. That is another thing therapy taught me.

I have to fight every ounce of my body's will to keep from jumping into his arms. He wouldn't catch me. He'd let me fall flat on my face and maybe offer a hand to help me up. I'm nothing to him except a reminder of mistrust and pain.

But I'm going to take a chance because I have to know if he's the one.

"Hi." I close my eyes and mentally chide myself for being ridiculous. Hi seems like such a simple thing to say and for this situation I need something profound and worthy of a response.

I look behind me and find Cole and Alex sitting at the bar. They aren't watching me fumble through this meeting. They're letting me fall on my ass without an audience.

I clear my throat and try again. "Hi, Ryan, it's good to see you."

His eyes rake over my body, up and down, back and forth. His lower lip is being torn apart as he gnaws on it. I so desperately want to reach out and pull it out of his mouth and soothe it with my touch, but I lost that right a long time ago.

"I never thought I'd see you again." His words stab me right in my heart. He's right. Why would he have any thought of ever seeing me again after what I did to him?

This isn't a conversation I want to have in a crowded pub with people lingering around listening but pretending not to. I nod and acknowledge that yeah, I didn't expect to see him either.

"You look really good." He looks down at himself and back at me. There is no hint of happiness in the way he's talking to me.

"Four years does that to some people."

Ouch. Clearly this was a mistake. He doesn't want to talk to me. I can finally close this chapter in my book. I was keeping it open in the hope that one day we'd cross paths again and could at least be friends, but I guess time *doesn't* heal all wounds.

I look over at his friend, Dylan, now clearly his girlfriend, only to find her staring at me. I can't tell if she's amused or threatened by me. Either way, she wins.

"It was good seeing you, Ryan." I nod slightly and sidestep, brushing him lightly as I walk by. I weave in and out of the tables, not bothering to call out to Alex and Cole. I just need to get away. I pull my coat off the rack and slide my arms into it as I walk out the door. I don't care about the weather. I just need to get out of here before I break down in front of everyone.

I don't need a reminder of what I did to him. It's fresh in my mind and my songs. The brief time we spent together, it's so vivid I could draw it out picture by picture. I have no doubt he's my soul mate. I'm just not his.

The pounding footsteps behind me make me walk faster. I've never felt unsafe in the city before and right now I feel very close to running except I'm at the steps to my apartment. With my foot on the first step, I tell myself not to look behind me.

"Hadley, wait," he says as he grabs my arm, stopping me dead in my tracks. I step back down and face him. He's wearing a sweatshirt. No hat or gloves to keep him warm. "I froze back there. I didn't know what to say."

"It's okay. I understand."

"It's good to see you too, by the way. A little shocking, but still good."

"How long have you been in New York?"

"Just over four years. We moved after graduation."

"We?"

"Dylan and I. Do you remember her?" He looks over his shoulder like she should be right behind him. She's probably lurking in the bushes, waiting to pounce on me for talking to her man.

"Yeah, I remember her."

"We have a place not too far from here. Well, five or six blocks away, but still close."

Great, they live together. The question is at the forefront of my mind. I'm dying to know so I ask. "How long have you been together?"

He laughs lightly and shakes his head. "We aren't together. We just live together. It's cheaper to have a roommate."

My body sighs with relief although I'm stupid to think he's single. He's far too good looking to be single. He steps forward, close enough that I can smell his cologne. His hands encase my cheeks so fast I don't know what's happening. Before I can react, his lips are on mine and I'm giving him all the access he wants. I'm no longer in control of my body. It's taken over and submitted to him.

He kisses me fast and urgent at first, before slowing down and taking his time. He places small kisses on my lips, resting his forehead against mine.

"I'm sorry," he whispers. I'm not. I'm so not sorry that he just kissed me and hate that he is. "I just had to know."

"Know what?"

"If you're the one."

chapter
forty-three

RYAN

If someone told me this morning that I was going to run into Hadley Carter today I would've laughed in their face. I haven't thought about her in years. No, that's a lie. Each time I began dating someone and things started getting serious, I would think of Hadley. I would compare them and end up ruining my relationship. I've had one serious girlfriend since Hadley and I'm not counting Dylan, because that was more of an exploration relationship.

I had met this girl in business class and she reminded me of Hadley. I thought it could work and it did for about a year. She started dropping hints about getting engaged and how a spring wedding in New York would be so beautiful. I didn't panic or freak out. I simply told her that she wasn't the one I saw when I closed my eyes at night. Since then I dated occasionally, nothing serious because there's no point in going head first into something if she isn't the one you see in your dreams.

During the winter our Friday nights are spent at O'Malley's. It's been tradition for about a year or maybe longer. It started when Dylan brought one of the O'Malley boys home. I liked John well enough and we've become friends.

I don't know what told me to turn around, but something did. Part of me is not sorry that I saw her, while the other part wishes I never turned around at all. I could've gone the rest of my life never seeing her again because living the nightmare from when she left me was enough the first time. But there she stands, staring at me. In shock, I'm sure. Just as I never expected to see her, I have no doubt she never expected to find me here, in her city.

I'm frozen. My legs don't want to move even though I'm begging them to step forward or back. Anything to let me relax from this rigid posture I've got going on. The cue stick in my hand is breaking from my grip. I can feel it splintering beneath my fingers.

Dylan reaches up and whispers into my ear. "I'm going to kick you in the balls if you don't smile right now."

I smile simply from the fear of getting kicked. I know she did it on purpose. She remembers everything clearly and doesn't want to see me going through it again. I watch as Hadley stares at Dylan and turns red when Dylan rests her hand on my arm a bit longer than normal. There's no doubt in my mind that Hadley is jealous of Dylan, just as I'm jealous of the guy she's with. I remember him from the magazine covers and photos I found online back when we broke up. I know who he is and know that he's looking over at me every few seconds wondering what I'm going to do with his precious girl.

She steps forward, one foot in front of the other, as she makes her way over here. It would be nice if I could move as well, but I'm cemented to the ground. Not too many things have changed about her in the last four years. Her features are softer and she's wearing less make-up. Her hair is down, the top hidden by a wool hat. She's wearing black boots and a dark gray skirt and black sweater. She's clearly dressed for the elements and not for the stage.

I remember that she used to wear cowboy boots and short dresses and she loved it because it felt more natural than that "leather contraption". The time I pinned her against the tree outside of my church flashes in my mind. Countless times I've replayed that image and wondered why I didn't trail my hands up her thighs when I had the opportunity. Her skin was begging to be touched, caressed, and she was allowing me to do it. I just didn't know it until it was too late.

"Hi." Her eyes close instantly like she's being forced over here to talk to me. I don't need her to talk to me. I don't need anything from her.

She clears her throat, but doesn't look at me. She doesn't look into my eyes when she says, "Hi, Ryan, it's good to see you."

Is it? I want to ask but can't find my voice. I hadn't realized how much anger I have pent up inside and I'm afraid to open my mouth. Afraid of what's going to come out.

I look her over just like I'd check out any other woman standing in front of me. At one time I wanted to know every inch of her body and had the pleasure of staring at my own map of discovery until things went south. I pull in my lower lip, a habit I've developed over the years and bite the shit out of it to help keep my mouth shut, but it doesn't work.

"I never thought I'd see you again," I blurt out with such acid I don't know where it came from. When I ran this line over in my head, it didn't sound like that. Thing is, I'm not so sure I want to take the words back either. I have so much to say to her, so much that I want to ask her, but I know she's not going to let that happen.

"You look really good." I look down at myself and think about how hard I've had to work to look this way. I'm finally getting noticed. When I walk into a crowded room, people stop and I like that. No longer am I the one sitting in the corner with no one to talk to. Those days are gone.

"Four years does that to some people." I'm snide with my remark and she knows it. She looks over my shoulder and I don't have to turn to know who's behind me. Dylan hates her.

"It was good seeing you, Ryan." She nods and brushes past me so fast I don't have time to react. I'm mentally kicking myself in my balls for being a dick. I watch as she grabs her coat and throws it on hastily. She pushes open the door to the pub and steps out before I know what's happening.

I've been looking for her in every girl I date and when I finally have her in front of me again not only do I freeze, but I'm a total prick. I grab my sweatshirt off the chair, dropping the pool cue and take off after her.

I step out, the harsh cold catching me off guard, making my eyes water as I look left then right for her. I see her crossing the street and walk after her. I don't want to startle her, but I also don't want to yell out her name on the street. She walks faster, cautious of someone following her. I reach for her arm, just as she takes the first step on a staircase leading to a well-lit building.

"Hadley, wait." My voice is pleading. I need for her to hear me out. The doorman looks at me and I instantly drop my hand. I don't want him coming outside and ruining the plan forming in my head. "I froze back there. I didn't know what to say."

"It's okay. I understand."

I wish I did. I wish I understood what's going on in my head right now. "It's good to see you too, by the way. A little shocking, but still good." Very good because staring back at me are the brown eyes that have haunted my dreams since I was seventeen years old.

"How long have you been in New York?"

"Just over four years. We moved after graduation." The shock on her face is evident. I've been in her city for a long time and not once have we run into each other.

"We?"

"Dylan and I. Do you remember her?" I look over my shoulder to see if Dylan followed me. I wouldn't put it past her, but hopefully John just took her home.

"Yeah, I remember her."

"We have a place not too far from here. Well, five or six blocks away, but still close."

"How long have you been together?" This question should shock me, but it doesn't. Hadley had told me once that Dylan liked me, but I didn't believe it. Even after Dylan and I got together, I didn't really think about Hadley's fears.

I laugh and shake my head. "We aren't together. We just live together. It's cheaper to have a roommate."

Her body visibly relaxes. I step closer, my body happy being this close to her. Her eyes close as she breathes in. Is she remembering what we had? Are her memories as vivid as mine? My hands cup her cheeks and I can't resist the temptation to kiss her.

The moment our lips touch, I know. The fire is back. The electric energy coursing through our bodies making us one is stronger than anything I've ever felt. My tongue seeks out hers and is met with the same heat and emotion that I remember so well. I know without a doubt that she is the one who can ignite desire within me.

I slow things down, careful not to open old wounds. I kiss her once more, before resting my forehead against hers.

"I'm sorry," I whisper. I should've asked if she had a boyfriend or a husband before I did that. For all I know, she's taken and I just assaulted her. "I just had to know," I say, pulling away from her.

"Know what?" she asks.

I don't hesitate this time. I'm not taking any chances. "If you're the one."

A smile breaks out across her freshly kissed lips and I fight every urge to kiss her again. But I hold back. If someone told me that I was going to end up kissing Hadley Carter after running into her, I would've laughed.

With utter reluctance, I let go of her. The connection is lost and I hate the feeling that I've had to suppress for so long. It's amazing what one person can do to you with just a simple touch. Hadley is my drug and for the past four years I've been jonesing for just the smallest taste.

"Do you want to come in?" she points to the apartment behind her. "We can talk. I think we should talk. I have so much I need to tell you."

I look at the doorman who's watching me like a well-paid hawk. The question still plagues my thoughts. "Are you married?"

"No."

"Boyfriend?"

"No, I'm single."

Those are the answers that I was looking for. "Okay," I say.

"Okay." She turns and I follow her up the stairs. The doorman opens the door for us and she nods as we pass them. We stand side by side, waiting for the elevator. When we step inside, she presses the button for her floor and we ride in silence.

When we step off, we only walk ten steps before she's opening the door. I step in and look around. She has a small Christmas tree in the corner and white lights hanging from the walls.

"It's probably not what you expected," she says as she steps next to me. "Alex and I like it, but she's moving next month so I'm not sure I'll stay here much longer or move closer to downtown. Can I get you something to drink?"

"Do you have a beer? I sort of left mine at the bar."

"Yeah, I do. Go ahead and sit."

I walk farther into the living room and look at her view. We're twenty stories up and while this isn't the best view, it's still very nice. I always imagined her living in a high-rise apartment for some reason.

She hands me a cold bottle and I notice that she has one too. She taps her bottle against mine, smiles and brings it to her lips. She sits down on the couch and I follow, letting my long legs stretch out on the side of the table.

There's too much silence between us. I know things need to be talked about, but who starts? I look over at her and find her staring at me. There is a stray tear on her cheek. I reach over and wipe it away. She holds my hand to her face and I fight every urge to pull her into my arms.

"I'm so sorry for what I did, Ryan."

I don't know what to say. Most people say 'it's okay' but it's not. She hurt me.

"I thought I was doing the right thing, but I wasn't. Not for me at least. Ian insisted he'd make your charges go away if you'd sign the paper and I kept thinking that it's only for a few weeks. But your birthday came and you didn't answer your phone. I knew you'd never forgive me."

"You called?"

She nods her head causing my thumb to rub up and down against her face. "I did every day for about six months until I finally gave up. I knew you had run away that night, but had hoped you had your phone and could tell me where you were."

I pull my hand away and her eyes drop, telling me she's disappointed that I'm no longer touching her. She just told me that she called me on my birthday. The same day I smashed my phone to bits and pieces and made a move on Dylan. Everything changed that day for me.

"I didn't run away, I went to live with Dylan. My dad..." I shake my head. I hate speaking about him and hate even more that we never were able to reconcile before he passed away. "My dad and I got into a fight that day and he tried to choke me. I fought back, but my mom sent me to Dylan's and I stayed there until we moved here after graduation."

I still can't get past the fact that she called. "You called?"

She nods and takes another sip of her beer. "I hated myself so much back then. We had this show the night before your birthday in Jackson. Ian did it on purpose and all I could think about was that night we met and everything that had happened. I messed up the show so bad. Alex had gone to your house to get you, but your parents told her you had run away. I was a wreck. Ian got so pissed at my performance that he told the press your name. I so hoped that they'd find you, but that didn't happen. The next day, I turned your phone back on and texted you and waited for something back, but nothing ever happened.

"Finally, about six or seven months later I started seeing a therapist and she has helped a lot. I've made a lot of changes in my life and I'm happy now, content."

Is one of those changes forgetting about me? I want to ask her but know I have no right.

I chug down my beer and set it down on her coffee table. "Do you have more?"

"Yeah, I'll get you one." She picks up my empty bottle and retreats to her kitchen. She's back with four more, determined to keep us talking. I notice that when she sits down, she's a little closer and asking for trouble if she thinks me and beer are going to make for a gentleman tonight.

chapter
forty-four

HADLEY

Having Ryan in my apartment is surreal. I thought about bringing him home so many times that to actually have him sitting on my couch is indescribable. He's like a fantasy come true.

I didn't mean to bring back four beers from the refrigerator, but I didn't want to keep getting up for more and I don't want to give him an excuse to leave.

"Are you still singing?"

I choke on my beer when he asks. How can he not know? "Don't tell me you still don't listen to music."

He looks at me like I've offended him. I set down my beer and face forward. His hand halts my movements, so still. "I don't listen to your music, Hadley. I listen to heavy metal or whatever's playing in the dugout. I don't watch MTV or awards shows and I definitely don't read magazines unless it's *Sports Illustrated*."

"Dugout?"

"I work for the Yankees."

My mouth drops in surprise. It's not that I didn't expect Ryan to do great things. I just can't believe he's working for the Yankees. "Wow, that's really great, Ryan. I'm proud of you!"

"Are you?" He doesn't hide the underlying tone in his voice. I lean closer just so I can feel the heat radiate between us.

"I am," I say quietly. I want him to kiss me again. I want him to take me and mark me as his own.

"You hurt me when you left. For the first time in my life, I cried. I hated myself for feeling weak. I hated you for making me feel that way. I told myself I'd never cry over another girl again, but sitting here with you, I feel like I'm going to cry because half of me wants to tell you to take a flying leap and I don't know if I could say those words to you and mean them. The other half wants to pick you up and do all the things I wanted to that night in the car, but I'm afraid that if we did, I'd walk out that door and never see you again and I'm not sure I can handle that either."

I move closer so I can thread my fingers through his hair. It's so soft. I've missed this. He closes his eyes and leans into my touch.

"I had a girlfriend. She had blond hair and brown eyes. She treated me well and I thought I loved her until I closed my eyes and thought about dancing with her at my wedding and when I opened them, she wasn't my bride."

"Who is?" my voice breaks when I ask.

He doesn't answer, just turns away from me. I sit back, breaking the connection we had going.

"To answer your earlier question, yes, I'm still singing. I just finished an overseas tour."

"That's good, and how's your manager?"

"She's great actually." He looks at me with his eyebrow raised. "Ian was fired a long time ago."

Ryan nods and takes another drink, finishing off his beer. He pops the top on the next and I can't help but wonder if this is usual for him.

"You said Alex is moving."

I look at him and smile. "Alex and Cole are getting married in two weeks."

"Isn't he your ex?"

"Yep," I nod and take a drink of my own beer. "Seems they're in love and they're good for each other."

"How does that make you feel?"

"Honestly, I'm fine with it. Cole and I haven't been together in a long time. He's lucky to have her. She's good for him, she's what he needed to make his life complete." I set my beer back down and wonder if we're going to continue being awkward around each other. He looks at his watch and frowns. "Do you need to be somewhere?"

"No, I'm just looking to see how long it's been since I've kissed you." He turns and looks at me. "The thing is, I'm sitting here and I have all these things to say to you and nothing is coming out. The only thing I want to do is kiss you."

Ryan gets up and starts pacing around the room. He pulls off his sweatshirt and I see dark lines on his arms that I didn't see before in the pub. I pull my legs up underneath me and watch as he mentally talks himself down from wherever he is.

"What's on your arm?"

He stops pacing, but doesn't answer me. He lifts his t-shirt over his head and I gasp at how much he's grown into a man. He was just a boy when I knew him last and now he's matured. He's carrying a clearly-defined six pack that is accented by a dark patch of hair leading into his boxers. Both arms are muscular and have thick black lines. He turns around and shows me what they belong to. On his back is a very large phoenix and its wings extend onto his biceps.

I swallow hard and fight the urge to strip down to nothing and lay here for the taking, because staring at the boy I fell in love with and seeing the man he became is enough to do me in. I stand slowly and walk over to him. I trace the lines of the bird with my fingertips.

"What's it for?"

"Because I rose from the ashes and made myself better."

"It's very sexy." I can't lie. It is. It's the hottest thing I've ever seen. I don't know if it's the tattoo or the man sporting the ink, but I have no doubt in my mind I've never seen something so sexy.

I lean closer and place my lips where my fingertips were, kissing my way up his back. My arms snake around him, my fingers tickling the hair on his stomach.

"Hadley," he croaks out my name. "I'm not going to be able to stop myself from taking you. I'm so in love with you. I've been in love with you for years. If you don't want this, step away please, I'm begging you."

"I want this. I want you."

He turns in my arms and picks me up. His lips are on me, his tongue thrusting into my mouth before I can react. His hands go under my skirt, pushing it up over my hips. I hate that I'm wearing tights right now. He cups my ass, pushing me into his erection. His fingers dig into my thighs, pulling my legs farther apart.

"Room?" he says, only breaking long enough to ask.

I hate pulling away, but have no choice. "Last door," is all I can get out before he's working me into a deep and frenzied kiss.

We stumble into the wall as he walks us down the hall. He twists my doorknob and pushes my door open, kicking it shut. I'm expecting him to throw me onto the bed, but he doesn't. He lays me down gently. His lips move down the column of my throat until he reaches my sweater, tugging lightly before giving up.

I start to laugh.

"You think this is funny? You're dressed like an Eskimo."

"It's cold out."

"I'll keep you warm," he says as he pulls me into a sitting position and lifts my sweater over my head. He slowly undoes each button on my dress shirt, including the ones on my wrists. He kisses each wrist and my shoulders as he slides it off.

"Another shirt?" he asks when he sees my camisole. I shrug. "I know, you're cold," he says as he lifts it over my head.

I unbuckle his belt, remembering the last time we were like this and how he stopped us. There's nothing stopping us now. My bra comes off and before I can catch my breath, he has me back on my back and he's hovering over me. His lips are dangerously close to my nipple that is all but screaming at him for attention.

"Last chance," he says against the valley of my breast before taking it in his mouth.

He has me squirming against him, looking for any type of friction I can get. I was desperate the last time and even more so now. He switches breasts as his hands work my skirt. I undo his fly and try to push his pants down. He slides down my body, painstakingly slow, the pressure increasing.

I lift my hips for him when he grips my skirt and pulls, taking my tights in one fell swoop. I sit up, bare except for my panties and watch him as he looks at me. He kicks off his shoes and drops his pants the rest of the way. I move up higher on my bed as he crawls over me. He's on the prowl and I'm his victim.

He kisses me at my core, over my panties. He moves them aside, feeling me. When his tongue touches me I clamp down on his hair, which he doesn't seem to mind. As many times as I thought of him, never did I imagine this.

He does everything perfectly and plays my body like a fiddle. I come undone from his fingers and tongue. My panties go flying across the room as he kisses his way up my body. I want him desperately. I need him.

He settles between my legs, pressing himself into my center, causing more of an ache. I can feel him, bare and against where I need him most. I wrap my legs around him, holding him there so he can't change his mind.

He enters, pushing slowly. I gasp and bite gently down on his shoulder. He hisses as he starts to move inside me. Our bodies sliding against each other, his forehead rested on mine.

"Oh God, fuck, fuck, fuck," he mutters, and before I know it he's off of me, leaning over the bed.

"What's wrong?"

"Condom. I don't have one. I don't even carry one in my wallet so I'm not sure why I'm looking for one." He covers his face with his forearm, taking deep breaths.

I want to cry from the emptiness I feel when his body leaves mine but instead I say, "Ryan, I'm on the pill."

He pulls his arm down slightly and looks at me. The nightlight in the corner is letting off just enough light that I can see that he is contemplating if he should or not. Thankfully, he doesn't think long, and hovers over me once again. He pushes himself inside me. I close my eyes, my legs wrapping around his waist as he goes deeper. Moving his mouth over mine, he kisses me hard, his hand gripping my hips as he stills inside me. Kissing down my chin and then up my jaw, my body clenches his before he slowly bites down on my shoulder.

Crying out, he chuckles against my throat as he moves his strong hands up to cup my breast. His mouth clamps over my nipple, biting softly before swirling his tongue devilishly against it. I can't stand it and I scream out, my nails cutting into his bare shoulder. Letting out a breath, his eyes wild with passion, he moves his mouth up the valley of my breasts, his hand moving down my body before gripping my thigh. Pushing my leg up, so that I'm open for him, he moves into me again, pushing to the hilt and taking my breath away. He pulls out and as he is about to slowly move into me again, I glance up at him, my eyes clouded with lust as I whisper, "Ryan."

He nods knowing that this is it. This is the moment when everything will change for us. I don't ever want him to leave. I want him to be mine for the rest of my life. I love him. Dropping my hands, I slowly grip his toned ass. His eyes close before I pull him into me. My body welcomes him and wants him, and when he squeezes my hips from the sheer pleasure of our bodies being connected, I want to scream, but I don't. He opens his eyes, looking down at me, and then so softly he whispers, "I've missed you."

I nod, my hands holding onto his wrist as I say, "I've missed you."

Dropping a kiss to my lips, he starts to move into me with earnest strides. Each thrust taking my breath away. Soon my body is quivering and I come undone, squeezing him so hard that he groans against my cheek. Pushing my legs forward with shaky hands, he starts to thrust wildly into me until he finds his own release, his fingers biting into my sides. I know he's leaving marks but I don't care. When he falls onto me, I can't breathe, but I'm smiling. His breath is labored against my neck as my hand moves up and tangles into his hair, holding him close to me. He kisses up my neck, then to my jaw before sitting up on his arms to kiss my lips. Looking down at me, he cups my face, his eyes searching mine as a small smile goes over his face. I smile back as he asks, "Can I take you to dinner tonight?"

"Really?" I ask, breathless.

He nods, "Yeah."

"Are you ready to be seen in public with me? Are you ready for the cameras, the life I lead, all of it? Because if you aren't I understand, but I want you in my life. I don't want to lose you ever again."

"I can handle it."

I hope he's right, because not having Ryan in my life isn't an option. It wasn't four years ago and it definitely isn't now.

chapter
forty-five

RYAN

"You're stupid."

"No, I'm not."

"YES. YOU. ARE!"

Dylan yells at the top of her lungs as she throws a glass at my head. I didn't expect this. Okay, maybe I did, but I thought things would be a bit milder.

Things have been going amazingly well with Hadley. I've seen her every night since that night at O'Malley's and was her date for Alex and Cole's wedding. That was the second time we were photographed together, except this time, there was no mistaking that she was with someone.

After the first night, I tried to take things slow. I didn't want to rush into having sex with her, unlike the first night, but I'm telling myself that it really didn't count. It's a guy thing. Just go with it. My resolve only lasted three days before I couldn't handle it anymore. We had plans, but when she answered the door in a tight black dress, I lost all ability to think clearly. Ironically, this was the night of my birthday.

I know things are moving fast. Faster than they should be, but I don't want to be away from her.

"What are you going to do about your job?"

"What about my job?"

Dylan stands with her hands on her hips. "You work non-stop from

February until October. You travel across the country. Are you going to give it up for her?"

I look at Dylan with confusion. "No, why would I?"

"Because she'll want you to go on tour with her, that's why. Because she'll want you to be her arm candy at all her awards shows and whatever." Dylan sits down on the couch and sighs. I know she means well, but this is a bit over the top. Hadley and I discussed our schedules and she's not going out on tour anytime soon. Besides, her schedule is more flexible.

"Look, I know you're protecting me, but this is right. It feels right, Dylan. If I don't do this, I'll regret it."

"You're making a mistake. She's going to hurt you again. You may believe her sad-ass excuses, but I don't."

"You don't have to."

"No, I just have to pick up the pieces again when she rips your heart to shreds."

"I don't feel that, in here." I put my hand over my heart and plead with Dylan to trust me.

She shakes her head, wiping her traitor tears away. She stands and grabs her purse. "I can't watch you do this. Not with her. Anyone but her, Ryan."

"It doesn't work that way and you know it."

"I *don't* know it, Ry. What I know is that when you were seventeen you were so lost in her that you couldn't see clearly. You haven't had a healthy relationship since her."

"Our relationship was good."

Dylan scoffs. "No it wasn't. I took advantage of you and you know it. You just don't want to admit it. We were always better off as friends."

I walk over to her and pull her into my arms. "I love you, D. I always have, but she's the one. I feel alive when I'm with her. Every fiber of my being is on fire when she's near. I know you don't want me to get hurt, but I don't feel like that is going to happen."

"And when it does?"

"Then label me a fool because that's what I'll be."

Dylan wraps her arms around my waist and holds herself to me. I don't want this to be goodbye, but I'm hoping after today things will change for Hadley and me.

"I love you, Ry. I hope you're enough for her. I'll be here if you're not."

Dylan lets go and walks out of the door. I look around our apartment, an upgrade from the one we lived in while I was in college. As soon as I was hired by the Yankees we moved here. It's a bit classier and definitely in a much nicer part of town. Dylan's in her final year of school and I know she doesn't need the stress, but this is something I have to do for me.

I pick up my keys and head out to Hadley's. We're supposed to meet up with her manager tonight, but I have other plans. I stop at the corner florist and pick up a couple dozen lilies and roses and carry them the ten blocks to her apartment.

I think that the worst discovery was that we only lived ten blocks from each other. I've jogged down her street many times and never once knew she was there. I climb the steps and meet the doorman. For the most part, her building is fairly secure. For the first few weeks, I had to show my ID to the doorman and the desk clerk before they'd even call her and let her know I was down there. Now they know me by name.

I ring her doorbell and wait. My nerves are starting to get the best of me. She doesn't know I'm coming. This is a surprise. When the door swings open I'm greeted with the most breathtaking smile I could ever hope for.

I kiss her, pulling her to me, smashing the flowers in between us. I know I'm making the right decision.

"What are you doing here?"

"I had to see you."

I shut the door behind me and lock it, handing her the flowers in the process. She brings them to her nose and takes a deep breath. Her eyes close as she inhales the fragrance. I could watch her all day and I'd learn so much about her.

She follows me into the living room and sits next to me. I kiss her again and again, thanking my lucky stars that I have her back in my life.

I clear my throat and pull her hand into mine.

"I was asked once to close my eyes and imagine I'm dancing. Play the song in my head and feel the person pressed against my body. Look at the person I'm holding and I'd know who my soul mate is." I reach into my pocket and pull out the black velvet box I bought three days after I saw her. Getting down on one knee, I kiss the inside of her wrist.

Her hand goes to her mouth to stifle her gasp. I can't help but smile. I know this is right.

"Ryan," she whispers.

"When I close my eyes, I see you. I've seen you since I was eighteen years old. I knew you were the one for me. If you would've asked me months ago if it was possible for me to find my soul mate, my answer would've been no. But you walked back into my life and I'm not willing to take any chances.

"I know our lifestyles are different and our jobs are crazy, but I can't see myself with anyone else but you. I don't want anyone else and I know you were in that bar for a reason."

"Will you marry me, Hadley?"

"On one condition," she says.

"What's that?"

"That we get married right away."

"Why the rush?" I ask as I slip the ring on her finger.

She picks up my hand and kisses it and then kisses my lips. "I don't want to live another day without being your wife."

I move over her, pushing her gently onto the couch. I hover above her, looking into her eyes and I know she's sincere.

"I love you, Ryan. I always have."

"You didn't say yes."

"What?" she laughs lightly.

"You didn't say yes. I asked you to marry me and you didn't say yes."

"Oh—"

"Will you marry me, Hadley Carter?"

"Yes, yes I will, but only if I can ask you something in return."

"You don't like your ring?" I sit back on my knees and look at her. I love her ring. The moment I saw it, I knew it was for her. That's how I knew I was making the right decision.

"What? No, I love my ring." She sits up and runs her hands up my chest. "Will you move in here?"

"I thought you'd never ask," I say as my lips come crashing down on hers.

Finally, my life is playing out like I planned all those years ago. I know things happened for a reason, but not knowing why is probably the hardest part. In the years I was away from Hadley, I grew as a person. I wasn't cynical or a hard-ass. I worked hard in college and at my job, paving the way for my future. I took care of Dylan as promised and even tried my hand at love once or twice, but nothing felt right until that night in the bar when I saw her standing there – and I knew. I felt it in my bones that if I didn't keep her, I'd never find the happiness I felt when I knew her the first time because, without a doubt, she and I are meant to be together.

THE END

SNEAK PEEK
OF

PRETTY LITTLE LIES

By Debut Author
Jennifer Miller

Chapter One

"Fashion tip: Stilettos are great when paired with a great pair of jeans skirt, or dress. Not only do they make your legs look longer and give your calves a great work out but they have the added bonus of coming in handy should you need to give a cheating husband a kick in the crotch!"

I blink hard and try to bring the papers in front of me into focus. I'm almost done. I just need to sign a few more of these freaking legal documents and then I can put this ridiculous mistake of a marriage behind me. When I met Deacon, I was a sophomore in college. I was vulnerable, and looking for an escape from the boring student I had become. Deacon offered me just the release I craved. The endless parties, tapped kegs, promises of hot sex, and occasionally other experimentation that I choose to forget, made getting involved with him a no-brainer. Add a side of studying and managing a fashion blog that took on a life of its own and you have my college life and relationship with Deacon in a nutshell.

My heart aches; anguish now courses through my veins just as steadily as blood. I'm really not sure at this point how or why I am still feeling pain. If I'm honest with myself, I can't really be surprised my marriage has ended this way. I mean, I got married in Vegas for god sakes; at a drive up chapel after a drunken late night proposal that I can barely remember. Spring Break during our senior year, a bunch of us had the brilliant idea to spend the week in Vegas. One night during our stay we did the traditional walk up and down the strip drinking the whole way. I vaguely remember Deacon making a production on the sidewalk, getting down on one knee and asking me to marry him, a rose he had bought from a street vendor in hand. Amongst the hoots and hollers of our friends, I impulsively accepted and we flagged down a taxi cab to take us to the closest chapel.

This bizarre wedding was only the beginning of what ended up being a marriage full of questions and contradictions. I spent years wondering what I had gotten myself into and questioning why I stayed as long as I did. So the question remains, why then am I still struggling? I've cried until I heaved from it over and over again and had nothing left. I've been so angry, that it felt like my insides were burning, and I was sure I was going to combust from the intensity of my fury. How my heart can still ache at a loss that frankly has been coming for a while, is unfathomable to me.

I stare again at the papers, and while the whole document is in the same font, the words **Dissolution of Marriage** seem to be screaming at me, taunting me with their meaning.

Dissolution of Marriage.

Divorced at twenty – five.

Single and just another statistic to add to the divorce rate.

Admitting I never thought this would happen to me is a gigantic understatement. My life wasn't supposed to go this way. At one time I had a plan, a dream, but little by little it all fell apart.

I briefly close my eyes and see myself on my wedding day, well what I remember of it anyway. Wearing my favorite designer jeans and Madonna t-shirt, giggling, with a cocktail in my hand; and while it may have been a crazy and an impulsive thing to do, I was actually elated and excited. When I woke up the next morning and realized what I had done, I knew things would never be the same. I had a brief sense of uncertainty and I wondered how I could have been so impulsive to make such a huge, life-altering decision but at the same time all I could see was the life I had always envisioned, more exciting and fuller because instead of just me… there would be an *us*. I wouldn't have to be alone, vulnerable and looking for an escape again. Maybe I could even resurrect the real me and get my life back on track. I would have a husband that would support me no matter what. Right? Any and all naysayers be damned, my life was about to start, and I would prove them all wrong. The world was mine! What a fool I was.

Now, just four years after saying I do, I realize my life is nothing but a horrible cliché. I remember the day it all came crashing down and the reality of what my marriage had become was laid out before me, refusing to be ignored.

With the eagerness of a child returning home after their long anticipated first day of school, delighted to have gotten off of work early and excited to see my husband, I exited the car. Bottle of wine in my hand and a sack of just-purchased groceries in the other arm, I intended on making Deacon a pasta dinner by candlelight. I opened the door and walked into our apartment, immediately overcome with the stench of pot. As I walked to the kitchen and placed my packages on the counter, I saw a trail of clothing leading to the closed door of my bedroom. I froze. Doom and dread instantly ran through my body and I felt a burning from my neck to the top of my head making me feel dizzy; sick. I knew without a doubt what I was going to find. I slowly started walking into my bedroom...

"Olivia...? Olivia?"

Blinking quickly and shaking my head trying to rid myself of the awful picture in my mind I look up at my attorney and attempt a smile. "I'm sorry, Clive. My mind wandered. You were saying?"

"That's okay, Olivia. I was just asking if you got everything signed? I am going to have my assistant make you a copy of the documents for your records."

Clive, whom I'm guessing is in his early 60s, has a pot belly, receding hair line and rather large ears. His kind and gentle personality never made me uncomfortable or feel stupid during this entire nightmare of a process. Once, during our conversation, he divulged he's been happily married for 30 years and has three grown children. I imagine seeing the ugly side of marriages and divorces up-close and personal has made him realize how lucky he is. I never doubted for a second that he would get my divorce done quickly and accurately.

"Thanks, Clive. That would be great." I tell him as I hand him the documents I've signed for copying.

Clive leaves his office and I'm left there with nothing but my thoughts once again. My mind flashes back to my apartment six months ago.

I picked up the articles of clothing littering my apartment floor as I walked closer to my bedroom --- a man's shirt with buttons missing, with lipstick in a shade I don't wear, on the collar. A woman's shirt in a very pale yellow, a color I didn't own. Given my skin tone, it would wash me out; my complexion is too pale to pull off such colors. Dark haired women like me should stick to bold colors.

I took a couple more steps and picked up an orange bra that must be a double D, two sizes bigger than I wear and in a color I did not possess. An orange bra under a pale yellow shirt? Really?

I tentatively, but steadily moved closer to the door and I heard the moans coming from the other side of the door. Apparently they were much too involved... the sound of my arrival did not even phase their sexcapade in the slightest.

Opening my bedroom door, I saw more clothes trailing up to my bed, an empty wine bottle on the side table and all I could think is that it's three o'clock in the afternoon, a bit early for wine. It took my mind a few moments to catch up before I fully comprehended the scene in front of me. A naked thin-bodied, extremely large busted peroxide blonde woman was in my bed, in our bed, riding the shit out of my husband. His head thrown back in apparent ecstasy, his eyes rolled back in his head. The bitch was fiercely slapping her body up and down against his. They had no idea I was standing there. None.

"WHAT THE FUCK?!" I screamed dropping the clothing I was somehow still holding in my hands to the floor.

I stared, completely dumbfounded.

Deacon practically threw the whore off the top of him in reaction to my scream and she went tumbling off the side of the bed.

Our bed.

Our desecrated bed.

Deacon yelled, "Oh my God! Olivia!"

"That's right you asshole! It's Olivia, your wife!" Before I even knew what I was doing I stalked over to the side of the bed where I saw the blonde bitch fall and dragged her up by her hair and bitch slapped her across the face. Deacon was standing there staring at me with his mouth open, eyes wide and a horror-shocked expression on his face. Before he could even comprehend what I was about to do I kicked him in the freaking balls as hard as I could.

"You bastard!" I shouted "How could you?"

With fury coursing through my veins I was shocked at my reaction. I'm not a violent person, had never hit anyone in my life. I was completely taken over by absolute disbelief and rage at what I was seeing. In an instant, literally the span of three minutes, my life had completely changed. I was filled with absolute agony. I didn't deserve this.

After my inner bitch did her thing, I stalked out of the room and headed to the couch, where I had thrown my purse when I came home. During that time, Deacon somehow miraculously recovered from the blow to his crotch and started screaming my name while holding his hand over himself and chased me into the living room. I snatched up my purse and headed to the front door. Before I could reach it, Deacon reached me, grabbed my shoulder and spun me around to face him.

"Olivia, wait… I can explain! It's not what you think!"

I laughed. I have no doubt it was a super creepy clown circus kind of laugh but still I laughed in his asinine face. He is unbelievable. Of all the things he could have said to me.

"It's not what I think? Are you KIDDING ME?! I think I just saw my husband jamming his dick into some bitch that isn't his wife! Don't even try to explain yourself Deacon, there is NO excuse. There is NOTHING that you can say that could make me not walk out of here right now."

I shoved him as hard as I could and made my way to the door.

Recovering quickly, Deacon caught up to me, grabbed my arm. Hard. The real Deacon was about to make an appearance. The begging lasted all of thirty seconds. "Olivia, I said to fucking wait. You are overreacting like a damn baby. Stop being a bitch and listen to me."

I looked at him and sneered, "Screw you Deacon."

I ripped my arm out of his grasp knowing I would definitely have a bruise above my elbow where his fingers dug into me hard. I opened the door, ran out, and slammed it behind me …Deacon screaming my name behind me.

I started to wait for the elevator, but when I heard my apartment door open behind me, I made a dash for the stairwell door and threw myself through the threshold knowing that he wouldn't follow me naked down the stairwell. I ran as fast as I could down two flights of stairs and then stopped, sat down on a stair and started to sob.

"Here you go Olivia. Your copies."

I jump slightly, startled by Clive's return.

"We will get these papers filed with the court and you can expect to get your divorce decree in the mail in about two weeks."

Clive hands me my copies of the divorce documents in a manila envelope. Wow. My four year marriage reduced to a few papers in an envelope.

"Thank you Clive. For everything."

"You're welcome, Olivia, and if you stop and see Jessica on your way out, she will give you your final invoice and make sure she has your forwarding address in our system. Best of luck to you."

I smile, give him a nod and step out of his office and walk to the reception desk to see Jessica.

After paying my bill, I take my manila envelope and walk out of the office.

The sun hits me in the face; I squint my eyes and start rooting around in my purse looking for my sunglasses. Popping them onto my face, I just stand there for a moment, take a deep breath and start walking to catch the next train. Pulling out my cell phone from the front pocket of my purse, I start dialing my best friend Pyper.

"Hi this is Pyper! I must be treating my clients like royalty at Shimmer & Soothe Salon and Spa! You should be jealous that you aren't here yourself! Leave me a message and I will get back to you to schedule the appointment I'm sure you want to make!"

I laugh at my friend's message as usual and wait for the beep.

"Hi, it's me. Well it's done. I just signed the papers and left Clive's office. Why do I feel…?" I stop talking and sigh. "Honestly, I don't know how I feel. Part of me feels empty and part of me wants to host my own divorce party. With cake. A cake that has a bride on top holding a knife with the bloody groom in a pool of his own blood at the bottom. They really make those you know. Crazy right? Anyway, give me a call when you can! I'm headed home to do some more packing. Kisses!"

I press end on my phone and shove it back into the front pocket of my purse. I walk through the subway entrance, scan my link pass, and wait for the T to arrive. I start reflecting on my life here. Deacon moved out a while ago. I had to threaten to call the cops if he didn't get his ass out. But I am leaving Boston for good. I still remember coming here seven years ago to attend the journalism program at Boston University. While it wasn't my first college choice, I will always look back, and love having lived here. In fact, once I married Deacon, I always thought I would stay here forever. Instead, I'm packing up and moving my life back to Chicago, Illinois. I'm going to move in with Pyper.

The T finally arrives and I step in looking for a seat. I take a seat towards the back and sit next to the window. Leaning my head back on the seat, watching the subway walls as they fly by, Deacon's handsome face comes to my mind. Willing to do anything to win me back, he brought me flowers over and over. He gave me sentimental cards pouring his feelings into them, telling me how sorry he was, that he made a mistake and of course he promised that it would never happen again. He bought me jewelry, offered to move away with me to start over, told me he couldn't live without me.

One time, after I had kicked him out I came home from work to find he had let himself into our old apartment, filled it up with flowers, made me dinner and once again pleaded with me not to leave him. I was so close to relenting. I can still close my eyes and remember the good times, the laughs we shared, all the times he tenderly made love to me and I felt like I was the center of his universe. As crazy as it seems, I know in his own demented way he truly loved me. I know I loved him.

That night, I almost gave in; it wasn't because of the flowers or the dinner, it was the pure anguish I saw in his eyes and the tears that trailed down his cheeks when he begged me not to leave him. I looked in his eyes, really looked and the sight astounded me. I had never seen him cry before; but it wasn't only that. I could see the love there. I could see that he truly wanted to work things out and was pleading for me to stay. Part of me wanted to give into him. I could see myself jumping into his arms and telling him we could figure it out and try… really try to make it work. I wanted to be able to tell him that I forgave him but in the back of my mind I had realized something in our time apart. Our marriage was a sham to begin with. The fact that we had made it for four years was a freaking miracle and believe it or not, choosing to stay would have been the easy way out. Staying was easy. Choosing to move on, the hard part.

I shattered his heart that night. I looked him in the eyes and told him once again to get out of the apartment and that I didn't want to see him again. I told him there was absolutely nothing he could do to make the situation right and that he needed to just stop. Stop trying. Stop buying me things. Stop coming over. Stop trying to fix "us," because it couldn't be done. We were broken. We were over; the marriage was over. When all of his efforts failed to work, and he felt desperate, he became mean.

Anger flashed across his face and he tried to hide it. His pleading ended up with him calling me names and storming out of the apartment. I had hurt his pride, set him off; a dangerous combination.

I know little miss blond slut wasn't Deacon's first betrayal; I just chose to ignore the signs that were right in front of my face. I chose to believe the pretty lies he told me. The excuses ranged from working late, to stopping at the gym or running into an old friend. When he realized the lies were becoming more frequent he tried to bury my questions and disappointments with flowers, shopping sprees or sex that was driven more by anger than passion. For a while, I desperately clung to the lies and the illusion that everything was fine. While his affairs mattered and of course they hurt, the simple truth was that they were only part of the problem. I didn't want to be in a marriage that only works when I played dumb and pretended to believe the lies and allowed things to always be on his terms.

I want more.

I need more.

I deserve more.

ABOUT THE AUTHOR

Heidi is the author of USA Today, Kobo, Digital Book World, Amazon and Barnes & Noble Bestselling novel, *Forever My Girl*.

Originally from the Pacific Northwest, she now lives in picturesque Vermont, with her husband and two daughters. Also renting space in their home is an over-hyper Beagle/Jack Russell and two Parakeets.

During the day Heidi is behind a desk talking about Land Use. At night, she's writing one of the many stories planned for release or sitting court-side during either daughter's basketball games.

Find Heidi on Twitter: twitter.com/HeidiJoVT
Facebook: https://www.facebook.com/HeidiMcLaughlinAuthor
Or her blog: http://heidimclaughlinauthor.blogspot.com/

ACKNOWLEDGEMENTS

I cannot thank the readers enough for the constant encouragement I receive daily. Interacting with each and every one of you has been such a blessing and I'm so thankful.

My brother, Ryan, isn't here to see this story. A lot of Ryan Stone is who my brother was. Shy, awkward, very cute (yes I can say that as his sister) and loved by everyone.

The word thank you seems so small when it comes to my best friend, Yvette, but without her, my stories don't work. She's my constant and for that I'll be in her debt forever.

There are plenty of people to thank that held my hand during *Lost in You*.

Miller & Cola – the late night chats and pre-reading helped me through that very rough patch.

Toni – I appreciate every encouraging word and most amazing help ever. I love knowing that I can just hand you a chapter.

Brandon – without your most spectacular images Ryan and Hadley would just be names. Thank you for the amazing promotions.

Jodie – thank you for taking the helms on this one. I owe you!

Sarah – your vision is one of the most amazing aspects of writing. You help create the story with what you make for the cover.

Tasha – thank you taking such an amazing photo and willing to let me put a story behind it. From the moment I saw it. I knew this was fate.

Fallon & Alyssa – good thing your red pen works wonders. Thank you both for the constant support and editing.

There are so many bloggers that I've become friends with, but my fear is that I'd forget someone. So… if we talk, text, email, tweet or Facebook – thank you for all your support. I can't even begin to tell you how much it means to me.

To my family – thank you for being so supportive and hashtagging our conversations – they make me laugh, even when I'm rolling my eyes. Mom; Dad & Beth book two - I'm on a roll.

This paperback interior was designed and formatted by

www.emtippettsbookdesigns.com

Artisan interiors for discerning authors and publishers.

Bruce County Public Library
1243 Mackenzie Rd.
Port Elgin ON N0H 2C6

CPSIA information can be obtained at www.ICGtesting.com
Printed in the USA
LVOW06s0226050915

452958LV00021B/1234/P